Film Noir and the Cinema of Paranoia

For Oyekan Owomoyela,
and all friends loved and lost

Film Noir and the Cinema of Paranoia

Wheeler Winston Dixon

Rutgers University Press
New Brunswick, New Jersey

First published in the United States 2009
by Rutgers University Press, New Brunswick, New Jersey

First published in Great Britain 2009
by Edinburgh University Press Ltd
22 George Square, Edinburgh

Library of Congress Cataloging-in-Publication Data

Dixon, Wheeler W., 1950–
Film noir and the cinema of paranoia / Wheeler Winston Dixon.
p. cm.
Includes bibliographical references and index.
ISBN 978-0-8135-4520-2 (hardcover : alk. paper) – ISBN 978-0-8135-4521-9
(pbk. : alk. paper)
1. Film noir–United States–History and criticism. I. Title.
PN1995.9.F54D59 2009
791.43'655–dc22
2008036417

Manufactured in Great Britain

Visit our Web site: http://rutgerspress.rutgers.edu

Contents

Acknowledgments

This volume would not have been possible without the help and advice of numerous colleagues and friends; of the many who contributed, I would like to single out Dennis Coleman, always an authority on films maudit; Mikita Brottman and David Sterritt, comrades in arms; Peter Brunette, a solid source of encouragement and guidance; Stephen Prince, who shares many of the concerns reflected in this manuscript; Steve Shaviro, whose writings have long been a source of both wonder and inspiration; Lucy Fischer, an astute judge of critical writing and a good friend; along with Patrice Petro, Jean-Pierre Geuens, Jonathan Rosenbaum, Dana Polan, David Desser, Marcia Landy, Stephen C. Behrendt, Maria Prammagiore, Valérie Orlando, Michael Downey, Miriam Linna, Billy Miller and a host of others who contributed, either directly or indirectly, to this project. Dana Miller, as always, did a superb job in typing the original manuscript from my customary handwritten draft, and thus earns my undying thanks. Jennifer Holan provided the index for this volume, and also did a superb job of correcting the final page proofs; my sincere thanks to her. Through all of this, Gwendolyn Foster provided an atmosphere of love and patience that made this work possible, and remains my best friend, staunchest critic, and constant ally.

While most of this volume is comprised of new material, there are some sections of this text that have previously appeared in either journals or collections of essays. For permission to use brief portions of these materials here, the author wishes to thank Yoram Allon and Wallflower Press for permission to reprint 'House of Strangers: The Family in Film Noir,' in A Family Affair: Cinema Calls Home, Wallflower Press; 2008; Leslie Mitchner and Rutgers University Press for permission to reprint 'The Endless Embrace of Hell: Hopelessness and Betrayal in Film Noir,' in Cinema and Modernity, Rutgers University Press, 2006, and 'Night World: New York as a Noir Universe,' in City That Never Sleeps: New York and the Filmic

Imagination, Rutgers University Press, 2007; James Peltz and State University of New York Press for permission to reprint 'The Eternal Summer of Harold Pinter and Joseph Losey's *Accident*,' in *The Films of Harold Pinter*, ed. Stephen S. Gale, State University of New York Press, 2001, 21–37; and pages 95–107, on the writer Jim Thompson, from my book *Straight: Constructions of Heterosexuality in the Cinema*, State University of New York Press, 2003; Felicia Campbell, editor of the journal *Popular Culture Review*, for permission to reprint 'The Commercial Instinct: New Elstree Studios and The Danziger Brothers, 1956–1961,' *Popular Culture Review* 9.1 (February 1998): 31–43; Robert King, editor, Classic Images, for permission to reprint '*The Invisible Man*, *Secret Agent*, and *The Prisoner*: Three British Teleseries of the 1950s and 60s,' from *Classic Images* 282 (December 1998); Margaret Walsh and the University of Wisconsin Press for permission to reprint 'Archetypes of the Heavy in Classical Hollywood Cinema' in *Beyond the Stars: Stock Characters in American Popular Film*, Bowling Green State University Popular Press, 1990; Rolando Caputo and the editors of *Senses of Cinema* for permission to reprint 'Fast Worker: the Films of Sam Newfield,' Senses of Cinema 45 (2007); Lloyd Michaels, editor of the journal *Film Criticism*, for permission to reprint 'A Cinema of Violence: The Films of D. Ross Lederman,' *Film Criticism* 30.3 (Spring, 2006); and finally John Brown and Taylor and Francis, for permission to reprint my article 'Hyperconsumption in Reality Television: The Transformation of the Self Through Televisual Consumerism,' in *Quarterly Review of Film and Video* 25.1 (2008). In all cases, these materials have been substantially altered from their original versions to incorporate new research, and only brief sections of the essays are used here.

For help in researching this book, it is my pleasure to thank Kristine Krueger of the Margaret Herrick Library, Fairbanks Center for Motion Picture Study, Academy of Motion Picture Arts and Sciences, for her help in locating information on some of the more obscure titles and production companies discussed here, as well as Janet Moat, Mandy Rowson and Ian O'Sullivan of the British Film Institute for their research assistance on the British noir-influenced films, particularly those produced by the Danzigers. Todd Geringswald of the Museum of Television and Radio, New York also provided invaluable assistance. The stills that grace this volume come from the personal collection of the author. Finally, I wish to thank the University of Nebraska, Lincoln Department of English for its support of my work through the years, and especially the chair of the department, Joy Ritchie.

The work of this volume is simple; it gestures towards an expanded vision of what constitutes a noir film, and so those readers who expect the visual catalogue of tough guys and hard-boiled dames will find them in these pages, but they will also find a host of other characters, from a variety of genres. Science fiction noir, horror noir, even musical noir are all present and accounted for, as well as those films that usually operate on the margins of cinematic discourse because of inadequate budgeting, distribution, and/or both. Noir *is* a state of paranoia, a zone in which nothing seems stable, no one can be trusted, and the world is a constant battleground. This book seeks a wider definition of that which we call film noir, following in the footsteps of Raymond Durgnat, Paul Schrader, Guy Debord and other theorists whose fascination with noir led them to path-breaking insights, of which the concept that noir is not necessarily a genre is perhaps the most intriguing, and the most mutable. What follows, then, are some variations on a theme.

'There ain't no answer.
There ain't never going to be an answer.
There never has been an answer.
That's the answer.'

Gertrude Stein
(as quoted in McFadden 1996: 9)

Introduction

This is the age of film noir. Though the genre dates from the late 1930s and early 1940s, its concerns of hopelessness, failure, deceit and betrayal are in many ways more prescient in the twenty-first century than they were at their inception. Then, too, most definitions of noir films are, it seems to me, excessively narrow. The classic archetypes of the lone protagonist in a dark, rainy alley, accompanied by an omnipresent voiceover on the sound-track, of doomed lovers on the run from the police, or hard-boiled detectives unraveling labyrinthian mysteries with cynical assurance represent only one manifestation of this pervasive film genre.

Film noir is the cinema of paranoia, of doubt and fear and uncertainty, which blossomed in the wake of World War II, as the Allies' victory was purchased at the cost of the specter of instant annihilation by forces seemingly beyond our comprehension. Returning veterans found that prices had spiked on the home front, that the world had moved on without them, that wives had acquired a new degree of independence and financial security through war work, and that behind the dream of the white house with the picket fence there lurked a nightmarish void hidden from public view. Noir served as the most authentic version of the inherent corruption and complacency of postwar life, when forced consensus and idealized conformity were prized above all other considerations. But as the 1940s gave way to the 1950s, the 1960s and beyond, the concerns and aesthetics of noir never left the screen, or the radar of both American and world consciousness. Each succeeding generation crafted films that were more bleak, more uncompromising, more fatalistic and despairing than the last. Often these films were not the dominant voice of an era – the late 1960s, for example, were at times shot through with a utopian impulse, coupled with a nearly desperate embrace of 'wholesome' entertainment.

But at the margins of society, speaking to a large yet phantom audience, a world of loners who seemingly coalesced into a group only when they went to the movies, another cinematic world continued to exist, and thrive. For every film like Robert Stevenson's *Mary Poppins* (1964), for example, there was also Herschell Gordon Lewis's *Blood Feast* (1963); for every vision of suburbia offered in such idealized television fare as *My Three Sons* or *Eight is Enough*, films such as Ray Dennis Steckler's *The Incredibly Strange Creatures Who Stopped Living and Became Mixed-Up Zombies* (1963) lurked in the cinematic background, as if to prove that there is no such thing as an uncontested zone of cinematic safety and certainty – all is in flux, and behind every halcyon facade there is an alternative universe, offering the very antithesis of the values the dominant culture seeks to uphold.

Noir persists in many forms, within many genres, and it's useful to note that for many observers, noir itself was never a stand-alone genre, but rather a pervasive world view that shot through works in a wide variety of cinematic staples; westerns, comedies, horror and science fiction films, teen exploitation films, and even musicals, to name just a few of the many genres that noir has influenced and continues to do so to the present day (see Durgnat 1970, reprinted in Silver and Ursini 1996: 49-56; Schrader 1972, reprinted in Grant 1986: 169-82; and Place and Peterson 1976, reprinted in Nichols 1976: 325-38, for more on the universality of the noir aesthetic in the cinema).

Durgnat's essay, in particular, was a groundbreaking enterprise, suggesting for the first time exactly how wide the definition of the noir aesthetic might reasonably be. From Robert Aldrich's *Kiss Me Deadly* (1955), with its Pandora's box of radioactive isotopes, ready to destroy all who come in contact with it, to Haskell Wexler's *Medium Cool* (1969), in which a news cameraman is forced to consider the consequences of filming scenes of violent carnage for nightly mass consumption on the evening news, Durgnat traces noir from its early iterations through a series of cycles, or thematic preoccupations, such as 'crime as social criticism,' 'gangsters,' 'on the run,' 'private eyes and adventures,' 'middle class murder,' 'portraits and doubles,' 'psychopaths,' 'hostages to fortune,' 'Grand Guignol: horror and fantasy,' and finds that noir, if anything, is spreading out from its original boundaries to embrace American, and international culture as a whole.

Partly this is a backlash to the saccharine view of life that Hollywood forced on viewers in the wake of the 1934 Production Code; partly it is because these newer films reflect emerging realities of life. Thus Erle C. Kenton's *Island of Lost Souls* (1932) fits comfortably next to Harry Horner's *Red Planet Mars* (1953), both films depicting a world of paranoia, psychic and/or physical pain, and an unfettered embrace of the darker side of human endeavor. Budd Boetticher's *The Rise and Fall of Legs Diamond*

(1960), Arthur Penn's *Bonnie and Clyde* (1967), and Anthony Harvey's filming of Le Roi Jones's (aka Amiri Baraka's) racial drama *Dutchman* (1966) all partake of the noir aesthetic, as does Jean-Luc Godard's pessimistic view of French pop life in the 1960s, *Masculine/Feminine* (1965).

Durgnat's central thesis, that noir is potentially everywhere, is one that this book seeks to endorse and expand upon; even Ernest B. Schoedsack and Merian C. Cooper's *King Kong* (1933) partakes of the noir tradition, not only in the violence that Kong wreaks, first on Skull Island and later in Manhattan, but also because of the economic violence of the Depression itself, in which the dreams of millions of men and women were destroyed in a wave of frenzied speculation, and the blandishments of those in authority proved counterfeit.

Even in such seemingly escapist fare as the Nancy Drew films from the late 1930s, to say nothing of later manifestations of resourceful heroines in television and films of more recent vintage, an aura of threat and menace is always present in the otherwise halcyon world that Nancy inhabits. Behind the facade, there always lurks another world, a society with codes and rules as strict as those of the dominant culture, and societal influence that often outstrips the bonds of recognized authority. As David Lynch is fond of demonstrating, behind the picket fence of well-manicured suburbia, there is another world – violent, self-contained, that operates by its own set of rules – coexisting with the idealized version of suburbia embraced by mainstream media. Lynch's *Blue Velvet* (1986) is the perfect exemplar of this dualistic tendency in American society; the brightly lit, artificially perfect veneer of middle-class complacency has more in common with the dark underside of suburbia than it cares to admit, and each side reinforces the other. There could be no light without the darkness; no day without the night.

Noir holds both promise and danger. If we view the domain of noir as a zone in which our inhibitions are loosened, we can also see it as a place without rules, where restrictions are relaxed, where people can pass us by unnoticed, until it's too late. Noir functions as a literal and figurative zone of darkness, a place that must be illuminated so that we can see. In all noir films, darkness surrounds the characters within the narrative, threatening to engulf them at any moment. The frame's blackness seeps into the faces of the protagonists in these doomed films, etching their features with fear and apprehension. In musicals and screwball comedies, the cinema functions as an arena of social release, a world where laughter and gaiety are unceasing. But in films that belong to noir as a central theme, it is despair and violence that dominate the screen. Indeed, the true domain of the noir is night, just as the inescapable terrain of the noir is the city. Rural noirs, such as Nicholas Ray's *On Dangerous Ground* (1952) and Delmer Daves's *The Red House* (1947), seem few and far between.

The world of noir is one of perpetual threat and contestation. Social conventions are stripped away to reveal the hard-scrabble realities underneath; even the family unit no longer functions as a zone of refuge. Families, small towns, churches, civic groups, doctors and lawyers, ministers and mayors; all are tested and found wanting. Examples are abundant; John Brahm, André De Toth, and Lewis Milestone's *Guest in the House* (1944), in which Anne Baxter destroys the family that takes her in out of charity; Jean Renoir's *Woman on the Beach* (1944), in which alcoholic impressionist painter Tod Butler, blinded by his wife Peggy in a domestic battle, battles the bottle, Peggy's chronic infidelities, and his own homicidal rage. Sam Wood's *King's Row* (1942) rips the lid off small-town American life, while simultaneously exposing the manners of polite society as a sham; John M. Stahl's superb Technicolor noir *Leave Her To Heaven* (1945) presents Gene Tierney as the psychopathic Ellen Berent, who destroys her own life and those around her through her implacable jealousy, and in Brahm's *The Locket* (1946), a young woman's kleptomania leads three suitors to their deaths. There is no safety zone in noir, no place to rest, or hide; no comfort or shelter; no friendship; no pleasure that isn't transitory, and usually purchased with one's money, or life.

Whom can we trust? No one. We cannot even trust ourselves; a little pressure, and we can easily be made to implicate our friends and associates in whatever manner the authorities wish. Or we could make a mistake; an error in judgment that might cost us our lives, trusting the wrong doctor, the wrong lawyer, the wrong associate who would eventually betray us for money, power, or influence. What has been termed neo-noir, in such films as Bryan Singer's *The Usual Suspects* (1995), John Dahl's *Red Rock West* (1993), and Larry and Andy Wachowski's *Bound* (1996), carries forward the thematic concerns of a genre whose authentic sense of menace and deception still holds us in thrall. Today, we have new fears to deal with, and a new set of escapist tools to transcend or confront them: video games, hyperviolent action films, Internet chat rooms, and interactive web sites. We are all 'connected,' yet we have never been more isolated from one another. This is the true message of noir; that today is horrible, and tomorrow will be worse; that hope is an illusion.

Such films as *Apology for Murder* (1945), *The Big Clock* (1948), *The Big Combo* (1955), *The Black Angel* (1946), *The Blue Dahlia* (1946), *Bodyguard* (1948), *Crossfire* (1947), *Decoy* (1946), *Detour* (1945), *Fall Guy* (1947), *Heat Wave* (1954), *In a Lonely Place* (1950), *The Mysterious Mr Valentine* (1946), *Raw Deal* (1948), *Roadblock* (1951), *Split Second* (1953), *Stranger on the*

Third Floor (1940), and *They Won't Believe Me* (1947) exemplify the sub-terranean world of true film noir, behind the surface of such canonical classic examples of the genre as *The Big Sleep* (1946), *The Maltese Falcon* (1941), and other films that have subsumed other, more authentic noirs. Created in such Poverty Row studios as Producers Releasing Corporation (perhaps the ultimate noir studio), Allied Artists and Monogram, these ultra-cheap visions of paranoid uncertainty more authentically portrayed the inherent sense of personal failure, betrayal, and hopelessness that informs the structure of the best noirs.

In many ways the Pre-Code films of the early 1930s were precursors of the true noir style that would flourish in the years after World War II. Before the Production Code was enforced in earnest in 1934, Hollywood presented a very different vision of American society on the screen, much at odds with the idealized world it would present between 1934 and 1945, the height of the Code's influence. In *Heroes for Sale* (William Wellman, 1933), for example, Richard Barthelmess, a World War I veteran, returns from the war with a morphine addiction, only to find that a man he saved claims Barthelmess's heroic war acts as his own. Duplicitous, smarmy, and thoroughly cowardly, this so-called friend is hailed as a great American hero as Barthelmess wanders from town to town, a hopeless bum, in a bleak and thankless effort to find a job in Depression-era America. The hypo-critical flag-waving America of the now classic *Heroes for Sale* is thus noirish in every respect. From the dark moody cinematography, to the out-rageous plot turns implicit in paranoid melodrama, the film paints the depths of American society in collapse, and particularly the plight of men during the era.

Men are similarly highlighted in the utterly blunt and despairing *Hell's Highway* (1932), a prison drama that is certainly as dark as the greatest noirs such as *Detour*. Memorable are the sequences in which the chain-gang members, including Richard Dix, are routinely whipped and beaten into submission. Meant as an exposé of the typical Southern chain-gang prison, the film features a horrifying sequence in which a young prisoner dies inside a metal box, fashioned something like a standing phone booth, in which the prisoner is hung and baked in the relentless sun. This scene, based on an actual real-life prison death, is typical of the utterly depraved depths to which the powerful, yet hypocritical authorities sink. The plight of African-Americans is also prominently on display in *Hell's Highway*, certainly by 1930s standards, and race prejudice is a theme throughout the film.

Reflections of the femme fatale glimmer in *Hell's Highway*'s attitudes toward women. Women are repeatedly blamed as the reason behind most of the men's prison terms. Over and over, it is implied that men, already up against it because of the Depression, were forced to steal, kill, or otherwise disobey the law in order to fulfill their role as providers. The all-male environment of the prison becomes a cauldron of barely suppressed rage and desire for masculinity, power, and any sense of entitlement to a place in the world. In a typical Pre-Code twist, the film features a flirtatious cook who is quite openly gay. It's clear that he trades sexual favors with the chain-gang bosses and leaders in return for a tiny bit of respect and a place over which to rule: the kitchen.

Many viewers are familiar with the better-known *I Am a Fugitive From a Chain Gang* (Mervyn LeRoy, 1932) in which Paul Muni plays an innocent man who is brutally oppressed by the crooked criminal justice system. The noirish stylization of a montage sequence in which Muni crisscrosses America is memorable for its use of high key lighting, giant shadows, and the bleak and repetitive visuals of signs pointing Depression-era men on the hunt for work to move on. There are no jobs here, no way to support yourself, no promise of the American Dream. This is the essence of noir in America, albeit in its early stages.

The American Dream is on trial in many Pre-Code dramas, as it is in the bizarre and twisted noir musical *Gold Diggers of 1933* (Mervyn LeRoy, 1933). The film is really two narratives in one: a standard love story featuring Dick Powell and Ruby Keeler; and another, barely buried film that directly addresses the harshness of the Depression, as gold-digging singers Joan Blondell and Aline MacMahon attempt to teach a lesson to snobby rich sophisticates Warren William and Guy Kibbee. The film features surreal spectacles that criticize the government for its lack of a response to Depression economics. These musical vignettes, famously directed by Busby Berkeley, include scenes of fallen and wounded veterans, desperate women prostituting themselves, murder, poverty, starvation, and class struggle. The film ends with an indictment of society at large in the famous 'Remember My Forgotten Man' musical number, which is a noir cry for help for forgotten men and women.

Women have it just as bad as men in Pre-Code vehicles, if not worse. Gilda Carlson (Dorothy MacKail), for example, flees to a remote island where she is surrounded by lecherous and slobbering men in *Safe in Hell* (William Wellman, 1931). The film's typically noir plot turns on her false, paranoid assumption that she cannot return to the United States, because she thinks she murdered her pimp. Gilda is subject to the daily sexual harassment of a gang of thieves on the island, who constantly spy on her and make her every living moment torture. Just when the viewer fully expects a gang rape, Gilda is blackmailed by the supreme legal authority on the island who offers her 'freedom,' if she will become his sexual slave. Instead, she opts for the death penalty, bravely and defiantly walking away from the camera in a typically bravura Wellman moment.

No rescue comes for her, no last-minute reprieve, just a violent and cruel noir fate. Perhaps if Pre-Code films had been more widely known and available to the French film critics who helped create the canon of film noir, the history and reception of noir would have included many of the great films of the Pre-Code era. But because of censorship and the lack of available prints, it is doubtful that the *Cahiers du cinéma* critics were able to see such films as *Baby Face* (Alfred E. Green, 1933) starring Barbara Stanwyck as a wayward woman who is forced into prostitution by her father and who literally sleeps her way to the top of a New York skyscraper.

Hobart Henley's 1932 film *Night World* is a sharp little fifty-eight-minute thriller that takes place entirely within the boundaries of a prohibition-era nightclub. *Night World* embraces the aesthetics of noir, both in visual stylization and in philosophical outlook, and features a truly eclectic cast, including Lew Ayres, Mae Clark, Boris Karloff, Hedda Hopper, George Raft, Louise Beavers, Jack La Rue, and numerous others in a hard-boiled story involving murder, blackmail, gambling, and illicit liquor.

In *Night World*, 'Happy' MacDonald (Boris Karloff) owns a prohibition-era nightclub, where his wife, known only as 'Mrs Mac' (Dorothy Revier), is a cashier. Unbeknownst to Happy, his wife is having an affair with Klauss (Russell Hopton), who works as the choreographer for the club. (The film's dance numbers were actually handled by Busby Berkeley, making *Night World* an even more bizarre concoction.) Happy is an atypical role for Karloff, as a smooth operator who runs his club with a mixture of persuasion, violence, and unctuous charm. Yet, it reminds us of the considerable range Karloff was capable of as an actor before he became hopelessly typecast, and performed almost solely in horror films.

The entire film takes place during one evening, as befits such an economically paced production. On this particular night, matters reach a crisis when Happy and his wife are killed by some disgruntled bootleggers, while the club's star attraction, Ruth Taylor (Mae Clark), falls in love with Michael Rand (Lew Ayres), a young man about town whose alcohol consumption is getting out of hand. At the end of the film, life goes on, irrespective of the various deaths, plot twists, and changed fortunes in which the film delights; *Night World* certainly qualifies as a noir, if only because the 'fun' in the film is empty and tinged with genuine danger, and Happy MacDonald's club is anything but 'happy.' It is a zone of despair and desperation, with only the slightest possible hope of personal renewal.

Mervyn LeRoy's *Heat Lightning* (1934), one of my favorite Pre-Code noirs, centers on two sisters (Ann Dvorak and Aline MacMahon) running a gas station and motel in the desert during the Depression, through which a number of people pass on a blazing hot summer day. People come and go, alliances are forged and broken; there is sex, violence, and death, all in one twenty-four-hour cycle, and yet life goes on for most of film's protagonists, like a sort of rundown version of Edmund Goulding's *Grand Hotel* (1932).

Pre-Code films thus provide a template for classic noirs, although they tend more towards a stylized realism that is mordantly humorous. They speak to an audience that was apparently thirsty for the truth, as harsh as the studios (especially Warner Brothers) could dish it out. Though Pre-Codes often have a silly or moralistic tacked-on ending, audiences were clearly aware that these endings were meant for the eyes of the prying censors, who were already demanding that the studios tone down the bleakness of these nihilistic, fatalistic, depressing, yet honest visions of despair, almost unparalleled in the years after the Pre-Code era.

In fact, one could easily argue that many Pre-Code films are actually *more* noirish than noir. Their central characters exist in paranoid, horrifying realities, there is often no escape. Extortion, rape, mistaken identity, murder, theft, sexual harassment, depravity of all kinds are dished out in rapid-fire plots, in films that often last as little as sixty-five minutes. Pre-Code audiences wanted their cruelties delivered without pulling any punches. They didn't know what was around the corner, so why should the characters know any better? Equally, fate had dealt them a cruel blow, so why shouldn't they see that reality reflected onscreen? No wisecracking voiceovers make light of the protagonists' fate, nor do they distance audiences from the characters in the Brechtian manner often found in more classic noirs.

Pre-Code films existed in a world of grab and greed, violence and brutality, where all that mattered was power, money and influence. Everything was for sale, if only one had the price. Often, one didn't. The most brutal Pre-Codes take the audience to hell, and only sometimes bring them back.

CHAPTER 1

The Dream of Return

What happened when the men came home from war? They returned to a world transformed into an alien landscape, something they didn't understand and didn't recognize as home, a place full of new and strange social customs, in which the fabric of prewar society had been torn asunder by massive social, economic, and political change. And a new kind of film was waiting for them, as well; the film noir, or 'black film,' which documented better than anything else the realities of this new social order.

Boris Ingster's *Stranger on the Third Floor* (1940) is often cited as one of the first unadulterated film noirs, and in its unrelentingly bleak and hallucinogenic structure, it is easy to see why. Shot on a shoestring budget by RKO's 'B' unit, *Stranger* tells the tale of a young newsman, Mike Ward (John McGuire), who fingers a taxi cab driver, Joe Briggs (perennial fall guy Elisha Cook, Jr), for a particularly brutal murder. Briggs, however, is innocent; the real killer is the psychotic Peter Lorre, billed only as 'the Stranger' in the film's credits. At the last minute, the Stranger's guilt is discovered almost by accident, and Briggs is set free. Director Ingster, largely forgotten today, would go on later in his career to produce the highly successful escapist teleseries *The Man from U.N.C.L.E.*, but in this film, he creates a nightmarish vision of urban life, set in a city of perpetual night. Lorre's part, almost wordless, is that of a restless psychopath, driven to kill by forces he is unable to control.

As Briggs, Elisha Cook, Jr is made to order to step off for the murder, and neither the police, the jury, nor reporter Ward is inclined to believe his protestations of innocence. The obligatory 'happy ending,' in which Briggs offers the services of his taxi to Ward and his new wife, Jane (Margaret Tallichet), apparently without any rancor for his false conviction through Ward's testimony, is a mere sop to the Production Code. In the real world of noir, *Stranger on the Third Floor* suggests Lorre will continue to kill, Briggs will go to the chair, and justice will fail all the film's protagonists.

Shot on a few cheap sets by the gifted cameraman Nick Musuraca, whose work defined the RKO 'B' look throughout the 1940s, *Stranger* offers a world without hope, escape, or even the illusion of a future.

H. Bruce Humberstone's *I Wake Up Screaming* (1941), also known as *Hot Spot*, the working title during the film's shooting, is another tale of big-city dreams shattered by the realities of daily existence. Vicky Lynn (Carole Landis) is a hash-slinger in a Times Square restaurant when fight promoter Frankie Christopher (Victor Mature) and his show business pals, ham actor Robin Ray (Alan Mowbray, perfectly cast) and gossip columnist Larry Evans (Allyn Joslyn) decide, almost on a whim, to promote Vicky as a rising star; Pygmalion in Manhattan. Vicky is all too willing to go along for the ride, though her sister, Jill Lynn (Betty Grable), remains suspicious. Why should Frankie and his friends take such an interest in Vicky? What are their true motives?

Vicky's career moves ahead smoothly, perhaps too smoothly. She soon decides to move to Hollywood for a screen contract, abandoning Frankie, Robin, and Larry. But at this point, things go terribly wrong. Vicky's brutally murdered body is found in her apartment, and obsessive homicide detective Ed Cornell (Laird Cregar, Jack the Ripper in John Brahm's *The Lodger*) steps in to solve the case. Ed is sure that Frankie is the killer, or so it seems. He grills Frankie relentlessly, and slowly but surely builds up a compelling chain of circumstantial evidence to convince the promoter.

But in a neat twist, mild-mannered bellhop Harry Williams (Elisha Cook, Jr again) is revealed as the murderer, a fact that Cornell has known from the beginning of the investigation. Ed Cornell's jealousy of Frankie's relationship with Vicky has driven Cornell to frame Frankie for the murder. With Frankie cleared, Jill and Frankie can begin a married life together. Frankie, it seems, never had any feelings for Vicky, viewing her only as an investment to promote, not a romantic partner. Thus, Cornell's jealousy has been completely misplaced. In the final moments of the film, Frankie discovers that Ed has created a shrine to Vicky in his apartment, complete with photographs, newspaper clippings, and a makeshift 'altar' to her memory. But Frankie was never a competitor; the real problem is that, weighing in at nearly 300 pounds, Ed Cornell never had a chance with Vicky at all.

I Wake Up Screaming abounds in ironies that extend beyond the framework of the film's narrative. Laird Cregar, the obsessed detective, was in reality one of Hollywood's first 'out' homosexuals, and his immense bulk at first prevented him from working in film, at all, until he found his niche as a screen psychopath. *I Wake Up Screaming* was Cregar's breakthrough film, but he would live only three years longer, dying in 1944 at the age of twenty-eight as the result of a crash diet and abuse of amphetamines, in a futile bid to remake himself as a matinee idol for John Brahm's *Hangover Square* (released posthumously in 1945; Katz 2005: 303–4). Carole Landis, the ambitious Vicky in *I Wake Up Screaming*, was equally ill-starred in real life, only rarely rising above 'B' films. After a tempestuous relationship with actor Rex Harrison, who was then married to actress Lilli Palmer, Landis committed suicide with an overdose of sleeping pills on 6 July 1948 (Katz 2005: 781).

Of all the principals, only Victor Mature emerged relatively unscathed from the making of the film. He continued to work in film and television, while moonlighting as a television repairman, until the early 1980s, playing his last role in the appropriately gaudy spear and sandal spectacle *Samson and Delilah* (1984), in the cameo role of Manoah. In the 1949 version of *Samson and Delilah*, Mature played the role of Samson, proving that in cinema as in life, you can't escape your past. Of all the members in the cast, Betty Grable decided she was out of her depth in dramatic roles, and returned to cheesecake vehicles and light musical comedies, though she acquits herself quite admirably here.

I Wake Up Screaming's vision of New York at night is handily reconstructed on the 20th Century Fox back lot, with the aid of rear projection and a few garish sets. Ed Cornell seems forbidding because he is forbidding; his sheer size, coupled with his patronizing, yet doggedly determined speech patterns, mark him as a man on a trajectory toward death. Victor Mature was cast for his 'beefcake' potential, just as Betty Grable trafficked in 'cheesecake'; to capitalize on this, *I Wake Up Screaming* contains an utterly gratuitous scene in which Frankie and Jill go to an indoor swimming pool, the Lido Plunge, the better to show off their perfectly proportioned bodies in skintight swimsuits. Vicky is foredoomed from the film's outset, both because of her ambition and her desire to 'class pass' above her waitressing milieu, and because Cyril J. Mockridge's extra-diegetic musical cues signal impending disaster.

As with many noirs, lighting in *I Wake Up Screaming* is noticeable more by its absence than its presence. During Frankie's initial interrogation by the police, we can see only Frankie's face, and the harsh light that shines on it. The policemen, especially Ed Cornell, remain in darkness. They belong in the dark. When Cornell first emerges into the light in the police station, his sheer physical presence terrifies Jill, who recognizes him as a 'peeping Tom' who has been hanging around the restaurant where Vicky worked. Steve Fisher's trashy source novel has given Humberstone and his cast a world devoid of light, hope, or any promise of the future; *I Wake Up Screaming* exists in a zone where all is a perpetual nightmare, from which one can never awake.

One of the most famous postwar noirs, Edgar G. Ulmer's legendary film *Detour* (1945), was made for Producers Releasing Corporation, or PRC, without a doubt the most marginal studio in Hollywood history. Shot for $20,000 (some sources say $30,000; still the budget is minuscule by any standard) in six days on a few threadbare sets and a car parked in front of an omnipresent rear projection screen, *Detour* tells the tale of Al Roberts (Tom Neal), who hitchhikes to California to marry his girlfriend, Sue (Claudia Drake). Along the way, Roberts is picked up by a fast-talking salesman named Haskell (Edmund MacDonald), who suffers from a heart condition.

When Haskell dies, Roberts assumes his identity, convinced that the cops will pin Haskell's murder on him anyway, and appropriates his money and car. But, in a masterful plot twist, Roberts, posing as Haskell, picks up Vera (Ann Savage), a young woman whom the real Haskell had given a ride the day before. Vera blackmails Roberts into selling the car and splitting the money, and then tries to convince Roberts to pose as Haskell for Haskell's dying father, so that Vera and Roberts can collect Haskell's inheritance. Roberts recognizes that the idea is insane, but Vera, in a drunken stupor, threatens to expose Roberts unless he plays along. In the film's climax, Roberts accidentally strangles Vera with a telephone cord, and now truly a murderer, disappears into the night. As a nod to the Production Code, Roberts is picked up outside a cheap roadside diner at the end of the film, presumably to face the death penalty for Vera's murder.

In his excellent book *Dark City Dames*, Eddie Muller recounts in detail the production history of *Detour*, as part of an interview with Ann Savage, the only surviving cast member of the film. As Savage noted,

If Edgar was under any pressure from the short shooting schedule, he never showed it. He was fast, decisive, and unflappable. You just couldn't make a mistake – there simply wasn't the time or money to do things over. (as quoted in Muller 2001: 162)

With only 15,000 feet of raw stock to work with, Ulmer directed Savage to speed up the tempo of her delivery to a machine gun pace, 'faster! faster! he really wanted me to spit out the lines' (as quoted in Muller 2001: 162). But because the film was a PRC film, Ulmer had to move through Savage's scenes with lightning speed, and her 'work on the film lasted a mere three frantic days – barely thirty hours of total work' (Muller 2001: 164). Three days later, the entire film was complete. But as with all true noirs, the ferociously tight budget and schedule of the film does nothing to detract from *Detour*; rather, it reifies the film's atmosphere of the endless embrace of hell

Figure 1.1 Hugh Beaumont as reporter Kenny Blake gets a light from Charles
D. Brown in Sam Newfield's *Apology for Murder* (1945).

alluded to in the title of this book. No one in this film will ever escape the
shabby PRC sound stages; the car, for the most part, is on a journey to
nowhere, its movement achieved through obvious rear-projection.

What emerges is a stark charcoal sketch of a film, with rough edges,
flimsy props, grinding music, and a relentlessly nihilistic scenario. A film
like *Detour* would never have been made at the majors, and it would have
suffered, rather than benefited, from the use of 'A' stars and a decent
budget. The domain of perdition is poorly lit and eerily inescapable; once
an actor appeared in a PRC film, they seldom went on to the majors. PRC
was, itself, a noir construct; the last stop before the gutter for a host of once-
famous Hollywood stars, working for a fraction of their former salaries in
films that were inherently compromised by their conspicuous lack of production values. Ulmer was PRC's most gifted director; the studio's main
house director, Sam Newfield, was so prolific that even PRC was ashamed
of his prodigious output, forcing Newfield to adopt two aliases (Peter
Stewart and Sherman Scott) to cover his tracks. Newfield, in fact,
directed Ann Savage in her only other PRC feature, the aforementioned
Apology for Murder, a typically low-rent PRC riff on Billy Wilder's
Paramount Pictures production of *Double Indemnity*, in which Hugh

Beaumont stands in for Fred MacMurray's character, and Savage for Barbara Stanwyck's.

Not surprisingly, Paramount took a dim view of *Apology for Murder* (for a time, PRC had actually considered calling the film *Single Indemnity* (Muller 2001: 167)), and the film played only two days at Graumann's Chinese Theatre before PRC pulled the film in response to a threatened lawsuit. Newfield's *Apology for Murder* is, indeed, a virtual carbon copy of *Double Indemnity*. Reporter Kenny Blake (Hugh Beaumont) falls for worthless Toni Kirkland (Ann Savage), who is married to an older, dyspeptic businessman (played by veteran smoothie Russell Hicks). Kenny and Toni stage an 'accidental' murder to dispose of her husband and collect the insurance, but Kenny's boss, Ward McGee (Charles D. Brown), figures out that the accident is indeed murder, and assigns Kenny to work on the story.

The end of *Apology for Murder* finds a mortally wounded Kenny returning to his office to type out his confession as a feature story, only to be interrupted by McGee as he finishes the last paragraph; an exact copy of the conclusion of *Double Indemnity*. The film is shoddy and cheap, and one is amazed that PRC had the nerve to try to get away with such obvious plagiarism. More than half a century later, *Apology for Murder* is still in legal limbo, although a clandestine screening of the film in 2002 at the Los Angeles Cinematheque revealed that *Apology*, while a much cheaper film, is in many ways more authentic than Wilder's original. In PRC films, the protagonists really need the money, as do the directors, grips, cameramen and other technical personnel. After PRC, there was nothing left but oblivion, and all the performers and technicians knew it. PRC, in contrast to the more established studios, offered absolutely no security to any of its employees. When a film was finished, PRC simply moved on to another low-budget project, like an assembly line in a sweatshop.

The classic, traditional (in a contemporary sense) noirs of the mid-to-late 1940s lived in a world that was something new for both the viewer and the people who actually made the films; never before had such an utterly nihilistic vision been displayed on the screen. Such films as Mervyn LeRoy's *I Am a Fugitive From a Chain Gang* (1932) or William Wellman's *Wild Boys of the Road* (1933) brought home the harsh realities of the Depression in a direct and uncompromising manner, but in many respects, these were 'actuality' films, based on desperate economic circumstances shared by almost everyone.

But now, in a time of real-time material wealth, in the postwar boom years, the cynicism ran much deeper; we had been through a horrible war and won it, our enemies were vanquished, order was being restored – and yet it still wasn't enough. Something was missing. Everyone seemed to be

Figure 1.2 Lana Turner and John Garfield in Tay Garnett's *The Postman Always Rings Twice* (1946).

on the take and the world was effectively split into two groups; suckers, and those who fleeced them. No one could be trusted, nothing was secure. It was as if the moorings of society had been permanently shaken by the conflict; America, in short, had lost whatever delusions of innocence it had ever had. Life was rough and tumble, and if you didn't watch your step, or expected something for nothing, or aimed too high too fast, you'd wind up in the gutter, or in extreme circumstances, the death house.

Tay Garnett's *The Postman Always Rings Twice* (1946) is for many the definitive postwar noir, starring the tragic John Garfield – a victim of the House Un-American Activities Committee (HUAC) blacklist, he would die of a heart attack only six years later, in 1952, at the age of thirty-nine – and the iconic blonde temptress of the era, Lana Turner, luring him on to his inevitable doom. Made for that most 'un-noir' of studios, MGM, where high gloss musical fantasies and Andy Hardy films were more the regular bill of fare, *Postman* is so unrelentingly bleak in its depiction of human affairs as to be almost insupportable. Tay Garnett, the film's hard-boiled director, had been a fan of James M. Cain's novel since it first appeared to considerable critical and commercial acclaim in 1934, but in the early days of the newly reinvigorated Production Code, no studio would touch it. Indeed, from 1934 to 1940, Shirley Temple was the top female star in Hollywood, as the country sought to escape the grim realities of the Depression in a wave of escapist musicals and small-town 'family' pictures – MGM's usual stock in trade.

Nevertheless, with an eye to the future, MGM paid $25,000 for the movie rights to Cain's novel in 1934, and for all intents and purposes put it in storage until a more propitious social climate arose. When Wilder scored a huge hit with *Double Indemnity*, MGM realized that the public was finally ready for a darker vision of American life. Ironically, Carey Wilson, a former radio announcer and producer of both the Andy Hardy films and a series of highly exploitable short subjects that, among other things, touted the prophecies of Nostradamus, was put in charge of the project. As Garnett later recalled, Wilson and MGM 'raised the tone' of Cain's novel a bit; 'I guess you could say [they] lifted it up from the gutter to, well, the sidewalk' (as quoted in Friedrich 1997: 235). Garnett revealed that he hit upon the strategy of dressing Lana Turner all in white to 'somehow [make] everything she did less sensuous'; as anyone who has seen the film can attest, this wardrobe 'malfunction' had precisely the opposite effect (Friedrich 1997: 235).

The film's plot is simple; drifter Frank Chambers (Garfield) floats into Nick's Diner one morning, and is hired by the affable owner, Nick Smith (Cecil Kellaway) and his mismatched wife, Lora (Turner), a twenty-five-year-old smoldering sexpot whose burgeoning femininity and unmistakable sense of desire are obviously not being satisfied by Nick, who seems more like her father than her husband. Together, Frank and Lora decide to kill Nick and make it look like an accident, so they can inherit the diner and live happily ever after. Naturally, things don't turn out that way.

Director Garnett insisted on shooting much of the film on location in Laguna Beach, roughly fifty miles away from the studio, for added authenticity, and had to contend with heavy fog rolling in on a daily basis, disrupting shooting; a later move to San Clemente to ameliorate the problem did little to improve the weather (Friedrich 1997: 236). The production fell seriously behind schedule, and Garfield and Turner, trapped on the set, found themselves initially repelled by, and then attracted to each other. 'Hey, Lana, how's about a little quickie?' Garfield greeted Turner on their first day of shooting. 'You bastard!' Lana shot back, an auspicious beginning to their on-set relationship. But as time wore on and physical proximity took hold, their on-camera love scenes had a sense of torrid passion that even the crew noticed was extraordinary (Friedrich 1997: 236).

But MGM was, predictably, unhappy with the fog continuing to roll in, and production costs mounting. Less and less film was being shot every day, and Garnett came under fire from the MGM studio brass, who threatened to pull him off the film. Garnett reacted as a self-respecting noir protagonist would; he got rip-roaring drunk, and almost shut down the entire project. A heavy drinker who had quit cold turkey just three years earlier, Garnett now sought escape from his troubles the only way he knew how. As Lana Turner later recounted,

> That's when Tay fell off the wagon . . . Nobody could control him. He was a roaring, mean, furniture-smashing drunk. The girlfriend he'd brought along stayed for awhile, then gave up. The studio sent nurses, but even they couldn't help. (as quoted in Friedrich 1997: 236)

Garfield also tried to reason with Garnett, but the director was so out of it that he didn't even recognize the actor. As he told Turner,

> It's terrible . . . when I tried to talk to him, he'd say, 'sure, Johnny boy, whatever you think.' But a moment later he'd start shouting, 'Who the Hell are you? Get out of my room.' Then he came at me with that cane he always carries. (as quoted in Friedrich 1997: 236–7)

Eventually, Garnett quieted down enough to admit that the whole thing had gotten out of control, and, amazingly, MGM shut the picture down for a week, and sent Garnett back to Los Angeles for treatment, rather than firing him. When production resumed, Garnett knocked out the rest of the picture (many of the later scenes, such as Frank and Cora's trial, were shot in the tightly controlled atmosphere of the MGM lot) with speed and efficiency, as if suddenly aware of the great opportunity he had almost let slip through his fingers. The finished film did spectacular business, was embraced by audiences and critics alike, and is easily Garnett's (and Turner's) finest work on the screen.

The electric effect of Turner's raw sexuality on postwar audiences was thrown into even sharper relief when director Bob Rafelson attempted a remake in 1981 with Jack Nicholson and Jessica Lange in the leading roles. Even with a script by David Mamet that was more faithful to Cain's novel than the 1946 adaptation by Harry Ruskin and Niven Busch, and with exquisite lensing from Sven Nyquist, Ingmar Bergman's favorite cinematographer, the film almost entirely failed to capture the urgency and passion of the original, because it was a film made out of its time. No one was this desperate in America in 1981; Nicholson and Lange's acrobatic sex scenes seem perfunctory and ultimately unnecessary. The 1946 version perfectly captured the pervasive mood of postwar pessimism, fatalism, and sexual repression needed to bring the novel successfully to the screen; anything else was simply an afterthought.

Michael Curtiz's *Mildred Pierce* (1945) was another cynical postwar noir based on a Cain novel; having recently been dismissed by MGM as someone whose pictures no longer commanded public attention, Joan Crawford as the title character of the film reinvented her screen persona so radically that she won the Academy Award for Best Actress for the film, her 'comeback' role. In a typical touch of star theatricality, Crawford accepted the Oscar in her bed, having contracted a heavy cold (perhaps) just a few days before the ceremony; the resultant extra publicity propelled Crawford through another twenty-five years of screen roles as a domineering, often brutal woman who took care of herself because no one else could be trusted.

In true noir tradition, almost the entire film is told in a flashback. The film opens with Mildred's attempted suicide; frustrated in the attempt by a passing policeman, and enmeshed in a complicated murder case, Mildred is picked up by the police, and tells her convoluted story to a homicide detective. As her story begins, Mildred rapidly disposes of her cheating, ne'er-do-well husband Bert (Bruce Bennett) in the film's opening moments, deciding that she can manage better on her own in what was then decidedly a man's world. Mildred has two daughters, the spoiled-rotten teenager Veda (Ann Blyth, in a role that typed her for life), and Kay (Jo Ann Marlowe), a ten-year-old tomboy who loves to play baseball and get dirty roughhousing with the neighborhood children. The children mean everything to Mildred, who restarts her career by waitressing in a hash house and supplements her income baking pies at home. When Kay suddenly dies of pneumonia at the film's midpoint, Mildred redoubles her efforts to succeed, so that Veda can have everything she wants.

After building up her business into a chain of Southern California restaurants and marrying a worthless gigolo (Monte Beragon, played brilliantly by

Zachary Scott) in the process, Mildred discovers that Veda and Monte are having an affair, and that Monte and the equally unscrupulous realtor Wally Fay (the usually genial Jack Carson; here a figure of opportunist greed almost unparalleled in the cinema) have cheated her out of her business, her house, and her future. When Monte rejects Veda's claim on his affections, Veda shoots Monte down in a hail of bullets, leaving Mildred to take the blame.

Mildred, having always protected Veda through a variety of tawdry affairs (including a quickie marriage, which Veda uses to extort $10,000 from her erstwhile husband) at first tries to protect Veda, but ultimately folds under police questioning, and inadvertently fingers Veda as the killer. True to form, Veda accepts this turn of events with singular self-possession, telling her mother passively 'I'll get along' as the police lead her away – and indeed, we never find out what happens to Veda, nor do we care. The film ends with Mildred and Bert broke but reunited in love, as they exit the police station at dawn with a group of scrubwomen in the foreground mopping down the halls of justice.

Many observers are fondest of Curtiz's romantic wartime drama *Casablanca* (1942), and consider it his finest film; as a conscientious studio craftsman, Curtiz tackled nearly everything from historical action pictures (*Captain Blood*, 1935; *The Adventures of Robin Hood*, 1938) to war films (*Dive Bomber*, 1941), horror films (*The Walking Dead*, 1936) and even musicals (*Yankee Doodle Dandy*, 1942, and Elvis Presley's *King Creole*, 1958). But Curtiz's true element was the world of noir, which reflected his own acerbic, cynical temperament.

Lewis Milestone's *The Strange Love of Martha Ivers* (1946) details how a childhood trauma (in this case, an accidental murder) can change the lives of three people irrevocably, binding them to each other for decades to come. Jacques Tourneur's superb *Out of the Past* (1947), one of the most fatalistic noirs, perfectly casts Robert Mitchum as drifter and small-time crook Jeff Bailey, who is sent by 'brains' racketeer Whit Sterling (Kirk Douglas) to retrieve his erstwhile girlfriend Kathie (Jane Greer), who has run away to Mexico with a bundle of Whit's money. Kathie is clearly up to absolutely no good, but Jeff falls in love with her anyway; as he tells her in one of the film's many memorable scenes, when she confesses her past sins in a torrent of remorse, nothing can alter his attraction to her. 'Baby, I don't care,' he says simply, thus sealing their fate: they are doomed lovers on the run. But when Jeff, tired of Kathie's endless double-crosses (and several needless murders), 'drops a dime' on her to the police as the couple attempt their final getaway in a stolen car, Kathie immediately reacts by shooting Jeff in the groin as they drive into the night. The car careens into a tree, killing them both.

Figure 1.3 Robert Mitchum, Jane Greer and Kirk Douglas in a tense moment
from Jacques Tourneur's *Out of the Past* (1947).

One of the most bizarre, brutal, and homoerotic films of the late 1940s
is Robert Wise's previously mentioned *Born to Kill*, a film that is miles away
in both soul and substance from the director's much better known *The
Sound of Music*. *Born to Kill* stars Lawrence Tierney as sociopathic killer
Sam Wild, who has such a hair-trigger finger that almost anything sets him
off into a homicidal mania. His sidekick, Marty Waterman, is played by the
omnipresent victim Elisha Cook, Jr, and the bond between the two men
seems closer than usual. In the first few minutes of the film, Sam becomes
enraged when he witnesses his girlfriend, Laurie Palmer (Isabel Jewell),
out with another man. In a jealous rage, he kills them both, and slips away
undetected. Marty, however, easily figures out that something is wrong
when Sam returns to their cheap rooming house in Reno, Nevada, and with
very little effort, Sam admits to the murders. 'Sam, Sam,' Marty remon-
strates, 'you can't just go around knockin' off people whenever you feel like
it! It ain't feasible.' But Sam is unmoved, and Marty loans him some money
to skip town until the heat dies down.

But on a train to San Francisco, Sam meets Helen Trent (Claire Trevor),
who, in a twist of fate, discovered the bodies of Laurie Palmer and her com-

panion the night before, but failed to report it to the police, so as not to get involved. Unaware that Sam is the murderer, Helen joins Sam in an unholy alliance, hoping to swindle Helen's adoptive sister, Georgia Staples (Audrey Long), a wealthy newspaper heiress, out of millions of dollars. While Helen is nominally engaged to the mild-mannered Fred Grover (Philip Terry), a wealthy steel heir, Helen can't keep her hands or her mind off Sam, attracted to his violent animal magnetism.

Helen is shocked when Sam starts dating Georgia, who also finds him attractive, and after a whirlwind courtship, the two are married, but Helen still lusts after Sam. Even though he is married to Georgia, Sam still wants to see Helen on the side, and when he mistakenly thinks that his pal Marty is having an affair with Helen, Sam lures Marty to an isolated stretch of beach and kills him with an ice pick. With Marty no longer around to calm him down, Sam's unreasoning rages and jealousies increase in intensity, along with his megalomania, and soon he is demanding to run one of Georgia's newspapers as editor-in-chief, although he has no experience in journalism whatsoever. Still smitten with Sam despite Marty's murder, Helen makes one last play for his affections. Rebuffed, she tells a disbelieving Georgia that Sam is a thief and a murderer, has only married her for her money, and is really still in love with Helen. Sam barges in, discovers Helen's double-cross, and instinctively pulls out his gun to kill Georgia. But the police, alerted by Helen, intervene, and Sam shoots Helen, killing her. The police then cut down Sam in a hail of bullets.

This remarkably downbeat and depressing film is perhaps the most nihilistic film of the era. None of the characters in the film inspires even a vestige of sympathy; Tierney, in real life, as on the screen, a taciturn tough guy and chronic alcoholic, stalks though the film like an errant angel of death, ready to strike at whim. Helen is a cold-blooded sensation seeker, without morals or scruples. Marty is what Elisha Cook, Jr's characters always are; the ultimate patsy.

Cook and Tierney's symbiotic relationship and physical closeness has a strong homosexual edge to it, as Marty clearly worships Sam, despite his unpredictable brutality. Georgia and Fred, the two most 'normal' people in the film, are insulated by their wealth from the realities of the world, and seem remote and distant, devoid of passion. This leaves only Laurie Palmer, whose death in the opening reel of the film underscores her victimhood; her death sets the plot in motion, with Sam's precipitous flight to San Francisco, and thus her death hangs over the entire film – as does the investigation of her murder by a corrupt detective, Arnold Arnett (the hefty screen villain Walter Slezak), who has been following Sam's trail from Reno. Complex, menacing, possessing not an ounce of humanity or

Figure 1.4 Joseph Calleia kneels next to the body of George Macready, as Stephen Geray, Glenn Ford and Rita Hayworth look on in Charles Vidor's *Gilda* (1946).

compassion, *Born to Kill* is one of the most unrelenting film noirs in existence, and one of the darkest. By contrast, Robert Mitchum in *Out of the Past* seems almost a decent fellow, betrayed by fate and circumstance. Tierney, with his real-life edge of sadism and truculence, makes *Born to Kill* a distinctly disturbing film, a true talisman of the late postwar era.

Nicholas Ray, best remembered for his teen noir *Rebel Without a Cause* (1955) which gave James Dean his most iconic role, also apprenticed in noirs with the desperately poignant *They Live By Night* (1948). This depicts the flight from the law of two young people, Cathy 'Keechie' Mobley (Cathy O'Donnell) and Arthur 'Bowie' Bowers (Farley Granger), who, thrown together by circumstance, forge an unlikely alliance on the run from the authorities. As the film's tag line proclaimed, 'Cops or no cops, I'm going through!' as if sheer willpower were enough to compensate for the stacked deck that inevitably humbles all noir protagonists. Like Bart Tare (John Dall) and Annie Laurie Starr (Peggy Cummins) in Joseph H. Lewis's masterful *Gun Crazy* (aka *Deadly Is the Female*, 1950), two violence-addicted misfits who reject conventional society for a life of crime, supporting themselves with a string of strong-arm robberies as they drift across the United States, 'Keechie' and 'Bowie' are doomed from the first frame of the film onwards. No one escapes from the true noir world; that would be too easy. But while the Production Code in the 1940s always extracted some sort of retribution for deviant, antisocial behavior, by the 1960s, noir protagonists, such as Lee Marvin's Walker in John Boorman's *Point Blank* (1967), were literally getting away with murder, and the fabric of society was frayed almost beyond recognition, as we'll see later.

Charles Vidor's *Gilda* (1946) is, of course, one of the key postwar noirs, a romantic death triangle between Gilda (Rita Hayworth), a nightclub singer with a shady past; Johnny Farrell (Glenn Ford), another of noir's aimless drifters who lucks his way into a job as manager of a Buenos Aires casino; and Ballin Mundson (George Macready), the ruthless, cold casino proprietor who takes Johnny in, and then competes with him for Gilda's affections. All the while detective Maurice Obregon (Joseph Calleia) and washroom attendant Uncle Pio (Stephen Geray) watch the interplay between Gilda, Johnny, and Ballin with bemused detachment. But as anyone who has seen the film knows, there is much more than that. For protection, Ballin carries an obviously phallic sword cane, which he refers to as 'my little friend,' and his relationship with Johnny is fraught with homo-erotic overtones.

For the first third of the film, the two men agree that whatever else might happen, there must be 'no women' in their lives to upset the delicate equilibrium of their gaming enterprises. When Gilda enters the film, it quickly becomes clear that she and Johnny had been romantically involved in the past, but Ballin seems unaware of this, or unwilling to admit it; catastrophe on every level almost immediately ensues. George Macready, as Ballin, is a glacial, impervious presence, often photographed in silhouette as a near shadow, shown in luxurious, feminine dressing gowns that reflect his moral laxity and indolent lifestyle. Shot in a brilliant, cold black and white, *Gilda* was a smash hit that shaped, for better or worse, the rest of Hayworth's career, and also stamped Macready as one of the screen's most hateful villains.

John Farrow's *The Big Clock* (1945) is another stylish noir thriller with distinctly homoerotic overtones, in which George Macready once again plays a principal role as Steve Hagen, confidant and assistant to megalomaniacal publisher Earl Janoth (a suitably over-the-top Charles Laughton), who is trying to pin a murder that he committed on one of his employees, George Stroud (Ray Milland). The victim in question is Janoth's mistress Pauline Delos (Rita Johnson), whom the publisher has killed in a jealous rage; but Stroud is made to order to step off for the crime, so Janoth conducts an elaborate campaign to frame him.

The film is full of memorable set pieces; Janoth threatening his staff to increase circulation or else lose their jobs at a tense board meeting conducted in a luxury penthouse; the murder itself, brought on by Janoth's insufferable ego when Pauline taunts him for his shortcomings as a lover; and finally Janoth's death, plunging to a well deserved doom at the bottom of his skyscraper's elevator shaft. Yet it is the small details that make *The Big Clock* so memorably sinister; Janoth's masseure and hit man Bill Womack (Harry Morgan) never says a word as he goes about his nefarious business, pummeling Janoth's massive body, and later eliminating or bribing Janoth's enemies; a throwaway scene in which Janoth docks a janitor's pay for leaving a light bulb on in a broom closet because 'it serves no apparent purpose'; and perhaps most remarkably, Janoth's confession to Steve Hagen shortly after he has murdered Pauline in Hagen's Manhattan penthouse. The dialogue is worth quoting at some length:

'Steve, I've just killed someone,' Janoth remarks languidly.

'Well, I must say she had it coming. She was a regular little comic,' Steve responds with false sympathy.

'How can you say that, Steve? She was the kindest, most generous woman I've ever known,' Janoth rejoins.

Hagen is momentarily astonished.

'Then why did you kill her?' he finally blurts out.

'I don't know, Steve, I just don't know,' Janoth wearily rejoins, thus neatly staging the central paradox of all characters who inhabit a noir universe.

Janoth is who he is; the ruthless, overweight, unattractive head of a gigantic news magazine empire (modeled, to some degree, on Henry Luce of *Time/Life* Incorporated) who will stop at nothing to expand his holdings, and reacts violently when anyone or anything opposes him. Janoth can't control his simultaneous power and impotence any more than he can stop himself from killing Pauline in a fit of pique. It's also natural for him to try to evade responsibility for his actions, to do anything to hold on to power, even as it inevitably slips away. The chilly camaraderie between Hagen and Janoth is really the center of *The Big Clock*'s amoral world, a world controlled by money, greed, power, and influence. Watching these two stunningly repellent figures plot to cover up the truth at the expense of an innocent man is what *The Big Clock* is really all about; leading man Ray Milland becomes a distant figure in our minds when confronted by the monstrous villainy of Janoth and Hagen.

Other classic noirs of the era, such as Robert Siodmak's *The Killers* (1946), Burt Lancaster's screen debut, John Cromwell's *Dead Reckoning* (1947), and Otto Preminger's *Whirlpool* (1949), all called into question the basic core values of the era. In *The Killers*, Lancaster's character, known only as Swede, waits in his shabby hotel room for two killers to gun him down in cold blood; he could run, but why bother? They'd only catch up with him somewhere else down the line. This sort of defiant fatalism was something new for the cinema of the period, a sense that there was a point where even bothering to continue to exist was more of a problem than it was worth. In *Whirlpool*, an unscrupulous psychiatrist (José Ferrer) hypnotizes the somnambulant Gene Tierney and frames her for a murder; Tierney's character doesn't know herself whether she's guilty or not. Did she do it, or didn't she? She can't be sure. *Dead Reckoning* offers us the fatalistic narrative of Humphrey Bogart caught up in a web of circumstances that he seems powerless to control, in stark contrast to his breezy self-assurance in Howard Hawk's *The Big Sleep* (1946) or John Huston's *The Maltese Falcon* (1941).

Richard Fleischer's paranoid police procedural *Follow Me Quietly* (1949) chronicles the brutal crimes of a serial killer known as the Judge. In one particularly unsettling scene, detectives chasing the Judge build a life-sized model of their quarry in the station house, clothing it with the same raincoat, shirt, pants, shoes, and hat the Judge has been seen in shortly after committing his crimes. Staring at the life-sized replica of the killer, they discuss the Judge's possible motivations for his crimes, methods of capturing him, and other essential details of their investigation; they leave the room to continue the chase.

But as the camera remains in the room after the detectives depart, we discover that the Judge himself has removed the mannequin, and taken its place, thereby gleaning useful information to keep himself one step ahead of the law, as he silently steals out of the room in pursuit of new victims. When the killer is finally apprehended, the Judge turns out to be not a monster, but rather an extremely ordinary, nondescript fellow, a mild-mannered Milquetoast who only becomes violent when it rains. Nothing about him is remarkable; indeed, it is his very 'ordinariness' which serves as his best defense.

Alfred Zeisler's no-budget Monogram film *Fear* (1946) is a modern retelling of Dostoyevsky's *Crime and Punishment*, as aspiring doctor Larry Crane (Peter Cookson) turns on his mentor, Professor Stanley (Francis Pierlot), when an anticipated scholarship fails to materialize, and kills him in a fit of rage, leaving numerous clues behind. Shortly thereafter, Larry's luck turns when one of his student articles is published in a prestigious medical journal, and he falls in love with a lovely young woman, Eileen (Anne Gwynne). But Larry's article, echoing Dostoyevsky's thesis that some men are above the law, convinces Captain Burke (Warren William) of the homicide squad that Larry may be the killer he is seeking.

As the noose tightens around Larry's neck in a series of hectic circumstances, he suddenly wakes up to discover that the entire episode has been a nightmare. Director Alfred Zeisler, yet another refugee of the Nazi regime, had a peculiar Hollywood career; working mainly for the minor studios, he produced a series of hallucinogenic, hypnotic narratives that brim with uncertainty and dread. The titles tell the whole story; in addition to *Fear*, he directed *Parole* and *Alimony* (both 1949), and the astounding *Enemy of Women* (aka *Dr Joseph Goebbels, the Life and Loves*, 1944), his personal attack on the head of the Nazi propaganda machine, with whom he had a number of unpleasant encounters before his forced departure from Germany.

Billy Wilder's brother, W. Lee Wilder, also specialized in vicious, uncompromising films, but unlike his more famous brother, he never graduated to the major studios, creating most of his work for independent, smaller studios, such as Republic Pictures. Wilder's *The Pretender* (1947), sumptuously photographed by the great John Alton on a nonexistent budget, is a crisply detailed examination of blackmail, deceit, and murder. It features noir fixture Albert Dekker as investment banker Kenneth Holden, a ruthless, charming sociopath and social climber, who steals money from one of his clients, Claire Worthington (Catherine Craig), and then proposes marriage to her, thinking himself irresistible. Needless to say, Holden's plan backfires in a series of increasingly convoluted episodes that drag him further and further down into an inescapable quagmire of violence and corruption.

Wilder savors all sixty-nine minutes of it, just as his more famous brother did, with his better known (and somewhat lengthier) films *Sunset Boulevard* (1950) and *The Big Carnival* (aka *Ace in the Hole*, 1951). W. Lee Wilder's films, including *The Glass Alibi* (1946), *The Vicious Circle* (aka *Woman in Brown*, 1948), *Once a Thief* (1950), *Three Steps North* (1951), *Killer From Space* (1954) and *The Man Without a Body* (1957, co-directed with Charles Saunders to fulfill English tax-incentive requirements), constitute a body of work so harrowing in its vision of the world that it's not surprising that few of W. Lee Wilder's films are available on DVD, and almost none are ever shown on TV.

Often, the plots of his films are preposterous; *The Man Without a Body*, for example, stars George Coulouris as unscrupulous Wall Street tycoon Karl Brussard, who revives the disembodied head of Nostradamus (Michael Golden) to get tips on the stock market; not surprisingly, there are unforeseen complications for all concerned. Even as the plot becomes more and more bizarre, Wilder never abandons the seriousness of his approach to the project, or betrays even a moment's hesitation, moving swiftly, even inexorably, from one scene to the next.

Sam Newfield is, in many respects, the ultimate noir director, not only for the films he directed, but also for the extremely impoverished, even desperate provenance of his work. He is also, in all probability, the most prolific auteur in American sound film history. The creator of more than 250 feature films, as well as numerous shorts and television series episodes, in a career that spanned four decades, from 1923 to 1958, Newfield directed across every conceivable genre, helming comedies, musicals, westerns, horror films, jungle pictures, crime dramas, and espionage thrillers, often on budgets of less than $20,000 per feature, and shooting schedules as short as three days.

But, as Martin Scorsese noted in a 1991 interview with critic Dennis Coleman, watching Newfield's work is difficult, because Newfield often seems absolutely detached from the images that appear on the screen, as if he is an observer rather than a participant: or as Scorsese put it, 'Newfield is hard, that's a hard one, you can't do too much of that.' Then, too, the conditions of extreme economy that Newfield labored under created a pressure-cooker environment in which the ultimate goal of all his films was simply to get them done on time and under budget. And if Newfield is the ultimate maudit director, his home studio, Producers Releasing Corporation, is arguably the ultimate hard luck studio, so deeply entrenched in the bottom rungs of the Hollywood studio system that there was never any hope that it would rise above its humble origins.

When PRC went out of business, the negatives for the entire PRC catalogue were sold to a television syndicator for a flat $1,750 each, and in the early days of the medium, when the majors shunned television as a threat to their hegemony, Newfield's films were ubiquitous. In time, the copyrights on all the PRC films lapsed when no one bothered to renew them, and the films entered the public domain, available for anyone to screen, copy, or sell to the public. With the advent of DVDs, nearly all of Newfield's work became available in five-dollar editions that flooded the market.

So, for better or worse, Newfield's work is everywhere. Perhaps surprisingly, many viewers have a great affection for Newfield's films precisely because of their compromised origins; films such as *Dead Men Walk* (1943) retain a certain sinister appeal in the grim certainty of their visual execution, while Newfield's many slapdash westerns are favored by aficionados of the genre for their utter disregard of narrative or character motivation; with Newfield, action always comes first.

Republic Pictures, on the other hand, was most famous for its Saturday morning serials, but also churned out a long series of sixty-minute programmers in a variety of genres. Among the most interesting, and certainly the most curious, of these brief films is Philip Ford's *The Mysterious Mr Valentine*. The first minutes of this brief film are so crammed with narrative coincidence as to almost defy description. While driving home on a lonely road late at night, a young woman, Janet Spencer (Linda Stirling), has an unexpected flat tire. Walking along the dimly lit road, Janet sights a chemical factory. Entering the building, she discovers research chemist John Armstrong (Tristram Coffin), and asks permission to use his telephone to call a garage. Unbeknownst to Janet, John Armstrong has just murdered his partner, and left the body in the back room. While Janet is on the phone trying to get help, Armstrong returns to the back room to discover that the body of his supposed victim has disappeared.

To relax his nerves, Armstrong suggests to Janet that they both have a drink. Moments later, Armstrong's wife and a police photographer break into the factory and photograph Janet and Armstrong in a seemingly compromising position. Janet flees, stealing Armstrong's wife's car. Driving away at high speed, Janet is blinded by the glare of oncoming headlights, and accidentally runs down a pedestrian. The driver of the other car emerges with an associate and offers to dispose of the body at the local hospital, telling Janet to go home and forget the whole thing. Frantic, Janet drives wildly through the streets in the stolen vehicle, sideswiping the car of private eye Steve Morgan (William Henry). Returning at last to her home, Janet discovers the first of a series of blackmail notes from a 'Mr Valentine,' demanding $25,000 for the return of her car, and for not implicating her in the hit and run fatality.

That's just the first six minutes of this fifty-six-minute wonder, which grows more complex with each passing second. In Janet's quest to extricate herself from the blackmail plot, she enlists the help of Steve Morgan, who has followed her home to collect on the damages to his car. However, Steve operates on the thinnest edge of the law, playing off the protagonists against each other in a series of jaw-dropping triple-crosses. These deceptions are all the more disturbing because of the breezy self-assurance with which Steve lies to each character to preserve his own interests. As Steve weaves his way through the increasingly Byzantine case, he repeatedly informs his prospective victims 'You know, I could use you . . . I mean, as a client.' At last, after numerous plot twists, insurance agent Sam Priestley (Kenne Duncan) is unmasked as the Mysterious Mr Valentine; the whole affair has been an elaborate insurance scam. In a final moment of what can only be described as heterotopic insanity, Janet agrees to marry Steve, despite the fact that he has been working against her interests (or, perhaps more accurately, only in his own interests) throughout the entire film.

Unlike PRC, the Republic lot occasionally served as a production facility for John Ford, Fritz Lang, and other 'A' list directors, but the bulk of its output consisted of Roy Rogers and Gene Autry westerns, the aforementioned children's serials, and a modest series of program pictures. Yet the superior production capabilities of Republic lent a sheen to even its most pedestrian work, while at the same time robbing its noir films of the true fatalism inherent in the genre.

Republic was even more famous for its serials, multi-episode chapter plays that ran for fifteen (and later, twelve) weeks on Saturday mornings at neighborhood theatres, offering a dystopian vision of a world of unremitting peril and violence, even though, in the final installment of each serial, the criminal mastermind behind each serial's particular disruptive project was summarily brought to justice. Spencer Bennet and Wallace Grissell's *Federal Operator 99* (1945) depicts the activities of smooth-talking master criminal Jim Belmont (George J. Lewis), who calms himself playing Chopin on his grand piano while planning a series of elaborate jewel heists.

In Spencer Bennet and Fred C. Brannon's *The Purple Monster Strikes* (1945), malevolent alien Roy Barcroft assumes the body and identity of eminent scientist Dr Cyrus Layton (James Craven) as part of his attempt to spearhead an invasion of the Earth from the planet Mars. William Witney and Fred Brannon's *The Crimson Ghost* (1946) chronicles the criminal career of its eponymous protagonist, who is (once again) a university professor, one Dr Parker (Joe Forte), who carries on a campaign of sabotage, murder, destruction, and violence behind the disguise of a particularly repellent skull mask and flowing crimson robes.

As with the other Republic films discussed here, mind control is once again a prominent theme. After capturing various members of the scientific community through the services of his henchman, the Crimson Ghost outfits them with slave collars that force his victims to commit whatever acts are deemed necessary to achieve the protagonist's aim of world domination: theft, murder, arson, whatever expediency requires. As Don Herzog notes, one 'can wear a mask of evil to disguise some other evil' (2006: 78). In short, you can't trust appearances, even malevolent ones.

But perhaps the most interesting aspect of serials is their structural nature. Each episode ends with a 'cliffhanger,' in which the life of the protagonist or one of his or her key associates lies in the balance, and only some last-minute interception can save them for imminent destruction. In each succeeding chapter, help inevitably arrives at the last possible second. The protagonists of these films thus live in an atmosphere of constant peril and paranoia, condemned by the circularity of events to repeat the same tasks, and run the same risks, within the confines of each film's narrative.

Dialogue is sparse and utilitarian; violence alone rules. Elaborate sets are built only to be destroyed, and force is always the first resort, not the last. Serials are compelling because they portray a world of constant danger, deception, and unrelenting action; the characters in a serial must keep constantly moving, like sharks, or risk extinction. The last serials appeared in 1956, as the format itself became an early victim of television, with its episodic half-hour programs that mimicked the continuity of the serials, with continuing characters and an overarching plot line.

Then, too, television in the 1950s was entirely free of charge, and commercials were less frequent. Serial audiences now stayed home to watch such serial-like dystopian children's programs as *Captain Midnight* and *Ramar of the Jungle* (see Dixon 2005: 1–66 for more on these early teleseries). The serial format had been around since the early days of silent films, in such epic chapter plays as Louis Feuillade's *Les Vampires* (1915–16), and continued through the sound era with several hundred offerings from not only Republic, but also Columbia Pictures and Universal Pictures, as well as numerous smaller companies. But although the serial format has vanished, the aura of menace, brutality, and deception that informed the creation of these films persists to the present day, particularly in the Star Wars and Indiana Jones films which are, in fact, much more physically ambitious 'serials' with commensurately larger budgets.

The central conceit of being unable to account for one's own actions informs numerous 1940s noirs, a period when psychoanalysis was just coming into vogue. Such films as Joseph H. Lewis's *So Dark the Night* (1946), in which French homicide detective Henri Cassin (Stephen Geray) is unaware that he is the murderer he seeks for a particularly vicious strangulation killing, speak to the essential mystery of the human psyche, capable of blocking itself off from interior knowledge that it finds disturbing or contradictory. Maxwell Shane's *Fear in the Night* (1947), Shane's *Nightmare* (1956; a remake of *Fear in the Night*), Harold Clurman's *Deadline at Dawn* (1946), Jack Hively's *Street of Chance* (1942), and Arthur Ripley's *The Chase* (1946), all derived from source material by Cornell Woolrich, explore similar themes of mistaken culpability and self-deception.

Edmund Goulding's *Nightmare Alley* (1947), a rare 'A' noir from 20th Century Fox starring Tyrone Power, presents Power as Stanton Carlisle, a sideshow barker with a gift of gab who bilks wealthy clients as a 'spiritualist,' with the help of an unscrupulous psychiatrist, Dr Lilith Ritter (Helen Walker). Budd Boetticher's *Behind Locked Doors* (1948) is just one of many films that treat mental hospitals as little better than fraudulent enterprises designed to bilk patients out of their life savings; *Behind Locked Doors* was later remade, after a fashion, by Samuel Fuller as *Shock Corridor* (1963), a

Figure 1.5 William Bendix, Hugh Beaumont, and Alan Ladd get a rocky
homecoming in George Marshall's *The Blue Dahlia* (1946).

late entry in the initial noir cycle. The public's distrust of conventional
authority figures (doctors, policemen, psychiatrists), coupled with a fear of
their own internal mental landscape, propelled the noir to national promi-
nence in the late 1940s, when returning soldiers, who had fought and killed
in battle, sought to readjust to a superficially calm but deeply repressive
postwar environment.

George Marshall's *The Blue Dahlia* (1946), another 'A' noir, tackles the
problem of 'socializing' returning veterans in a dark and sinister film, based
on an original screenplay by Raymond Chandler. In the film, returning soldiers Johnny Morrison (Alan Ladd), Buzz Wanchek (William Bendix) and
George Copeland (Hugh Beaumont) discover that Johnny's wife Helen
(Doris Downing) has been unfaithful to him during their enforced separa-
tion. When Helen is murdered shortly thereafter, suspicion falls on Johnny,
and then Buzz, who has come home from the war with a steel plate in his
head. Buzz is given to frequent headaches, bouts of amnesia, and violent,
erratic behavior, which George and Johnny try to cover up, as the trio
attempts to adjust to postwar society.

Chandler had originally intended Buzz to be, in fact, the murderer,
but the War Office intervened, protesting that the proposed narrative

conclusion unjustly maligned returning servicemen. The film's producers immediately capitulated, and Chandler was left with the task of finding a new killer, even as the film was being shot. At the last minute, Chandler decided to pin the murder on down-at-heel house detective 'Pop' Newell (Will Wright), seen skulking in the shadows throughout the film.

The revised ending was hastily photographed in a single office set; Chandler was so upset with the final result that he wrote the last scenes of the film literally in a drunken stupor (see Houseman 1976: 7–23). *The Blue Dahlia* projects a world of utter hopelessness, treachery, deceit, and betrayal, in which, once again, one of the protagonists cannot recall his whereabouts at the time of the murder. The nominal romance between Johnny and nightclub singer Joyce Harwood (Veronica Lake) that brackets the film is merely a cynical re-teaming of two of Paramount's biggest stars of the postwar era, fresh from director Frank Tuttle's surprise box-office hit *This Gun for Hire* (1942). The true center of *The Blue Dahlia* is a world of terminal despair.

In the paranoid world of postwar film noir, even innocence is no defense against the misguided judgments of society; indeed, the entire fabric of conventional justice has been called into question. Irving Pichel's *They Won't Believe Me* (1947), from a screenplay by noir novelist Jonathan Latimer, tells the story of ne'er-do-well Larry Ballentine (Robert Young), interestingly cast against type as an amoral social climber, who marries his wife Greta (Rita Johnson) solely for her wealth and position. Larry forthrightly admits that he has no love for Greta, and conducts a series of tawdry affairs right under her nose, despite his wife's continued protestations of love for him. Desperate to salvage their marriage, Greta relocates Larry to a brokerage firm in Los Angeles, where she purchases a partnership for him. But Larry immediately falls for his scheming secretary Verna Carlson (Susan Hayward), and the two impulsively run off to Reno for a quick divorce so Larry can marry Verna.

On the way to Reno, however, the couple are involved in a car crash, and Verna is killed. With the body burned beyond recognition in the flaming wreck, Larry passes off Verna's body as Greta's, and returns home to kill his wife for real, so he can inherit everything. But when he arrives at their ranch, Larry discovers that Greta has committed suicide, driven over the brink at last by his repeated infidelities. Fearful of being blamed for Greta's death, Larry hides Greta's body at the bottom of a deep canyon on their property, hoping to pass off her death as a riding accident. But his 'deception' is discovered, and Larry is put on trial for Greta's murder, a crime that he did not, in fact, commit.

The entire film is structured as a flashback, as Larry relates his story to a skeptical judge and jury from the witness box, and then disconsolately waits for the verdict. When the jury returns, Larry is convinced they have found him guilty of first-degree murder, and is shot dead by a guard while trying to jump from a courtroom window, essentially committing suicide before the verdict can be read. But against all odds, the jury has believed Larry's story, and acquitted him of Greta's murder. The last shot of the film is a close-up of the court clerk (Milton Parsons, who usually specialized in playing ghouls, undertakers, or police informants) reading the verdict: 'Not guilty.'

They Won't Believe Me's astoundingly bleak scenario created considerable controversy at the time of its initial release, and as Alain Silver and Elizabeth Ward note, 'contemporary reviews suggested that the popularity of Billy Wilder's adaptation of James M. Cain's *Double Indemnity* had had a deleterious influence upon American films, as illustrated by *They Won't Believe Me*' (1988: 286). Against such a backdrop of unrelenting fatalism and despair, there is no defense. One either capitulates, or is dragged under the wheels of a new social order in which everything and everyone is suspect.

Jack Bernhard's *Decoy* (1946) is an even more vicious and cynical film, which for some reason almost slipped between the cracks of film history. Produced by Monogram Pictures, the film is cheap in every respect, but is more than salvaged by the remarkable performance of British actress Jean Gillie as the psychopathic Margot Shelby. As the film's tag line promised, 'She Treats Men the Way They've Been Treating Women for Years!' The ultimate *femme de désastre*, Margot stops at nothing to retrieve $400,000 in stolen bank funds hidden by her former boyfriend, the gangster Frankie Olins (Robert Armstrong), who is sentenced to die in the gas chamber for the murder of a policeman.

Olins, fearing a double-cross, refuses to tell Margot where the money is hidden, so Margot concocts an elaborate plan to revive Olins after his execution with the aid of the crooked doctor, Lloyd Craig (Herbert Rudley). When Olins is successfully revived, Margot systematically murders all of her accomplices as she races to find the missing loot, including the hapless Jim Vincent (Edward Norris), whom Margot runs over with her car to obtain Vincent's section of the treasure map. During her search for the treasure, Margot is shadowed by Sergeant Joe Portugal (Sheldon Leonard, who usually played criminals, but is entirely at home here in a world that is absolutely corrupt, as a strong-arm cop who doesn't know when to quit).

Appropriately enough, Olins's 'treasure,' once located, is utterly worthless. It contains a single dollar bill and a note saying that Olins has left 'the rest of the money to the worms' (as cited in Silver and Ward 1992: 87). The decay and corruption of *Decoy* is evident from the first shot of the film, a close-up 'of hands being washed in a filthy service station sink . . . and then a tilt-up to a fragmented mirror that reveals the disheveled face of Dr Lloyd Craig, [thus setting] the tone for the entire film' (Silver and Ward 1992: 87). Almost never shown, even on television, but recently released on DVD as the result of efforts by the Los Angeles Cinematheque, *Decoy* is one of the key noir films of the late 1940s, along with *Detour*, *They Won't Believe Me*, and *The Blue Dahlia*.

Anthony Mann, who labored as a director for PRC, Republic, and Eagle Lion on such bizarre 'B' noirs as the hallucinatory *Strange Impersonation* (1946), *Railroaded* (1947), *T-Men* (1948), and *The Great Flamarion* (1945), created one of his most enduring visions of urban hell in *Raw Deal*. This featured second-string leading man Dennis O'Keefe as Joe Sullivan, a gangster whose plans for revenge against his double-crossing associates are complicated when he falls in love with Ann Martin (Marsha Hunt), and inducts her into his world of violence and mayhem.

Mann's signature Dutch angle shots, deep focus compositions, and stark lighting, masterfully executed by John Alton – perhaps the most accomplished noir cameraman in noir history – create a claustrophobic world of betrayal and homoerotic sadism, as in the scene where heavy Rick Coyle (Raymond Burr) tortures Joe with a lighted match to demonstrate his hold over his criminal associates. Sordid, violent, and unremittingly nihilistic, *Raw Deal* consolidated Mann's reputation as a director of hard-boiled offbeat films, and paved the way to his later career as the director of such noirish epics as *The Fall of the Roman Empire* (1964), an interesting conflation of ancient history and stylishly choreographed brutality. Clearly, for Mann, a house is never a home; it's just a place to stop and rest awhile, before moving on with one's inexorable journey.

The postwar bubble was multifaceted; inflation was spiraling out of control, society was in flux, but at the same time there was an enormous outpouring of activity in Hollywood, in the years just before television became a serious threat, as the majors and the minors competed to produce enough films to fill the nation's burgeoning movie palaces. Unlike today, where people go to the movies to see a specific film, postwar audiences went to the movies each week to sample whatever might be playing; this week a romance, next comedy, then a melodrama, or a western, or a crime thriller.

Yet unlike the 1934–40 era, and even the 1941–5 period, in which most American films were either escapist (hence the use of Abbott and Costello, as well as the numerous wartime musicals) or overtly patriotic (Ray

Enright's *Gung Ho* (1943) is an excellent example of this, chronicling the exploits of a team of American guerrilla fighters who volunteer for a nearly suicidal mission against Japanese forces in the South Pacific), the films of 1945 to the early 1950s, no matter what their genre, are in many instances shot through with a sense of despair and longing, yearning for a time past when social issues were less complex.

Who was right, who was wrong; what were 'right' and 'wrong,' anyway? Wasn't almost anything justifiable in a world that had newly experienced the horrors of the German death camps, Hiroshima and Nagasaki, and the deaths of millions of people, both soldiers and noncombatants, in the greatest global upheaval in modern history? Peace had come, but at what price? Could we be sure of anything, anymore?

As veterans painfully reintegrated themselves into postwar society, cracks were starting to show. Mothers weren't always going to be there for their children; during the war, they might have been doing defense plant work, but now, with a new sense of freedom (and in many cases, a new career), the time of sacrifice was over; it was time to have fun. Children seemed less obedient, more apt to question authority; businesses became more stripped down and predatory, in a climate that seemed more competitive by the day.

What would the future bring? One thing seemed certain; there was no possibility of returning to the past. The future had promise, perhaps, but it also held danger and uncertainty. Out with the old, in with the new; but what was the 'new'? As rhythm and blues began to turn into rock and roll, and the big bands of the 1940s faded into memory, it seemed as if one had to strive continually against the tide of change just to keep up. Fortunes were being made, new technologies were being developed, and an entire new America came into being.

Television would be, perhaps, the most important harbinger of social change, as the community fractured into isolated family units, each with its own glowing electronic hearth, forsaking the social experience of 'going out to the movies' as a group. People began to look inward, and placed increased importance on material possessions; after all, the war was won. Why not indulge yourself? It was nothing less than an entirely new way of looking at the world, an atmosphere of constant unease and dread brought on by the threat of nuclear weapons and the internal danger of the supposed Communist conspiracy at home.

Social engineering films, popular in classrooms since the 1920s, began to aggressively model behavior for teens and young couples, teaching them rules to live by – codes of etiquette and public presentation, regulations and rules that had to be obeyed according to gender, class, and economic status. In all of these films, there was an emphasis on preserving the status quo, of finding some sort of stability for the family as a social unit in a new and transformed America. But these 'guidance' films really represented an attempt to impose the societal norms of the past on the constantly changing landscape of the uncertain present. There was no solid ground anymore, no small-town America to return to. The postwar era marked the definitive turning point for American society in the twentieth century; the war was over, but so was the dream of the past.

CHAPTER 2

The Postwar Bubble

When noir came along, it changed everything. Women were among those who eagerly embraced the new world of noir, having been cut out of the film industry since the 1920s, and none did it with more style and verve than Ida Lupino. An actress since the 1930s, she had always wanted to work behind the camera to tell the stories that simply weren't being shown on the screen; in 1949, she got her first chance to direct. Significantly, Lupino got her chance to direct *Not Wanted*, a story of children born out of wedlock, only when the initial director of the film, Elmer Clifton, suffered a heart attack after the start of shooting, and Lupino was pressed into service. Lupino took over the production, delivered it on time and under budget, and thus began a series of feminist noirs that constitute a remarkable body of work, particular given the repressive tenor of the times.

Although there had been numerous women directors working in Los Angeles in the 1920s and 1930s, including Lois Weber, Ida May Park, Ruth Stonehouse, Cleo Madison, Dorothy Arzner and a number of others, by 1943 women had effectively been dismissed from the director's chair. Dorothy Arzner was the only woman director working in the Hollywood film industry in the early 1940s; her last film, *First Comes Courage* (1943), was a powerfully feminist production starring Merle Oberon as a Norwegian freedom fighter, working undercover. The film retains Arzner's individual stamp, although Columbia took the film out of her hands as the end of production neared, and it was completed by noir director Charles Vidor, who in just a few years would have his biggest hit with the dark and brooding *Gilda* (1946).

After *First Comes Courage*, Columbia terminated Arzner's contract, and from 1943 to 1949, there was not a single film directed by a woman made in Hollywood. Lupino was angered by this blatantly unfair situation, and she set about putting her vision on the screen with typically unwavering energy. *Not Wanted* was made for the relatively small company Eagle-Lion, rather than Warner Brothers, the studio that most often employed Lupino's skills as an actress in the 1940s. At Warners, Lupino had learned from noir masters Raoul Walsh, William Wellman, and other gifted auteurs of the Hollywood system. Now she got a chance to do it on her own, and made it work. 'Believe me, I've fought to produce and direct my own pictures . . . [I] always nursed a desire to direct pictures' she told Robert Ellis in a 1950 interview (Ellis 1950: 48). Clearly, Lupino's films formed a personal statement for her.

Lupino went on to direct *Never Fear* (1950), in which a young woman battles polio; *The Outrage* (1950), the first serious film about rape told from a feminist viewpoint; *Hard, Fast and Beautiful* (1951), in which Claire Trevor ruthlessly pushes her daughter to superstardom on the professional tennis circuit; *The Hitch-Hiker* (1953), a tense examination of machismo in the Arizona desert; and *The Bigamist* (1953), a noirish vision of family life which is surprisingly sympathetic to its protagonist/malefactor. Lupino's films are very much a product of her personal vision, and remain as resonant today as they were when first produced; perhaps even more so, inasmuch as they represent the sole voice of feminist consciousness in 1950s Hollywood, and tell us much about the prejudices and mores of that repressive era in American history.

The image of home and hearth was a lie from the start. Traditional romance films end with the ideal heterotopic couple living 'happily ever after'; family noir films show the viewer the real 'ever after.' Frank Capra's sentimental Christmas film *It's a Wonderful Life* (1946) captures our attention most during the scenes of Bedford Falls in social collapse, as the result of George Bailey's attempted suicide. It seems that the structure of small-town America needs constant verification in order to survive; pull out the peg, and the entire edifice collapses. In Edgar G. Ulmer's *Strange Illusion* (1946, also known as *Out of the Night*), Paul Cartwright (Jimmy Lydon), the wealthy son of an important California family, is haunted by a dream that an impostor has replaced his deceased father, Lieutenant Governor Albert Cartwright, in his mother's affections. In a modern-day variation on *Hamlet*, the dream intimates that Paul's father has been murdered, and that Paul must avenge his death.

The killer is the suave Brett Curtis (Warren William, in one of his last roles), a psychopathic sex killer who courts Paul's mother, Virginia (Sally Eilers), with a view towards marriage, and eventual control of the estate. Ostensibly a friend of the sinister Professor Muhlbach (Charles Arnt), Curtis is actually Claude Barrington, a criminal well known to Paul's late father as an exceptionally clever and dangerous man. Everyone seems fooled by Brett Curtis's masquerade, especially Paul's sister Dorothy

(Jayne Hazard), and Paul's only ally is his friend Dr Vincent (Regis Toomey), the family's physician.

Paul's father communicates from beyond the grave through a series of letters written before his death, delivered to Paul on a regular basis, warning him of the potential danger to Paul's mother and sister. Only at the end of the film, when Brett tries to rape Paul's sister, Dorothy, is the killer's real nature unmasked, and the sanctity of the home preserved. *Strange Illusion* was made for Producers Releasing Corporation in a mere six days on a budget of less than $40,000, beginning production on 10 October 1944, and ending on 16 October (Silver and Ward 1992: 266). Despite the film's tight budget and schedule, Ulmer brings both grace and style to *Strange Illusion*'s complex narrative, giving Paul Cartwright's privileged world a genuine sense of substance and splendor.

Lewis Milestone's *The Strange Love of Martha Ivers* (1949), on the other hand, is an 'A' noir that documents Martha Ivers's (Barbara Stanwyck) tyrannical control of an entire Midwestern town, through the local factory that she inherited as a child. Like Paul Cartwright, Martha is a child of wealth and power, but in Milestone's film, Martha's hold on those around her has corrupted her completely; Martha believes that her money can buy her anything, whether it be the love of old flame Sam Masterson (Van Heflin), who drifts into town on a whim, or her putative husband, the weak and ineffectual district attorney Walter O'Neil (Kirk Douglas), whom Martha despises. When Masterson's old affections for Martha are aroused, Martha's husband is understandably annoyed, and attempts to have Masterson driven out of town through the machinations of femme fatale Toni Marachek (Lizabeth Scott).

Masterson, however, realizes that what is really holding Martha and Walter O'Neil together is a shared secret of murder – the true source of Martha's vast inheritance. In the film's harrowing conclusion, both Martha and Walter, fearing exposure, kill themselves, leaving Sam and Toni to flee Iverstown without a backward glance. Money, power, influence – everything has a price, and Martha's life has been a charade that she and her husband can no longer maintain. Behind the surface, all is rotten. The sleekness of Milestone's mise-en-scène, coupled with the dark interiors of Martha's palatial yet claustrophobic mansion, do nothing to persuade us that Martha has made a good bargain in trading murder for instant wealth. What is repressed will inevitably be exposed in a rupture of violence; in this case, violence that destroys Martha's unstable, artificial domestic milieu.

In such a world, someone has to pick up the pieces, and do the dirty work that no one else wants to attend to. Richard Fleischer's *Bodyguard* (1948), from an original story co-written by Robert Altman (later to become a major director in his own right), Harry Essex, George W. George and Fred Niblo, Jr, presents Lawrence Tierney as Mike Carter, a brutal cop, suspended from the police force for his strong-arm tactics. Hired as a bodyguard to a rich woman who owns a meat-packing plant, Tierney soon discovers he's being framed for murder.

Pushing his way through the brief sixty-two minutes of *Bodyguard* with violent assurance, Carter has to unmask the real killer in a world where no one can be trusted, and all appearances are merely that – surface impressions, without any real depth or veracity. Contemptuous of authority ('One side, Dracula,' he barks at an astonished butler, who tries to block Carter's entry into a particularly palatial estate), Carter regards the world around him with perpetual, justified suspicion. At the film's end, Carter discovers that the murder he must solve merely functioned to cover up another crime; the owners of the meat-packing plant are spiking their beef with salt water to increase the weight. Thus corporate greed becomes murder, and only Carter's lack of faith in humanity prevents him from becoming the fall guy.

Indeed, Reginald LeBorg's *Fall Guy* (1947) is emblematic of one of the central concerns of the noir: misplaced blame. In this brief sixty-four-minute programmer, a young man, Tom Cochrane (Clifford Penn), is arrested for murder solely on circumstantial evidence. The victim, a young woman, has been brutally stabbed to death, but Tom has no memory of the evening of the murder, and thus is unable to defend himself. In a typically convoluted narrative, Tom discovers that he has been drugged and then framed for the murder; the real killer is revealed as a distinguished member of the community. Based on the short story 'Cocaine' by Cornell Woolrich, *Fall Guy* was shot in a mere six days on standing sets at Monogram Pictures, one of the most impoverished Hollywood studios. But although the technical execution of the film suffers from haste and lack of money, in many ways *Fall Guy* is the perfect noir; desperate, shabby, and unrelentingly bleak.

John Brahm's *Guest in the House* (1944) is another kind of noir, in which the corrosive force is not greed, or the lust for money and power, but rather madness, and possessive jealousy. As Evelyn Heath, Anne Baxter offers a performance of such exquisite treachery that it almost seems a rehearsal for her star turn as Eve Harrington in Joseph L. Mankiewicz's backstage drama *All About Eve* (1950), in which Eve successfully derails the career of aging star Margo Charming (Bette Davis), while all the time playing the role of the long-suffering supplicant. In *Guest in the House*, Evelyn Heath is brought to the seaside house of a rich family to recuperate after a nervous breakdown. Soon, she sets her sights on Douglas

Proctor (Ralph Bellamy), who is happily married to Ann (Ruth Warrick). But happiness is a relative word to Evelyn, who immediately begins an effective and insidious campaign to replace Ann in Douglas's affections, with apparent success.

As *Guest in the House* unfolds, Evelyn's malice and deceitfulness takes a decisive toll on the entire household, while Evelyn herself remains the serene center of the storm she has created. The film's tag line neatly summarizes the narrative's inexorable trajectory, 'No girl has ever been called more names! That's Evelyn . . . the guest . . . who manages to throw her pretty shadow around where any man near must see it – and when it comes to a man she grants no rights to anyone but herself!' (IMDB), and director John Brahm was certainly no stranger to this noirish psychological territory.

In fact, *Guest in the House*, while principally the work of Brahm, had uncredited directorial assists from two prominent noir auteurs, André De Toth and Lewis Milestone, indicating an equally troubled authority structure behind the camera, as well as in front of it. De Toth also wrote a good deal of the film's dialogue, although he received no credit for it, with the final screen credit going to Katherine Albert for the original story, Dale Eunson and Hagar Wilde for their stage play adaptation, and Ketti Frings, who adapted the play for the screen. In many ways, *Guest in the House* betrays its theatrical origins, and Evelyn's scheming is transparently on view almost from the film's outset.

In her portrayal of Evelyn, Baxter touches on a genuine vein of uncertainty and instability in her performance. As in *The Strange Love of Martha Ivers* and *House of Strangers*, the Proctor family in *Guest in the House* is no match for the forces that seek to destroy the domestic tranquility of their genteel, well-appointed home. Werner Janssen's appropriately ominous music, coupled with Lee Garmes's moody cinematography and Nicolai Remisoff's baroque production design, combine to create the vision of the summer house by the sea as the ineluctable domain of madness; a home waiting to be torn asunder by Evelyn's invading intellect.

In many ways, *Guest in the House* can be seen as a parable of the last days of World War II, when social changes were threatening the stability of the traditional family unit. As with many of his other films, Brahm was ahead of his time with this little known work, which nevertheless reminds us that once invited, a guest may easily overstay her or his welcome, with disastrous results. At the same time, *Guest in the House* can be seen as a confirmation of the isolationist doctrine that preceded World War II: or, whatever is happening in Europe is none of our affair; let's keep this war out at all costs. But Evelyn is a force that cannot be denied, and until the

Figure 2.1 D. Ross Lederman (seated) directs Ralph Bellamy in a scene from one of his films from the 1930s.

Proctors finally realize that their home front is in danger of imminent collapse, Evelyn operates unchecked by normal social rules. Only a last-minute intervention stops Evelyn's relentless campaign of destruction, leaving the family members shaken, and arguably scarred for life. Will they be as welcoming to the next stranger who comes to call?

As with Sam Newfield at PRC, certain directors became closely associated with low-budget noir films, but one of the most overlooked and yet astonishingly prolific auteurs in the noir universe is the largely unheralded D. (David) Ross Lederman. Working at Warner Brothers in the 1940s, Lederman specialized in noir genre films, and created his films swiftly, compactly, and with authority. His films stand out because they all display Lederman's uniquely dystopian view of life, combined with a relentless, inexorable narrative drive; rapid, nearly Eisensteinian camera set-ups; and a willingness to alter or change the course of his character's destiny at a moment's notice. In his best films, Lederman not only bent the rules of genre cinema, he all but abolished them. The sheer intensity of Lederman's imagistic and editorial pacing, coupled with his encyclopedic knowledge of genre filmmaking, allowed him to transcend the conventions of the typical program film, no matter what the genre, and make it a personal statement, while still staying firmly within the prescribed schedule and budget.

Lederman's 1942 film noir *Escape from Crime* is surreal, violent, and hard to classify. In the film's first scene, Red O'Hara (Richard Travis) is stuck in prison for a crime he didn't commit, and despairs of ever getting out. In the next scene, one of his prison buddies rushes to tell Red that he's been paroled, effective immediately, for no apparent reason. Thirty seconds later, Red is driving away from the prison with his erstwhile criminal associate, Slim Dugan (Rex Williams), exulting in his newfound freedom. Not thirty seconds after that, Red is demanding that Slim 'hand over his rod,' so that Red can murder his wife, Molly O'Hara (Julie Bishop), for being unfaithful. 'I hope you know what you're doing,' Slim laconically intones, but of course, Red has no idea what he's doing; he's simply a pawn in the film's bizarre and often contradictory narrative, pursuing one objective in one shot, only to change his mind in the next.

Abruptly convinced of Molly's fidelity by the presence of a redheaded young boy whom Molly claims is his child, Red abandons his plans to murder her ('Gee, that's swell!' Slim comments, upon hearing of Red's change of heart), and decides to pursue a job as a newspaper cameraman. At this point, the film becomes a compressed remake of Lloyd Bacon's James Cagney vehicle, *Picture Snatcher* (1933), as Red claws his way to the top of the tabloid news photographer's trade.

Wherever Red goes, things happen. His first big break occurs when his former associates, including Slim, stick up a bank while Red is passing by, his Speed Graphic camera at the ready. Convincing Cornell (Frank Wilcox), the editor of a sleazy daily, to hire him despite his prison record on the strength of his exclusive photos of the hold-up, Red plunges into a maelstrom of pictorial violence. Planes crash at air shows, cars are wrecked in automobile races, fires consume entire tenement blocks, and Red is always on the scene, dutifully recording it all for posterity.

At length, however, the senior editor of the newspaper, Reardon (Charles Wilson) presents Red with an assignment that is too tough for even Red to consider; photographing the execution of Slim in the electric chair, for his part in the robbery that got Red his first break with the paper. Red is understandably reluctant to accept the assignment, which is in direct violation of prison rules, and will result in the revocation of his parole. But, as always, in D. Ross Lederman's world, money is the ultimate arbiter of all social intercourse, and Red agrees to clandestinely photograph the execution for a fee of $1,000. (The incident itself is based on the true-life story of the execution of Ruth Snyder, who was put to death in the electric chair for murder on 12 January 1928; *The New York Daily News* sent a photographer to cover the execution, and then ran the photo as a full-page spread on the front page of the morning editions, selling an extra 750,000 copies of the issue because of the grisly photograph.) Red arrives at the prison at the appointed hour, and cheerfully gives Slim a 'thumbs up' as he trudges to the chair, then snaps a picture of Slim's death, unobserved by the other reporters.

As in *The Picture Snatcher*, Red accidentally drops the camera on his way out of the prison, and is thus unmasked by his rival news hounds as a 'rogue photographer.' Though the other reporters give chase, Red eludes them, and successfully collects his bonus. However, as Red had predicted, his parole officer, Lt Biff Malone (Wade Boteler; Boteler was a fixture in numerous Lederman films) takes a dim view of Red's perfidy, and arranges to have him returned to prison as a parole violator.

Yet, as Ledermanian chance would have it, on the way back to the prison, Red and Biff stumble upon the hideout of Dude Merrill (Paul Fix), mastermind of the gang that pulled the fateful bank job. Convincing Biff to let him capture Dude and his associates, Red in a matter of seconds infiltrates Dude's gang, and in a remarkably violent machine gun battle in which half the city's police participate, brings Dude to justice, assures Biff's promotion to captaincy, captures another photographic 'exclusive' for his newspaper, and by the order of the governor, is issued a full pardon for any and all past criminal offenses.

One is astonished at the audacity of the film's mise-en-scène, which is simultaneously frenzied and improbable. Aside from the fact that Lederman's films for Warner Bros. in the 1940s were all constructed from recycled scripts, existing sets, contract players, and pre-existing music scores, the stark economy of Lederman's production methods placed him firmly under the radar of studio interference. If Lederman was directing a film, Warners could be assured that it would come in on time and probably under budget; why bother him, since he clearly knew exactly what he was doing? Thus, Lederman functioned virtually without studio interference at Warners during the early 1940s, even though Jack Warner had declared that the studio would no longer produce 'B' films after 4 October 1941.

Undeterred by this announcement, Lederman kept churning out program films until 1944, including the comedy *Passage From Hong Kong* (1941); the bizarre murder mystery *Shadow on the Stairs* (1941, co-directed with Lumsden Hare), in which the entire narrative and its protagonists are revealed to be the figments of a playwright's imagination in the last two minutes of the film; *Across the Sierras* (1941), a William 'Wild Bill' Elliot western Lederman made on loan-out to Columbia; the family drama *Father's Son* (1941), based on a story by *Penrod* author Booth Tarkington, featuring the reliable character actors John Litel and Frieda Inescourt; *Busses Roar* (1942), a violent action thriller involving Axis spies, and a bus rigged to explode, with passengers still inside, at a vital oilfield; *Bullet Scars* (1942), a typically vicious crime thriller with Howard Da Silva as Frank Dillon, a psychopathic gangster with a Napoleon complex; *I Was Framed* (1942), of which the title tells all (a reporter is framed by crooked politicians); *The Gorilla Man* (1942), a World War II espionage thriller with distinctly sadistic overtones, in which a group of Nazis pose as psychiatrists, tricking downed commando Captain Craig Killian (John Loder) into believing that he has become a dangerous psychopath; *Adventure in Iraq* (1943), perhaps Lederman's best known film, no doubt due to its title, and one of the few available on DVD, in which a group of British nationals crash-land in the Iraqi desert, and are captured by the smooth-talking sheik Ahmid Bel Nor (Paul Cavanagh), who intends to sacrifice them to appease his bloodthirsty, 'devil worshipping' constituents; and finally *The Last Ride* (1944), which was actually Warner's final program picture, in which wartime rubber shortages lead to the illicit manufacture of substandard automobile tires and, predictably for Lederman, violent death.

All of these films tell us much about 1940s American society at its most unvarnished; filled with fear, desperation, and a fatalistic view of both people and events not shared by Warners' glossier productions, Lederman's brief 1940s program films are precisely geared to their target audience, a wartime public weary of conflict, afraid of the disruptions in society that it caused, and deeply insecure about the future of the American political and social system.

Lederman had been like a mad alchemist in his final days at Warners, grafting together sections of screenplays from one film, and then another, incorporating stock footage with near-Vertovian abandon, shifting from comedy to tragedy in a matter of seconds, borrowing stock music scores from other Warner Brothers films to underscore his violent visuals, until his final, frenzied films for that studio became almost a genre unto themselves – the violent, chaotic, unmistakably singular works of a genre artist in overdrive.

Jean Renoir's American masterpiece, *Woman on the Beach* (1947), is easily the best Hollywood film by the resolutely humanist director of such classic films as *Rules of the Game* (1939) and *Boudu Saved From Drowning* (1932). When Renoir fled France with the advent of the Nazi onslaught, he initially landed at 20th Century Fox, where he directed the torrid melodrama *Swamp Water* (1941), shot on location in Georgia. The film failed to click at the box office, and Renoir left Fox for Universal, where he began work on a Deanna Durbin musical, but walked off the film after a few weeks, upset with Universal's factory production methods. The film was eventually released as *The Amazing Mrs Holiday* (1943), with writer/producer Bruce Manning taking sole directorial credit. Leaving Universal, Renoir landed at RKO, where he was able to direct the noirish French resistance drama *This Land Is Mine* (1943), starring Charles Laughton as a meek schoolmaster, though the film was marred by a stage-bound, Hollywood 'studio' look, in contrast to Renoir's best, more naturalistic films.

Renoir then left RKO, and made a brief propaganda short, *Salute to France* (1944), before creating *The Southerner* (1945) and *The Diary of a Chambermaid* (1946), both independent productions with modest budgets and shooting schedules. Renoir's American odyssey was coming to an end when he returned to RKO for his last Hollywood film, the brutally vicious *Woman on the Beach*, which effectively ended Renoir's ties with the American film industry.

Joan Bennett, then at the height of her box-office fame after her memorable role as the duplicitous prostitute Kitty Marsh in Fritz Lang's *Scarlet Street*, heard of Renoir's interest in making a film for RKO, and insisted that Renoir direct her new project, then titled *Desirable Woman*. However, as the film was being readied for production, RKO's production chief, the gifted Charles Koerner, died on 2 February 1946 of leukemia (Bergan 1992: 261), and Jack Gross took over as producer, much to Renoir's chagrin. Koerner, said Renoir, was 'an understanding man, a man who knew the film market, who understood the workings of it very well, but who allowed for experimentation just the same' (as quoted in Bergan 1992: 261). Gross was much less given to individual nuance in his films as producer, but nevertheless Renoir found that with Joan Bennett as his star, he could afford a relatively luxurious production schedule.

Still, the scenario and production of *Woman on the Beach* bothered Renoir, if only because it was unlike any other film he had ever attempted. As he noted at the time,

I wanted to try and tell a love story based purely on physical attraction, a story in which emotions played no part . . . In all my previous films I had tried to depict the bonds uniting the individual to his background . . . I had proclaimed the consoling truth that the world is one; and now I was embarked on a study of persons whose sole idea was to close the door on the absolutely concrete phenomenon which we call life. (as quoted in Bergan 1992: 261)

This, of course, is the very essence of noir, and whatever his misgivings, Renoir embraced this new emotional terrain with his customary skill and insight.

Woman on the Beach tells the tale of Tod Butler (Charles Bickford), an extremely successful American artist, whose career has been cut short by an accident, in which he was deprived of his eyesight. His wife, Peggy (Joan Bennett), loves and hates Tod in equal measure, but remains bound to him, because it was she who blinded Tod during a lovers' quarrel. The two live in a seaside cottage near a US Coast Guard base, in a state of perpetual disharmony; Tod keeps his paintings locked up in a closet as his only link to the past, while Peggy wants to sell the paintings and move to New York, seeking the fast life the two once shared when Tod could see. Into this uneasy marriage comes Lieutenant Scott Burnett (Robert Ryan), a young officer who has recently survived a torpedo attack, and is now recovering from his physical wounds, but is still mentally unbalanced. Peggy immediately seduces Scott, much to the displeasure of Scott's fiancée, Eve Geddes (Nan Leslie).

Scott becomes obsessed with 'freeing' Peggy from Tod, whom he believes is not really blind, but rather manipulating Peggy so that she will stay with him out of guilt. Scott creates a series of cruel tests for Tod, in one instance standing by while Tod walks off a cliff, in an attempt to prove his theory. Convinced at last that Tod really is blind, but unable to free himself from Peggy's grip, Scott battles with Tod for Peggy's affections, culminating in an astounding final scene, in which Tod sets his house and paintings on fire, in a desperate attempt to free himself of his past life. As the house explodes in flames, Tod renounces his past ways, and tells Peggy to go with Scott. But Peggy chooses to stay with Tod, who now intends to pursue a career as a writer; Scott returns to Eve, and domestic tranquility.

While the shooting of the film went smoothly, the release of *Woman on the Beach* was fraught with difficulties. The film was given a 'sneak preview' in Santa Barbara before a crowd of young students who greeted the film with derisive catcalls, and Renoir was forced by RKO to recut the film. Scenes with Joan Bennett were reshot, and the love scenes with Ryan and Bennett were also revised (Bergan 1992: 262). The final result pleased no one, and the film was released in May 1947 to 'general public indifference' (Bergan 1992: 262). Renoir, sensing that the political landscape in the United States was about to change for the worse, with the House Un-American Activities Committee hearings on the horizon, left Hollywood shortly thereafter; his next project would be *The River* (1951), a Technicolor feature shot entirely on location in India. From *The River*, Renoir returned to postwar France, making the gently elegiac *French Cancan* (1955) and other films before his final retirement from the director's chair. Summing up his Hollywood period, Renoir commented that 'Although I don't regret my American films, I know for a fact they don't even come close to any ideal I have for my work . . . they represent seven years of unrealized works and unrealized hopes. And seven years of deceptions too . . .' (as quoted in Bergan 1992: 264).

Even if that is so, *Woman on the Beach* is still a remarkable film, the only true noir that Renoir ever made, and one of the most economical and relentless examinations of a marriage in collapse ever filmed, along with Jean-Luc Godard's 1963 masterpiece *Le Mépris* (*Contempt*). As Tod Butler, Bickford gives the most nuanced performance of his career, at once tender and yet dangerous, while Robert Ryan brings an intensity to the role of Scott Burnett that is both haunting and achingly realistic. Joan Bennett's foredoomed femme fatale is essentially a reprise of her role in *Scarlet Street*, but in *Woman on the Beach*, she seems more tragic and human than in Lang's much colder moral universe. At seventy-one minutes, the film has little time to waste, and is harrowingly compact. Not available on DVD or VHS, or even in 16mm rental format, *Woman on the Beach* is Renoir's one true American masterpiece, into which he distilled all his disdain for the Hollywood studio system and American culture.

Sam Wood's *King's Row* is another matter altogether, although it, too, looks behind the scenes of domestic life and finds a great deal to abhor. The film began life as a wildly successful popular novel by Henry Bellamann, published in 1940, and soon the studios were engaged in a fierce battle for the rights to the book. But filming *King's Row* would be difficult. This muckraking novel of turn-of-the-century Americana featured insanity, murder, gratuitous amputations, homosexuality, premarital sex, suicide, and incest; not exactly what the Hays/Breen office had in mind when it instituted (and finally enforced) the Motion Picture Production Code in 1934. Warner Brothers finally secured the rights to Bellamann's novel, but then wondered how on earth they were going to adapt it to the screen. When he was originally assigned the project, associate producer Wolfgang Reinhardt wrote to Warner Brothers' production chief Hal Wallis in dismay on 3 July 1940 that

I prefer not to kid myself or you regarding the enormous difficulties that [a film version] of this best seller will undoubtedly offer . . . the hero finding out that his girl has been carrying on incestuous relations with her father, a sadistic doctor who amputates legs and disfigures people willfully, a host of moronic or otherwise mentally diseased characters, the background of a lunatic asylum, people dying from cancer, suicides – these are the principal elements of the story . . . in my opinion the making of a screenplay would amount to starting from scratch . . . (as quoted in Behlmer 1985: 135)

Indeed, Joseph Breen wrote to Jack Warner on 22 April 1941 that the entire undertaking of filming *King's Row* was inherently suspect. Noted Breen, in part,

before this picture will be approved under the provision of the Production Code, all illicit sex will have to be entirely removed; the characterization of Cassandra will have to be definitely changed; the mercy killing will have to be deleted . . . [and] the suggestion that Dr Gordon's nefarious practices are prompted by a kind of sadism will have to be completely removed from the story . . . to attempt to translate such a story to the screen, even though it be re-written to conform to the provisions of the Production Code, is, in our judgment, a very questionable undertaking from the standpoint of the good and welfare of the industry. (Behlmer 1985: 136–7)

Nevertheless, Warners pressed ahead, with significant changes in the novel's plot line, and much suggestion, rather than direct explication, of other narrative points in the original text. In *King's Row*, Parris Mitchell (Robert Cummings) is an idealistic young man, who is cared for by the kindly Madame von Eln (Maria Ouspenskaya), who studies to become a psychiatrist. His best friend, Drake McHugh (Ronald Reagan), is the town hellraiser, always in trouble of one sort of another, and a perennial ladies' man. Cassandra 'Cassie' Tower (Betty Field) is the daughter of Dr Alexander Q. Tower (Claude Rains), who serves as Parris's first teacher; Parris falls in love with Cassie, but before the relationship can progress, Cassie begins exhibiting symptoms of an inherited insanity from her mother. Parris and Cassie engage in unprotected premarital sex, Cassie becomes pregnant, and in a rage, Dr Tower kills both Cassie and himself. Most of this is suggested; as critic Tim Dirks notes, in the novel, Dr Tower's motivation was even more sinister.

In Bellamann's original text,

Cassie was afflicted with nymphomania, not insanity. Dr Tower's diary revealed that the warped doctor had eliminated his wife and then committed incest with his daughter in order to study its psychological effects. He then killed Cassie when she threatened to leave him and go to Parris. (Dirks)

As Breen made clear in the letter cited above, *King's Row*'s original source material would never have made it past the censor's office in 1942, so this, and other elements of the story, were significantly revised in Casey Robinson's still-daring screenplay. In *King's Row*'s other main narrative strand, Drake, who has been living handsomely from an inheritance, suddenly finds himself bankrupt, and involved with two women; Randy Monaghan (Ann Sheridan at her no-nonsense best), and Louise Gordon (Nancy Coleman), the daughter of Dr Henry Gordon (Charles Coburn), a sadistic local doctor who specializes in performing operations without anesthesia. Unfortunately for Drake, when he is injured in an accident at work, he is taken to Dr Gordon's for surgery. Knowing of Drake's relationship with his daughter Louise, Dr Gordon amputates both of Drake's legs as an act of revenge. After the operation, Drake looks down at his mutilated body and utters the film's most famous line, 'Where's the rest of me?,' which would eventually become the title of Ronald Reagan's 1965 autobiography.

Generally a competent but unmemorable actor, Reagan gives the performance of his career here, easily outshining the mannered Robert Cummings in what is ostensibly the film's leading role. Sam Wood's utilitarian direction concentrates on the performances of the actors, rather than on any visual impact the film might possess, but the film is given a paranoid, claustrophobic air by the alcoholic, gifted set designer William Cameron Menzies, who designed *Gone With the Wind*, and later directed and designed the paranoid science fiction classic *Invaders From Mars* (1953).

Wood, a lifelong Republican, can hardly have been in sympathy with the novel's intent; indeed, he kept falling behind in production because of a labored, slow pace, and seemed more interested in Robert Cummings's portrayal of Parris than any other element of the film. As production manager T. C. Wright noted in an internal office memo, *King's Row* completed shooting on 7 October 1941 (just months before the attack on Pearl Harbor, which would have probably shelved the production of *King's Row* completely), 'twenty-three days over schedule and very considerably over the [b]udget' (as quoted in Behlmer 1985: 141). The film was released to solid business and respectable reviews, but will probably never be embraced as an American classic; even watered down at Breen's behest, *King's Row* is a stinging indictment of American society.

Indeed, as a dystopian vision of the dark underside of Midwestern small-town life, *King's Row* has never been equaled. Gorgeously photographed by

Figure 2.2   Jeanne Crain and a contemplative Gene Tierney in John Stahl's
Leave Her to Heaven (1945).

James Wong Howe, with a sweepingly romantic score by Erich Wolfgang
Korngold, *King's Row* remains in the memory as a vision of puritan hell,
unrelieved by any ray of light. Parris, as a budding psychiatrist, offers Drake
words of consolation at the end of *King's Row* that are sufficient to bring
Drake out of his self-pity, and renew Drake's interest in life. But, even as
Parris recites the lines of the poem 'Invictus' to Drake in an attempt to make
him whole again, in spirit, if not in body, and Drake reunites with Randy to
plan their future together, *King's Row* remains an unstinting indictment of
the ignorance, insularity, and small-mindedness of Midwestern America, as
true today as when it was written and subsequently filmed.

Leave Her to Heaven has another distinction, as the first true
Technicolor noir. In this justly famous film, psychotically possessive Ellen
Berent (Gene Tierney) falls in love with novelist Richard Harland (Cornel
Wilde), even though she is engaged to attorney Russell Quinton (Vincent
Price). Spiriting Richard away to her lavish family ranch in the desert,
Ellen impulsively announces that they are betrothed. When Russell arrives,
Ellen coldly sends him away. After their marriage, Richard begins to notice
that Ellen is too attentive; fixing his breakfast, making his bed, watching
him type his new novel – never leaving him a moment's peace. Anyone who
intrudes on their relationship is ruthlessly eliminated.

When Richard's paralyzed brother Danny (Darryl Hickman) threatens to monopolize Richard's time and attention, Ellen lures Danny out into a deep lake and lets him drown. When she becomes pregnant, Ellen is repulsed by the idea that her unborn baby will soon have a claim on Richard's affections. Ellen throws herself down a flight of stairs, and successfully induces a miscarriage. When Richard finally realizes what a monster Ellen is, it is too late. Richard has fallen in love with Ruth Berent (Jeanne Crain), Ellen's cousin, as he has drifted away from Ellen. In response, Ellen commits suicide, knowing she can never regain Richard's love, but frames Ruth for her 'murder.' Only a last-minute courtroom maneuver by Richard keeps Ruth out of the gas chamber and, after a short stint in prison (for not reporting Ellen's infamous deeds to the authorities earlier), Richard and Ruth are reunited at his hunting lodge, Back of the Moon. The entire story is told in flashback, that time-honored noir structural tradition, by family friend Glen Robie (Ray Collins), who has witnessed the tragedy from first to last.

In contrast to most of the other films discussed in this volume, *Leave Her to Heaven* is shot in gorgeous Technicolor by the gifted Leon Shamroy, with a sumptuous and suitably ominous symphonic musical score by Alfred Newman. The sets, by Lyle Wheeler and Maurice Ransford, are worthy of a Douglas Sirk melodrama, which in many ways *Leave Her to Heaven* resembles; ornate, carefully color coordinated, and ostentatiously lavish. At a running time of 110 minutes, the film has a narrative sweep eschewed by most noirs, which are compactly structured, offering little time for reflection. In *Leave Her to Heaven*, based on Ben Ames Williams's wartime bestseller (the title itself is spoken by the ghost of Hamlet's father on the battlements in Shakespeare's *Hamlet*, in reference to Hamlet's adulterous mother), the audience is immersed in a world of unremitting luxury and visual splendor, and then brought up short by the viciousness of the film's narrative.

Perhaps the most shocking scene is Danny's death. With great cunning, Ellen has been taking Danny for therapeutic swimming lessons for several weeks, building up Danny's trust in her, as well as his confidence in himself as a recovering victim of paralysis. Danny bravely asserts that he can swim to shore, but Ellen, clad in appropriately dark sunglasses, knows that he has gone too far from the shore, and impassively watches him drown, as he pathetically screams for her assistance. The brutality and cruelty of this sequence – unaccompanied by any music – in such a bucolic setting is deeply distressing, and made even more disturbing by Ellen's 'desperate' attempts to rescue the drowning Danny, but only when she knows that he is beyond help.

Worse still, Ellen's pathology is no secret to her mother, Mary (Mary Philips), who tells Richard that 'there's nothing wrong with Ellen . . . it's just that she loves too much . . . perhaps that isn't good . . . it makes an outsider of everyone else . . . you must be patient with her . . . she loved her father too much' (as quoted in Renov 1991: 233), the father whom, we discover late in the film, Ellen drove to suicide with her unceasing demands for his attention, and her impossibly high expectations. As Ruth tells Ellen during a final, angry confrontation, 'With your love you wrecked your mother's life, with your love you pressed your father to death, with your love you've made a shadow out of Richard' (as quoted in Renov 1991: 233).

Yet what Ellen fears most is the loss of identity that her marriage will bring, a loss of self that matrimony anticipates in the very act of the wedding ceremony itself. Richard and Ellen's marriage is not real, can never be real, because Ellen, a product of postwar American culture, seeks a life for herself above all other considerations and refuses to be subsumed in any relationship. Yet unable to declare her true intentions because of the social conventions of the period, Ellen must lie continually about her relationships, about her actions, and, eventually, even about the manner of her death. As she commits suicide with a lethal dose of poison, Ellen leaves incriminating evidence to frame Ruth for the crime, so that Richard and Ruth will be prevented from marrying (and, the narrative implies, having children).

But nothing can quite prepare the viewer for the experience of watching John Brahm's *The Locket*, famous for its 'flashback within a flashback within a flashback' structure, perhaps the most convoluted narrative in the history of noir. The plot itself is relatively simple: Nancy (Laraine Day) is a kleptomaniac, driven to steal anything that strikes her fancy (the original title of the film was *What Nancy Wanted*). Nancy's compulsion springs from a childhood incident, in which she was given a locket as birthday gift, which was then taken away from her by the cruel Mrs Willis (Katherine Emery), her mother's employer. When the locket goes missing, Nancy is suspected of having stolen it to recover the trinket for herself. Although it is later discovered that the locket simply fell in the hem of a garment, Nancy is never truly exonerated. Now, twenty years later, Nancy is poised to marry John Willis (Gene Raymond), and thus regain admission to the household she was banished from as a child; Mrs Willis does not recognize Nancy, having only known her as a child (played by Sharyn Moffet).

Within this seemingly straightforward narrative, there are numerous obstacles. The film itself begins on the day of Nancy's wedding to John Willis. Just as the ceremony is about to begin, psychiatrist Dr Harry Blair (Brian Aherne) breaks in demanding to see John. Dr Blair, it turns out, was one of Nancy's former husbands; Blair knows that Nancy is insane, and pleads with Willis not to marry her. As Blair recounts the tale of his marriage with Nancy in a flashback voiceover, he unfolds the tale of another of Nancy's husbands, the late Norman Clyde (Robert Mitchum), a moody artist who ultimately committed suicide because of Nancy's compulsive thefts, and her participation in a murder. All this unfolds in reverse, back to Nancy's childhood and the incident with the locket, and then reverses to end in the present, where the still doubting John Willis, having heard Mr Blair's tale, confronts Nancy, who predictably denies everything.

Only Nancy's collapse at the altar, brought on by Mrs Willis's 're-gift' of the locket Nancy briefly had as a child, saves John Willis from a similar marital fate. As *The Locket* ends, Nancy is taken off to an asylum ostensibly for a cure, but the camera remains within the gloomy precincts of the Willis family's Fifth Avenue mansion. What has transpired has left a mark not only on Nancy, but on all who knew her, and even Dr Blair's supposed skill as a psychiatrist is useful only after the fact. For most of the film, Nancy's mania eludes detection, and everyone who discovers her secret is summarily destroyed. Thus, all surfaces are suspect, all appearances deceiving, and nothing is to be taken at face value, especially protestations of innocence.

Director John Brahm keeps a firm hand on the proceedings, and effectively stages *The Locket* so that most of it happens at night, on claustrophobic studio sets. Mitchum, a rising star at the time, is oddly convincing as Norman Clyde, a Bohemian artist with attitude to spare, and Nicholas Musuraca's moody lighting leaves the characters, and the viewer, in a state of continual confusion and suspense. Most intriguing, of course, is the triple-flashback structure of the film, which brings into question the reliability of the film's narrative. When Dr Blair bursts in on John Willis and begins his recital of Nancy's crimes, Blair's flashback contains Norman Clyde's reminiscences, which in turn contain Nancy's own memories of her childhood, as told to Norman, containing the incident of the locket.

Thus, we have only Nancy's word, through Norman, and then through Dr Blair, that any of this is really true, and yet we unquestionably believe in the veracity of all three statements. Why? The entire story is so fantastic that one can understand John Willis's lack of trust in Blair's accusations; Nancy seems like a 'nice girl.' The failed wedding that climaxes the film is proof enough of Nancy's affliction, but are all the details of her illness quite correct? For this, we have only the word of three narratives that enfold each other like Chinese boxes, refusing to give up their secrets, opening only when the proper pressure is applied to the correct location.

There are other noirish narratives of family rupture: in Douglas Sirk's *Shockproof* (1949), parolee Jenny Marsh (Patricia Knight) invades the house of her parole officer, Griff Marat (Cornel Wilde), with disastrous consequences; in Irving Reis's *All My Sons* (1948), based on Arthur Miller's stage play, Edward G. Robinson is the head of yet another dysfunctional post–World War II family, this time as a munitions manufacturer who allowed faulty airplane parts to be transported to the front lines of combat. As Joe Keller, Robinson is all bluster and bravado; when his crime is discovered, Keller frames his partner for the crime, so that his family can continue their complacent lives.

In all these films, the message is the same. The relationship you thought would last forever is doomed. The person you brought into your house as a guest seeks to destroy it, and you. Your friends don't believe you. The police don't believe you. You are powerless before the forces of fate, which have once again capriciously decided to deal you a new, much more unpleasant future from the bottom of the deck. The world of the postwar noir is the domestic sphere in peril, in collapse, existing outside the normative values of postwar society, values that are themselves constantly in a state of flux. The family unit is constantly celebrated in the dominant media as the ideal state of social existence, but is it, when so much is at risk, and so much is unexplained?

The sense of manipulation and despair prevalent in these noirs persists today, and will continue tomorrow, with the representational stakes raised with each succeeding generation. Cops become thieves, judges are corrupt, politicians take graft, lawyers militate against their clients, accountants embezzle, family friends desert you in time of need, husbands beat their wives, and wives retaliate by murdering their abusive spouses. Notch by notch, the family has become a new kind of hell, far removed from the ersatz world of *My Three Sons* and *Leave It to Beaver*, which was never real in the first place. No, say these films; leave it to heaven, and in the meantime, let us sort things out here on earth as best we can.

CHAPTER 3

1950s Death Trip

Film noir and its various iterations were certainly not confined to America. In the late 1950s and early 1960s, there was still a market, and a social need, for the British 'B' feature, whose birth had been brought about by the government-enforced Quota System. In 1956, Edward J. and Harry Lee Danziger opened their New Elstree Studios on Elstree Road, Elstree, Hertfordshire, which consisted of six sound stages dedicated to the production of low-budget films and teleseries (Warren 1995: 92). The budgets for these features were astonishingly low, running from £15,000 to £17,500 at the most (Pitt 1984: 15).

Typical of the Danzigers' films were such 'B' features as Frank Marshall's *Feet of Clay* (1960), Montgomery Tully's *Man Accused* (1959), Godfrey Grayson's *High Jump* (1958), Max Varnel's *Sentenced for Life* (1959), and Grayson's *The Spider's Web* (1960), *An Honourable Murder* (1960), and *Date at Midnight* (1959), to name just a few of the many feature films made at the studio between 1956 and December 1961, when New Elstree closed its doors for good.

Viewed today, the Danzigers' films offer a fascinating microcosm of British social values in the 1950s, as seen through the lens of American commercialism. Thus, the Danzigers' telefilms and modest program pictures can correctly be seen as early examples of inverse-colonialism in the production of imagistic commerce; the vision that Harry and Edward Danziger presented on the screen was simultaneously rooted in the British colonial past, and yet aware of the newly encroaching forces of change which were shortly to rip asunder the fabric of this inequitable system.

A typically intriguing project is *High Jump*, which stars Richard Wyler and Lisa Daniely in a tale of a circus acrobat who loses his nerve during a high-wire performance, and is subsequently reduced to being a TV repairman in a run-down shop in East London, while he attempts to assuage his pain with alcohol. The film opens with near-documentary footage of a series of grotesque clowns during a circus performance; the lighting is harsh and stunningly bright, making the working-class entertainment of the shabby circus seem simultaneously unappealing and garish. The film's main titles are slammed over this newsreel material seemingly without care or concern; as the clowns douse each other with water, or parade around the center of the one-ring 'big top' on stilts, the pageant we witness seems degrading and dehumanizing to both audience and performer. Once again, the reliable Jimmy Wilson serves as director of photography, with Brian Clemens and Eldon Howard providing the film's script, and Godfrey Grayson the direction.

As the opening credits fade out, the camera swings up to observe an aerial act in progress. All seems well, until one 'catcher' misses his connection, and his partner plunges to earth. Several spectators react with justifiable horror, but we are never shown the result of the accident. Instead, Grayson fades out on the scene, and then fades back into a publicity still of one of the aerialists, Bill Ryan (Richard Wyler), staring mockingly at the audience at the height of his fame as a circus performer.

The camera tracks back to reveal the alcoholic wreck of an apartment, with chairs overturned, cigarette butts overflowing in ashtrays, and the figure of Bill passed out on his bed in a stupor. At length, Bill rouses himself and reports to the TV shop where he now works; Kitty, a young secretary, hopes for a relationship with Bill, but Bill is almost immediately attracted to the dubious Jackie Field (Lisa Daniely), a customer whose television is always in need of repair. While Kitty (Leigh Madison) is presented as obedient, wholesome, blonde, and modestly dressed throughout the film, Jackie Field accessorizes her wardrobe with costume jewelry, a trench coat, perfume, and a dangerously ripe French accent.

As the film progresses, we realize that Jackie Field's trip to the repair shop had a hidden motive; aware of Bill Ryan's prowess as an aerialist, she wants to recruit him for a dangerous robbery that requires a 'high jump' between two buildings. The job goes awry, with predictably disastrous results, but Ryan manages to escape serious consequences by cooperating with the police in the aftermath of the abortive heist. *High Jump* presents the viewer with a world which is at once drab, rife with temptation, and hermetically sealed, as if offering no real escape to either its protagonists or its audience. Jackie Field's 'luxury flat' is nothing more than a trap for the unsuspecting Ryan; Kitty, the one sympathetic character in the film, toils thanklessly at her job in the TV repair shop in the midst of poverty and squalor.

The 'high jump' that Bill Ryan is being asked to make is in fact a leap from the seedy gentility of his dead-end existence into the realm of criminal wealth, but even this leap is an illusion. As Ryan discovers, the mastermind of the robbery is Jackie Field's putative lover; they intend to double-cross Ryan the moment that the loot is in their possession. Brutality in the film is rampant, both psychic and physical. Ryan callously stands up Kitty for numerous dates throughout the film, without any apology for his behavior; during the robbery itself, two guards are senselessly shot down for the pure thrill of killing. Everything about *High Jump* presents a world devoid of hope, the desire for ambition, or the possibility of advancement; indeed, the only aspect of the production which rings false is the obligatory happy ending, which, while meeting the demands of conventional narrative closure, undermines the noirish despair of the rest of the film.

Feet of Clay (1960), another Danziger second feature of the period, deals with the murder of a social worker known as 'the angel of the police courts,' whose activities are really a front for a group of recidivist criminals. Boasting a superb 'cool jazz' score by Bill Lesage, scripted by Mark Grantham, and shot by Jimmy Wilson, this brief but effective thriller was directed by Frank Marshall. As with *High Jump*, the stark sets and claustrophobic interiors add to the no-apologies intensity of the film, which effortlessly conveys the shabby gentility of the working-class milieu of the period. Angela Richmond, 'the angel of the police courts,' is found shot dead in an alleyway of a London slum as the film opens; the rest of the narrative unravels the circumstances of her existence.

Far from being a benefactor to newly paroled criminals, Angela in fact runs a 'hotel' whose sole purpose is to force the men and women put in her charge back into a life of crime. Angela Richmond's social status as a legitimate probation officer further adds to her veneer of respectability, but, as *Feet of Clay* makes abundantly clear, Angela Richmond and her associates are utterly unscrupulous in their exploitation of the unfortunate women and men put into her custody. The hotel itself is a drab, cheerless domain, whose staff enforce their regime with blunt displays of brute force. In this instance, it is not so much the narrative of the film that is of interest, but rather the situation into which *Feet of Clay*'s protagonists are placed. As the surface of Angela Richmond's respectable existence inexorably erodes before us, we see the vision of an empire in collapse, a system of government in which even legitimate authority has been compromised. *Feet of Clay*'s brief sixty-minute running time is admirably suited to the world the film depicts; indeed, one could barely stand to endure being trapped in Angela Richmond's 'hotel' much longer.

In another British independent studio, Diana Dors, then the reigning 'bad girl' of British cinema, memorably starred as a violent killer in J. Lee Thompson's modestly budgeted *Yield to the Night* (1956). Loosely based on the true story of Ruth Ellis, the last woman sent to the gallows in Britain for murder, on 13 July 1955, the film has an odd double resonance; Dors, who plays 'Mary Price Hilton,' the role similar to the true-life story of Ruth Ellis, once actually appeared in a film with Ellis, Frank Launder's *Lady Godiva Rides Again* (1951), in which Ellis played an unbilled bit part as a beauty pageant contestant. Now, five years later, Dors was starring as the murderous Ellis herself, in a suitably cheap and violent thriller. Ellis's story would be told again in Mike Newell's *Dance With a Stranger* (1985), but Dors, who embraced her noir celebrity with every fiber of her being, was far more convincing in Thompson's film than Miranda Richardson was in Newell's mannered retelling of Ellis's sordid life. As critic Dylan Cave notes,

> The film's greatest creative coup is the inspired casting of Mary Hilton. Despite good reviews in numerous supporting roles, Diana Dors was most famous for a sensational private life. Her image in the press as a worldly young blonde kept her in the public eye, but seriously limited any consideration of her acting ability. As Mary, Dors brought an expressive sexuality to the role, allowing us to believe her capacity for romantic adventure and passionate revenge. But beyond this, in the scenes in her prison cell, she revealed a truly compassionate understanding of her character.

In her uncompromising performance, Dors captures the essence of this misguided young woman, who guns down her rival for the affections of another man in broad daylight, and then waits dispassionately for the police to arrive, feeling fully justified in her actions. The film's mood is something like Robert Wise's *I Want To Live*, but Thompson's vision is far more harrowing. Wise left open the possibility of his protagonist's guilt; here, we know that Mary Hilton is guilty of the crime, and the only question is whether or not society will have any mercy on her. But the film is as much a class drama as it is a social justice tract, and there is no reprieve. Mary will pay for her crime with the her life, but the case raised such a row in Britain that the death penalty was abolished soon after; the impact of Thompson's film, and Dors's performance, thus extend far beyond the boundaries of the film itself.

British television in the 1950s also embraced a strong sense of noir in service to the fading Empire, which seemingly existed under the continual threat of annihilation from a variety of external forces. In 1958, Ralph Smart created a British teleseries, *H. G. Wells' The Invisible Man*, ostensibly based on the character created by Wells. But Smart's version had very little to do with the 1933 classic James Whale film from Universal, or even with any of its many sequels for that company. In direct contradiction to

Figure 3.1 A foreign minister consults with *The Invisible Man* in this
scene from the 1950s British teleseries.

the source material, the hero of Smart's series, Dr Peter Brady (whose
identity was never revealed by Smart as a publicity gimmick; the actor was
'voiced' by performer Tim Turner), lives in the lap of bourgeois luxury in
the English countryside near Elstree with his sister, Diane Wilson (Lisa
Daniely), and her daughter Sally (Deborah Watling). Unlike the protagonist of Wells's narrative, Brady becomes invisible by accident, while

working on an experiment into the qualities of refracted light on a guinea pig. For the most part, the 'invisibility' special effects are handled by wires holding various objects such as car keys, test tubes, guns, and the like; 'matte' photography is used very sparingly. Quite often, first-person camera work from Brady's point of view lends artificial presence to his 'invisible appearance' on screen; Brady's asynchronous 'voice' and his transparent 'look' thus replace any other personal physical characteristics.

In one of the most prescient and/or paranoid episodes of *H. G. Wells' The Invisible Man*, entitled 'The Big Plot,' parts to produce a nuclear bomb are discovered in the wreckage of an otherwise ordinary aircraft crash. Confronted with the evidence, Brady immediately leaps to the remarkably paranoid conclusion that an international gang of terrorists plans to plant nuclear devices in every major capital of the Western world, and extort vast sums of money from capitalist countries to underwrite the activities of the Soviet regime. Further, Brady theorizes that these activities are being carried out under cover of an international 'peace' organization.

As subsequent events will prove, his bizarre theory is correct on all counts; the narrative thus reads something like an updated version of Hitchcock's *Foreign Correspondent* (1940). Indeed, a newspaper article of the period ('TV Film "Could Cause Hatred,"' in the *Chronicle* [London] for 17 November 1959) noted that the series was seemingly designed to heighten international political paranoia. The Labour Peace Fellowship, an organization campaigning for world disarmament, noted that the plot lines in the series were 'calculated to foment hatred against Russia' and went on to call the series 'a danger to East-West relations' in general.

Producer Ralph Smart subsequently expanded upon this vision of colonial empire in his subsequent and even more successful series, *Danger Man* (aka *Secret Agent*, an espionage drama featuring Patrick McGoohan as John Drake), in much the same role (defender of the empire) as Peter Brady. *Danger Man* began as a series of thirty-nine half-hour shows, debuting on UK television on 11 September 1960. After a successful one-year run, the series was revamped into an hour-long show beginning in the United Kingdom on 13 October 1964. It was the hour-long series that was exported to the United States under the title *Secret Agent*.

Both *Invisible Man* and *Secret Agent* were unusually successful for British television productions, attracting network interest in the United States against competing Hollywood product. *H. G. Wells' The Invisible Man* ran for thirty-nine half hours on the CBS network from 4 November 1958 to 22 September 1960, as part of the prime-time evening block; *Secret Agent* ran for forty-five hour-long episodes in CBS prime time from 4 April 1965 to 10 September 1966. Both series have since been successfully

Figure 3.2 Patrick McGoohan in a noirish scene from the teleseries *Danger Man*, aka *Secret Agent*.

syndicated throughout the world. Thus, ostensibly disguised solely as entertainments, these two teleseries effectively promulgated the social aims of British society in the late 1950s and early to mid-1960s.

Interestingly, McGoohan himself followed up on the latter series with his own creation, *The Prisoner*, in which the character of John Drake from *Secret Agent* finds himself detained in a military compound called 'The Village,' as his superiors attempt to extract information from him, which Drake may or may not have passed to the Russians. This seventeen-hour series has become something of a cult favorite, owing in large measure to its aggressive op and pop art design strategies, its liberal use of 'Swinging

Figure 3.3 Tony Wright menaces Patricia Dainton in Montgomery Tully's *The House in Marsh Road* (1960).

London' iconography, and its elliptical, semi-Beckettian dialogue, which relies almost entirely upon puns, impersonations, and Pirandellian situations which are seemingly never resolved.

Other British production studios, such as Butcher's Film Service, also specialized in noir thrillers made for a modest price, such as Lance Comfort's *The Breaking Point* (aka *The Great Armored Car Swindle*, 1961), which chronicles the downward spiral of Eric Winlatter (Peter Reynolds), a young husband so deeply in debt to a group of nefarious gamblers that he hatches a plan to hijack the entire new currency supply for a foreign country – easier to do than one might suspect, given that his father is in the currency engraving and printing business. Shot in a matter of days on cramped sets, the film's inevitable air of doom is highlighted by the hermetically sealed atmosphere of the entire work; as in all true noirs, there is no escape.

Moving into the world of supernatural noir, Tully's *The House on Marsh Road* (aka *The Invisible Creature*, 1959) deals with a similarly unscrupulous young married man who, failing to make a living as a writer, drifts into a relationship with his tawdry blonde typist, Valerie Stockley (Sandra

Dorne), and determines to murder his too-trusting wife, Jean (Patricia Dainton), and thus inherit her property and not inconsiderable bank account. But the house Jean owns is protected by a poltergeist, whom the cleaning lady, Mrs O'Brien (Anita Sharp Bolster), calls 'Patrick,' and with each new attempt on Jean's life, 'Patrick' invisibly comes to her and prevents her from falling down an elevator shaft, or tumbling down a flight of stairs. Finally convinced that David means to kill her, Jean escapes to London, and the solace of a sympathetic male friend, Richard Foster (Derek Aylward). With the house all to himself, David invites Valerie over for an evening of illicit passion, but 'Patrick' sees to it that the lovers are trapped in the attic room, as a lightning storm outside sets fire to the house.

In the film's grim conclusion, Jean arrives back from London just in time to see her house burn to the ground, as her husband screams for help through the barred attic window. David and Valerie both perish in the blaze, and in the stern moral universe the film inhabits, their violent deaths are seen as entirely deserved. Jean, it is implied, will move on through life with her new love, Richard. But more distinctly American genre films were also taking on a noir edge, and nowhere was this made more manifest than in the violent and unrelenting westerns of the postwar era.

Westerns in the 1950s became more and more noirish in their construction; even amiable Roy Rogers's program films in the Cold War era were exceptionally violent for the normally easygoing genre star. Perhaps the most memorable noir western of the era was Anthony Mann's *Winchester '73* (1950), in which Jimmy Stewart obsessively trails his own brother, who has killed their father in cold blood years earlier. Gone are the drawling, stammering, endearing mannerisms that marked Stewart's earlier films; in their place, Stewart has been transformed into an implacable force of vengeance with a hair-trigger temper.

The presence of such noir veterans as Stephen McNally and Dan Duryea further strengthens the link to the world of noir, as does Mann's direction, which is brutal and economical. In the early days of his career, as we've seen, Mann was heavily immersed in the world of film noir, even creating a noir set during the French Revolution, *The Black Book* (aka *Reign of Terror*, 1949), featuring production design by William Cameron Menzies, and a grimly paranoid performance by Richard Basehart as the crazed Maximilien Robespierre. When Mann moved to westerns in the early 1950s, he began a string of fatalistic, violent films such as *Bend of the River* (1952), *The Naked Spur* (1953), *The Man From Laramie* (1955) and *Man of the West* (1958), definitively demonstrating that the concerns of noir easily translated into the domain of the western; hopelessness, a sense of rootless despair, and the overarching law of a cruel destiny.

Late in his career, Mann was transformed into a director of historical spectacle, such as *El Cid* (1961) and the sprawling epic *The Fall of the Roman Empire* (1964), which, along with Tinto Brass and Bob Guccione's much later, and far more violent, *Caligula* (1980), offers one of the most compelling visions of complete societal collapse ever committed to film – an empire imploding under its own weight in a maelstrom of greed, ambition, ruthlessness and treachery. No matter what the pictorial backdrop – the big city, the old west, or ancient Rome – Mann was a noirist at heart, in thrall to the inevitable and complicated corruptibility of the human psyche above all other considerations.

Budd Boetticher, another director with several effective noirs to his credit, including *The Missing Juror* and *One Mysterious Night* (both 1944), *Behind Locked Doors* (1948), and *The Killer is Loose* (1956), deftly moved to a string of low-budget westerns with Randolph Scott – the 'Buchanan' films – in which Scott, an aging gunfighter, must deal with a rapidly changing frontier, rife with treachery, deceit and murder. *Seven Men From Now* (1956), *Decision at Dawn* and *The Tall T* (both 1957), *Buchanan Rides Alone* (1958), *Ride Lonesome* and *Westbound* (both 1959), and *Comanche Station* (1960) all reflected Boetticher's view of the west as a lawless and unforgiving moral universe, devoid of the sentimentality and 'codes of honor' one finds in the westerns of John Ford or Howard Hawks made just a few years earlier.

If one had to search for a single word to describe Boetticher's westerns, it would be 'hostile' – people treat each other with wary suspicion, the land itself is barren and cruel, and violence is everywhere. When Boetticher relinquished the old west for a more modern era, he created one of the most nihilist gangster films of the mid-twentieth century, *The Rise and Fall of Legs Diamond* (1960), which featured Ray Danton as the title character, a ruthless and manipulative hood who uses people and then discards them on his way to the top of the underworld, only to be cut down in a barrage of bullets by rival mobsters in the film's final minutes. Typically for a director of Boetticher's sophisticated savagery, we see Diamond's murder from his point of view; we *become* Diamond as one bullet after another is shot directly into the camera.

As critic Philip French astutely commented of the western in the post-World War II era, the formerly 'black and white' morality of the classic western was transformed into a more complex and fatalistic zone of engagement in such films as Raoul Walsh's *Pursued* (1947), which cast noir icon Robert Mitchum as a psychologically unbalanced gunman haunted by the knowledge that he was an adopted child; in 1948, the normally stalwart Glenn Ford was effectively cast as a 'psychotic judge' in Henry Levin's *The*

Man From Colorado (French 1977: 49). John Wayne emerged as a psychotic cattle drive boss Thomas Dunson in Howard Hawks and Arthur Rosson's epic noir western *Red River* (1948), tangling with his on-screen adopted son, Matthew 'Matt' Garth, played by the tormented Montgomery Clift.

Other films of the era – such as John Ford's atypically pessimistic 'chamber western' *The Man Who Shot Liberty Valance* (1962), featuring Lee Marvin, another noir specialist, as the title character, psychopathic killer-for-hire Liberty Valance – also carry over the noir aesthetic to the world of 'manifest destiny' and national westward expansion. Valance is an irredeemable killer, motivated primarily by financial gain, but who also takes an undisguised delight in sadistically humiliating and then violently murdering his victims. While the film does present John Wayne, back in form as Tom Doniphon, an aging authority figure who eventually figures in Valance's destruction, Ford's melancholy, black and white (in itself, an odd choice for a director who had been making westerns in color since the late 1940s, most famously with his sweeping epic *The Searchers* in 1956) film seems almost an anomaly in the director's long career, an acknowledgment that an aura of claustrophobic violence best suited a more contemporary vision of the 'code of the west.'

Arguably the most authentically noir vision of the western appears in an unlikely form; the films of one of the last undeniable stars of the genre, Audie Murphy. The most decorated Allied soldier of World War II, Murphy overcame a hard-scrabble existence in Texas to enlist in the US Army, and went on to make forty-four films, thirty-three of them westerns, upon his return to civilian life. His breakthrough film as an actor, although it was poorly received at the time, was John Huston's truncated version of Stephen Crane's Civil War novel, *The Red Badge of Courage* (1951). As a certifiable hero of the century's greatest conflict, Murphy was idolized by millions of fans and admirers. Murphy's 1949 autobiography *To Hell and Back* (actually ghostwritten by David McClure) became an international bestseller, and was made into a hit movie of the same title in 1955, directed by Jesse Hibbs, with Murphy playing himself, recreating his heroic war service in a rather conventional film.

But the real story of Audie Murphy is that of the returning veteran who discovers that war has changed him utterly, and that he is a stranger to himself, and others. When the Korean War erupted in 1950, Murphy felt that his new life as an actor was fraudulent; 'in Korea guys are dying – the real McCoy. And here I am playing at it,' he said in disgust (Graham 1989: 193). At the same time, he was plagued with chronic bouts of depression, insomnia, and an unquenchable anger that often erupted on the set of his films, and in his turbulent private life.

Murphy's numerous marriages and affairs brought him little satisfaction, and he became, in the words of his biographer, Don Graham, 'insomniac, secretive, suspicious, paranoid, a tireless pursuer of women, a man in touch with the dark underside of America' (Graham 1989: 210). Naturally comfortable with guns – too comfortable as far as many observers were concerned – Murphy prided himself on his quick draw and the accuracy of his marksmanship. But there was something disquieting about Murphy's love of guns, as actor Michael Dante, who made two films with Murphy, attested.

Dante recalled 'watching him fondle [his weapon] when he worked with a gun. He was very, very smooth. He fondled it and treated it like it was something very precious. Very smooth. No panic. Very cool, very quiet. I'd never seen anybody handle a six-shooter like him' (Graham 1989: 220). On the set, Murphy was known as a 'practical joker' with a mean streak, who liked to bully people to see how far he could push them before they'd explode. After working with him on one film, Kirk Douglas pronounced Murphy simply a 'vicious guy' (Graham 1989: 221), and gave the veteran a wide berth.

Nor were Murphy's early westerns satisfying to the fledgling actor, who had blossomed under Huston's empathetic direction in *The Red Badge of Courage* (ironically playing a coward who finds himself as a 'man' in battle), but was now relegated to a seemingly endless series of 'B' westerns, such as Nathan Juran's *Gunsmoke* (1953), a film that even its director remembers with little relish. As he recounted in an interview near the end of his life, Juran felt that his westerns with Murphy were fatally compromised from the start. Said Juran,

> When you finished it, that was it. Also you didn't dare take too many takes of any particular shot because you didn't have time, it would be at the expense of the show. So most often if the scene was okay, and the part that you knew something was wrong with it, you'd say, well, 'I'll cover that in the close-up and fix it with a close-up,' and very often you'd settle for a scene that's really not good and in the projection room it looks terrible and it's got some holes in it. But then you cover pieces that need to be covered, and there's no options for the cutter except to use those pieces and bridge the gap . . . (Graham 1989: 229)

Murphy was thus a commodity, the decorated war hero as western star, his dark side carefully hidden from public view. His home studio, Universal, pushed him through one violent western after another in rapid succession; Juran's *Tumbleweed* (1953), Hibbs's *Ride Clear of Diablo* (1954), Hibbs's *Ride a Crooked Trail* (1958), and numerous other program films followed one another with monotonous regularity, with little or no thought of anything but profit.

Occasionally, Murphy would draw a director of more than average skill, such as Jack Arnold, best known for his riveting science fiction films, which also explored the dark side of the American dream. Arnold's *The Incredible Shrinking Man* (1957), for example, is one of the most intelligent and despairing of all 1950s films, regardless of genre. In *The Incredible Shrinking Man*, an average American 1950s male, Scott Carey (Grant Williams), is enveloped in a mysterious mist while on a boating vacation, and subsequently begins to gradually shrink in size, until he is smaller than a blade of grass by the film's end.

Along the way, Scott's wife Louise (Randy Stuart) deserts him, the medical profession fails to help him, his brother Charlie (Paul Langton) urges Scott to exploit himself as a freak for quick cash, and the home Scott thought to be a sanctuary turns into a series of deadly traps; the cat that tries to kill him, a spider that attempts to devour him, a basement staircase that can never be scaled again, due to his minute size. *The Incredible Shrinking Man*, in short, showed the 1950s as total nightmare, a world of false security, and even less certain humanity, in which men lose their stature within society and the domestic sphere, and are eventually abandoned to the whims of fate.

With Arnold, Murphy made the taut little western *No Name on the Bullet* (1959), in which he plays a hired killer, John Gant, who drifts into town on an assignment, but won't disclose who his intended victim is. The film is a constant battle of nerves, as everyone in the small, insular community has something to hide, something in their past they fear will be discovered. Has the killer come for them? Murphy strides through the film with cool, calm assurance, toying with the townspeople, engaging in philosophical discussions with his potential targets, including the town's doctor, Luke (Charles Drake). Gant is death personified, and tells the doctor that he's wasting his time trying to save the townspeople's lives – 'they're going to die anyway. Best you can do is drag out their worthless lives. Why bother?' Incensed, the physician responds

> Gant, I'm a healer. I've devoted my life to it and I intend to continue. Right now I've got one big public health problem, and I'm looking at it. (as quoted in Graham 1989: 273)

In the final minutes of the film, Gant confronts his prey, 'an old, corrupt judge dying of consumption' (Graham 1989: 273). When the judge refuses to defend himself, Gant confronts the judge's young daughter, and rips off her blouse, presenting it to the judge as 'proof' that he has raped her, which he has not. The judge is taken in by Gant's deception, and moves to draw on him, but dies of a heart attack before he can remove his gun from his holster. Gant's response to all of this, as described in the film's script, is 'a terrible smile, insinuating anything . . . everything' (as cited in Graham 1989: 273).

Murphy's life in the ensuing decade predictably unraveled. His friend Casey Tibbs commented after Murphy's death that 'he didn't really like things when they was [sic] going good' (Graham 1989: 302). He gambled recklessly, and ran up huge debts he had no hope of paying. His last film, the appropriately titled *A Time for Dying*, shot in 1969, and released in Europe in 1971, but amazingly never shown in the United States until 1981, was directed by Budd Boetticher as a favor to an old friend in trouble. As Boetticher told me in our interview shortly before his own death in 2001,

> I'd known Audie for a long time. When I was working at Universal in 1951, I made a small picture there called *The Cimarron Kid*, and Audie was in it. He was just a kid then. But when we made *A Time for Dying*, Audie got in real trouble with some people in Las Vegas, and he needed a director to make a picture, and he would be the producer. He was a friend, and he was in trouble; so I made the picture for him. But then Audie was killed in a plane crash [on 28 May 1971] shortly after the film was finished, so the whole thing was just tragic. (Dixon 2007: 55–6)

Murphy was just forty-six years old; but as Boetticher told me during our talk he had really 'died many years before.' The war and its aftermath had turned Audie Murphy into one of the walking dead, even as Universal's publicity machine ground out fan magazine copy extolling him as the boy next door, the fresh-faced kid who'd come through the horror of war and beaten the odds to become a movie star.

One of the most compelling dystopian visions of the 1950s can be found in Martin Ritt's overlooked domestic drama *No Down Payment* (1957), which chronicles the lives and fortunes of four couples living out the southern California suburban nightmare in the last years of the decade. Jerry Flagg (Tony Randall) is an impulsive and impractical dreamer, always ready with another get-rich-quick scheme, much to the consternation of his long-suffering wife, Isabelle (Sheree North). Troy Boone (Cameron Mitchell) is a psychotic, macho veteran, whose good-time wife Leola (Joanne Woodward) can't see how dangerous he really is. David Martin (Jeffrey Hunter) is a straight arrow married to the submissive and timid Jean (Patricia Owens). Herman Kreitzer (Pat Hingle) is doggedly determined to succeed in postwar America, and is arguably the most practical of the group, along with his no-nonsense wife Betty (Barbara Rush). As the title clearly states, all the couples live in a 'no money down' housing development, something like Levittown in the early 1950s, where all the houses look alike, and backyards are so close together that they become a shared space.

Each couple seems dissatisfied in their own way; Jerry wants instant riches, while Leola just wants to party. Herman and David want to build something of a life, but the temptation of easy credit and installment plan living makes them perpetual wage slaves in a world they will never own. Through it all, sexual tensions simmer, and finally come to a boiling point when David goes out of town on a business trip, and Troy, obsessed with David's wife, Jean, rapes her, because he feels Leola slipping out of his grasp. Retribution of a sort comes when Troy, a perennial grease monkey, is killed when a car he is working on falls off a car jack onto his chest, crushing him to death. Leola reacts to this by simply picking up and leaving, looking for some place else, someone else, while the other families dutifully file off to church. No one will miss her; no one ever knew her.

Nobody really knows anyone else in *No Down Payment*; wives and husbands are strangers to each other, relationships with 'friends' are as disposable as Kleenex. The surface is all here; maintaining the illusion of an orderly world of bright promise, when the much darker reality is that these people have nothing in common except their proximity. No one has any money, and yet money is everything; everything the characters want, everything they hope to be, everything they dream of alone or together. *No Down Payment*, in fact, functions as an antidote to the idyllic fictions that ruled other then-contemporary entertainment, and 'exposes the illusory character of the typical Hollywood fantasy and presents Hollywood itself as the biggest illusion of them all' (Mann 2008: 143).

Credit cards had just been introduced, and the protagonists of *No Down Payment* embrace it with a passion; they can pay for everything later, some time in the future that may never come. As with *My Son John* and other phantom films of the 1950s, *No Down Payment*, a major film for 20th Century Fox at the time – its producer was Jerry Wald, known for his glossy, escapist entertainments – has become a phantom film. Unavailable on DVD, the film survives through occasional cable screenings and bootleg discs circulating on the web, as if it were a forbidden, secret text, something that the twenty-first century doesn't want us to examine too closely.

For here are the roots of twenty-first-century materialism laid bare, the mechanisms of supply and demand examined in detail, the truest picture of the dark side of the American dream. Shot in lurid black and white CinemaScope, and written by a blacklisted writer, Ben Maddow (Philip Yordan took the official credit), *No Down Payment* shows us an America desperately trying to adjust to peacetime, haunted by the aftermath of World War II and Korea, uncertain of how to behave in postwar society, making up the rules as it goes along, going on a spending spree that can only end in disaster. Whatever emotional life there is here is bartered for, and all allegiances are temporary; the couples in *No Down Payment* keep chasing after happiness, but have no idea how far they are from any real understanding of themselves, or the new world they inhabit.

Like children with charge accounts, Leola, Jerry, Troy, and the rest have no idea what they really want, or how to get it. This is the true noir vision of American social collapse; the war is over, you have your home and your neighbors, but there's no real connection to anything. Some elect to stay, because there's no other way out for them; some leave, because life has become unbearable. Much, much later, *No Down Payment* would ironically serve as the template for the watered-down television series *Knots Landing* (1979–83), as well as the now-forgotten teleseries *90 Bristol Court* (1964–5), which both documented the intertwining lives of a group of dissatisfied suburbanites, living on other people's borrowed money, drifting through life, searching for something to hang onto, afraid to look too deeply into their own hearts.

No Down Payment, though, through its noirish black and white lighting, sparse sets, too neatly manicured lawns and brutal mise-en-scène, paints a far more harrowing vision of suburban life than either of these two later iterations; this is the real world of the 1950s; instant 'communities,' empty, fearful, always on a knife edge. It's Updike and Cheever territory by way of Cornell Woolrich; in 1950s suburbia, you've got to wing it, and hope that something works out, and always keep your guard up. Best not to look too closely; after all, the neighbors are watching you, too. In the world of *No Down Payment*, privacy is impossible.

This loss of self is eerily echoed by Irvin S. Yeaworth's remarkable science fiction film *4D Man* (1959), shot in garish color on a low budget in Pennsylvania, in which scientist Scott Nelson (Robert Lansing) discovers a way to alter the molecular structure of his body so that he can pass through walls, doors, concrete, anything at all at will. Scott, who had once entertained notions of a romance with Linda (Lee Meriwether), finds that Linda prefers Scott's brother, Tony (James Langdon). Without any con-nection to the world around him, Scott steps up the pace of his experi-ments, and is soon walking through bank vault doors to gather stolen cash with impunity.

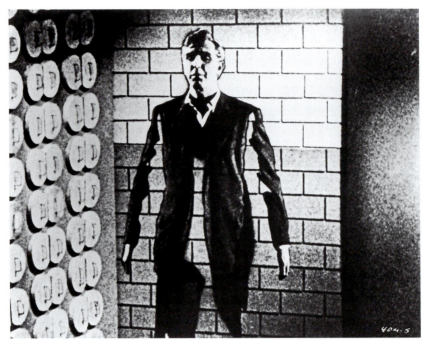

Figure 3.4 Robert Lansing can walk through stone walls in Irvin S. Yeaworth's
4D Man (1959).

The bank robbery scene is beautifully built up during a long sequence
shot at night, as Scott strolls through the deserted streets of town, reaching through a glass supermarket window to steal an apple, purloin-
ing objects at will by simply reaching through locked doors, delighting
in his new-found powers, and his detachment from society. At one
point, Scott walks *through* a door into a room, surprising his boss, who,
in true noir fashion, plans to steal Scott's process and patent it for
his own profit. 'Scott! How did you get in here?' he asks in alarm.
'Through the door,' Scott answers laconically, by now used to his non-
corporeality.

But this power comes with a terrible price; Scott finds that with each use
of his 'fourth dimensional' (hence the title) ability, his life force drains
away. At first, Scott is content to simply destroy those who opposed him,
or sought to steal his work, or mocked his ambitions. But by the film's end,
he is reduced to reaching out to anyone just to continue living; in one of
the film's most compelling scenes, he drains the life out of a young girl,
Marjorie (Patty Duke, three years before Arthur Penn's *The Miracle
Worker* (1962) shot her to stardom) simply by embracing her. Robert
Lansing plays Scott as a tortured, perpetually dissatisfied malcontent, a

failure both at the office (his boss exploits him mercilessly, and never gives Scott any credit) and in his personal relationships.

As Linda, Lee Meriwether seems convincingly torn between Scott and Tony; she likes Scott, but he's just too much of a loner, too temperamental – in short, he doesn't fit in. Thus, Scott creates a space for himself where there is no space or room to breathe in a world that is slowly suffocating him. Tony, Scott's brother, is a go-along-to-get-along rationalist, willing to compromise himself to get ahead in business, and in life. Scott is driven, uncompromisingly, not a team player; a prescription for personal disaster in the 1950s.

The film's special effects are surprisingly good, using a great deal of moving matte work to depict Scott's invasion of the existing world, set to a moody jazz score that highlights Scott's outsider status within conventional society. Scott Nelson, like other 1950s antiheroes, is never really part of the world he exists in, even if he can walk through walls. He exists in a dimension all his own, and his life, and eventual death, are that of an isolated man, cut off from the places and people that surround him. He doesn't really exist in any dimension, and his destruction as a disruptive force in 1950s society is thus assured. Scott Nelson was never really alive; now, he has become one of the undead, not real in any sense, corporeal or otherwise.

One of the most influential 1950s noirs was almost completely silent: Russell Rouse's experimental feature film *The Thief* (1952), starring an anxious Ray Milland as Dr Allan Fields, nuclear physicist and spy for the Soviet Union. Shot entirely without dialogue, and using location shooting whenever possible, *The Thief* charts Fields's downward spiral as his treachery becomes known to the authorities, and the law closes inexorably in on him, despite all his efforts to escape. Throughout the film, we hear background noises and street sounds, and much of this sound was actually recorded live during the making of the film. But except for one anguished cry of spiritual agony from Fields at the lowest point in the film, throughout the entire length of *The Thief*, not one character utters a single word.

Fields's reputation, his career, the many honors he has amassed working for the United States; none of this matters now. Fields scrambles edgily from one drab 'drop location' to the next, until, on the run, he lands in a cheap rooming house where he meets an unnamed woman (Rita Gam, in her first screen role), and comes to terms with his tortured conscience. At the end of the film, Fields turns himself in to the authorities, because there's nowhere else to run to; it isn't so much patriotism but rather exhaustion that compels him to surrender. Grim and unrelenting, *The Thief* is almost unique in motion picture history, as one of the only films

Figure 3.5 Ray Milland looks grim, as Rita Gam beckons, in Russell Rouse's
experimental 'silent' feature *The Thief* (1952).

that succeeds without any spoken words in conveying an atmosphere of
menace, betrayal, and social isolation.

Joseph H. Lewis, a noir veteran, began his career in the 1930s, directing
westerns for Universal and Columbia, and became known by the crew as
'Wagon Wheel Joe,' for his habit of dragging half a broken wagon wheel
from shot to shot, urging the cameraman to frame each scene through the
spokes of the battered wheel for an added Brechtian effect. Abandoning
westerns, Lewis began a frenzied round of freelancing that took him from
Poverty Row to the majors, with such films as the disquieting horror
Universal film *The Mad Doctor of Market Street* (1942), and the astonish-
ing *Secrets of a Coed* (aka *The Silent Witness*, 1942) for PRC, which opens
with a continuous ten-minute take of a courtroom scene that predates
Alfred Hitchcock's experiments in *Rope* (1948) by a number of years.

Lewis designed the shot starting off in a wide shot, then moving across
the jury box to get close-ups of the witness stand, the judge, and various
shots of the spectators – all in one continuous take. *My Name is Julia Ross*
(1945) is equally dazzling, but working for Columbia's 'B' unit, Lewis had
much better technical facilities and capable performers (Dame May Whitty
and George Macready) at his disposal. The film is a remarkably inventive

Figure 3.6 Peggy Cummins and John Dall plot a new caper in Joseph H. Lewis's *Gun Crazy* (1950).

psychological thriller, in which a young woman is drugged and forced to assume the identity of a psychopathic killer's dead wife; for sixty-five minutes it creates a genuine mood of suspense. Nina Foch is excellent in the title role; as the film's tag line aptly summarized it, 'She went to sleep as a secretary . . . and woke up a madman's "bride"!' Lewis then went on to direct his two most famous works, *Gun Crazy* (1949) and *The Big Combo* (1955). Both projects were done on a shoestring, and both use long takes for the sake of economy, achieving a near-documentary feel in certain sequences that adds to the verisimilitude of each film.

Noir aficionados have long hailed Lewis's *Gun Crazy* (aka *Deadly Is the Female*, 1950) as the director's masterpiece, a film shot on a non-existent budget for the notorious King Brothers, who specialized in producing low-budget tales of violence, such as Max Nosseck's *Dillinger* (1945), starring Lawrence Tierney as the famed gangster. *Gun Crazy* tracks the codependent relationship of Annie Laurie Starr (Peggy Cummins) and Bart Tare (John Dall), both of whom have been obsessed with guns since childhood. The couple first meet at a carnival where Annie is performing a trick-shooting act, and Bart is immediately taken with her. Soon, they are the stars of the carnival, but are fired when the owner reveals that he has romantic designs on Annie. They hit the road, and soon are robbing liquor stores and gas stations, and eventually banks. Perhaps the single most famous sequence in the film is a one-take bank robbery shot on location without the use of process screens or studio sets.

Bart and Annie's momentary idyll is shattered when a meat-packing plant robbery goes awry, and Annie senselessly guns down two employees. Hunted, the couple flee into the swamp, pursued by the police. As the authorities close in, Bart kills Annie with his gun, and then shoots himself. The *Cahiers du cinéma* critics (particularly Jean-Luc Godard and François Truffaut) were astounded by the film when it first appeared, and Lewis became a darling of the Nouvelle Vague.

The Big Combo, photographed by noir specialist John Alton from a screenplay by Philip Yordan, is another 'syndicate' film, in which the organization is all, but with a difference. Lewis is an eccentric, and he depicts a universe that is as out of kilter as his often imbalanced camera set-ups; the camera sweeps in on the protagonists in their most intimate moments, frames them as silhouettes in wide shots that effectively use fog and a few shadows to disguise the fact that there is really no set at all, and indulges in sinuous tracking shots that seem to entrap his characters in even tighter compositions.

The Big Combo's plot is simple; Cornel Wilde plays Leonard Diamond, a hard-nosed detective on the trail of Richard Conte's Mr Brown, who has combined all the local racketeers into a far-flung conglomerate. But his associates are all marginalized from society, and marked for their 'differences' in one way or another. Brown's two key enforcers, Mingo (Earl Holliman) and Fante (Lee van Cleef), are clearly homosexual lovers; Brown's former boss, McClure (Brian Donlevy), is for all intents and purposes deaf, and relies upon a bulky hearing aid to keep apprised of the gang's activities.

Sadism is everywhere apparent. In one key scene, Mingo and Fante take great delight in torturing Diamond with McClure's hearing aid, with the volume at full blast amplifying a drum solo to the point of excruciating pain. Later, when McClure tries to double-cross Brown, Mingo and Fante shoot him down without compunction on orders from Brown, but only after taking away his hearing aid in a final, sadistic touch, so that, as they tell him in his final moments, 'at least you won't hear it' when the blast of a machine gun claims his life.

Running at a taut eighty-nine minutes, *The Big Combo* is one of the bleakest and most perverse of all 1950s crime films; it exists in a world of perpetual menace and double-cross. As Richard Conte's character 'Mr Brown' repeatedly reminds his associates throughout the film, life has become a fight to the finish: 'first is first, and second is nobody.' But despite the film's rapturous reception abroad, Lewis remained a maverick, and *The Big Combo* did little to advance his reputation in Hollywood, where it mattered most.

When Fritz Lang directed *The Blue Gardenia* in 1953, he was coming off a period of blacklisting that nearly ruined his career. Lang, who had fled Germany in 1933 in order to avoid becoming complicit with the Nazi regime, and then directed a series of anti-Nazi films in America such as *Man Hunt* (1941), *Hangmen Also Die* (1943) and *Ministry of Fear* (1944), suddenly found himself unemployable because of his supposed 'Communist' connections, which in his case consisted of signing a few peace petitions in the 1940s, and collaborating with writer Thomas Mann, producer Walter Wanger, and playwright Bertolt Brecht. Despite his universally acknowledged opposition to any form of authoritarianism, except perhaps his own as director on a film set, Lang was summarily blacklisted. As he told Peter Bogdanovich,

> My lawyer went to New York and he talked, I think, with the head man of the American Legion. It was such an insidious thing [. . .] No one ever said: 'He is on a list.' I just didn't get any offers. Howard Hughes' man said: 'We are not working any more; this script is not good for him; we would love to have Lang, but there is just nothing here at the studio that would fit his great talent [. . .] Well, finally, after a year and a half, Harry Cohn [the head of Columbia Pictures] gave me the first job. The only thing I can tell you about [*The Blue Gardenia*] is that it was the first picture after the McCarthy business, and I had to shoot it in 20 [actually 21] days. Maybe that's what made me so venomous. (Bogdanovich 1967: 84)

A tangled tale of murder, betrayal and the mechanics of lust when all hope of love is gone, with Anne Baxter, Richard Conte, Raymond Burr, and *Superman*'s George Reeves in the leading roles, *The Blue Gardenia* launched Lang on a streak of noir thrillers at Columbia, including the previously mentioned *The Big Heat* (also shot in 1953), in which tough cop Dave Bannion (Glenn Ford) goes on a rampage when his wife is killed in an automobile explosion staged by syndicate boss Mike Lagana (Alexander Scourby, better known as the go-to, 'Voice of God' voiceover artist during the 1950s and 1960s).

In *The Big Heat* Bannion threatens, strong arms, bullies, and batters his way to the center of Lagana's corrupt universe, with the aid of Debby Marsh (Gloria Grahame), the girlfriend of Lagana's key triggerman, Vince Stone (Lee Marvin). The film is perhaps most infamous for the scene in which an enraged Vince flings a pot of boiling hot coffee in Debby's face after discovering that she has betrayed him; she later returns the 'favor' by flinging a pot of boiling coffee in Vince's face, only to receive two fatal gun-shots to the abdomen for her attempt at retribution.

What makes *The Big Heat* so compelling, finally, is the absolute slimi-ness of its milieu; everyone is on the take, and corruption is not only encouraged, it is a given, an inescapable feature of the film's moral uni-verse. Lang's shooting schedule on the film was certainly not luxurious; just twenty-nine days, only eight more than *The Blue Gardenia*. Despite international acclaim as an auteur for more than twenty years, the director of the dystopian science fiction epic *Metropolis* (1927) had become just another program director in the corporate 1950s.

Despite, or perhaps because of, the film's bleak world view, *The Big Heat* became a solid critical and commercial hit. Nothing speaks louder in Hollywood than box-office success, and Lang was suddenly 'employable.' Pushing ahead, Lang made a series of equally corrosive films for a variety of Hollywood studios; *Human Desire* (1954), a remake of director Jean Renoir's *La Bête Humaine* (*The Human Beast*, 1938); as well as one of the first serial killer films, *While the City Sleeps* (1956), in which a young mes-senger boy, Robert Manners (John Barrymore, Jr; Drew Barrymore's real-life father), terrorizes New York with a series of brutal murders of young women; and finally *Beyond a Reasonable Doubt* (1956), in which Tom Garrett (Dana Andrews), seemingly an upstanding member of society, is secretly guilty of murder.

In all of Lang's films, issues of moral culpability are always extreme; life gives one choices, but fate always plays the deciding hand. Once his own master at the German film conglomerate UFA (Universum Film AG), Lang now had to contend with continual cost-cutting interference from his producer Bert E. Friedlob, on both *While the City Sleeps* and *Beyond a Reasonable Doubt*. It was too much. After making films in America from MGM's lynching drama *Fury* in 1936 onwards, Lang finally threw in the towel. With the final day's shooting of *Reasonable Doubt* in the can, Lang walked off the picture, out of the Hollywood studio system, and out of America. As he told Bogdanovich,

> I was disgusted. I told my cutter, Gene Fowler [Jr, who would be the direc-tor of *I Was a Teenage Werewolf* just one year later], what I wanted so I knew the picture would be in good hands, and I left. Then, when everything was finished, the producer suddenly started to be sweet again: 'But you don't want to leave me now?' I said, 'Yes, I am sick and tired of you.' I left. I looked back over the past – how many pictures had been mutilated – and since I didn't have any intention of dying of a heart attack, I said, 'I think I'll step out of this rat race.' And I decided not to make pictures here any more. (Bogdanovich 1967: 110)

Thus does Hollywood dispose of its most accomplished artists; use them, and then throw them out when they're out of fashion, or even if they're not out of fashion, but rather just too troublesome, too individualistic. Lang, always his own man, knew too well from his experiences in Nazi Germany what totalitarian fascism could do to an artist; he returned to Germany, made a few more films, and finally appeared as himself in Jean-Luc Godard's superb commentary on the commercialization of the cinema *Le Mépris* (*Contempt*, 1963), battling the vindictive and ignorant producer Jeremy Prokosch (Jack Palance), in his quest to make a film of Homer's *Odyssey*.

The 1950s were thus a period of crisis and contestation, in which all the values of the preceding decades were called into question and found wanting. Mickey Rooney, who as Andy Hardy played the ultimate small-town teenager in a string of modestly budgeted but utterly pervasive paeans to the simple life from 1937 to 1958, finally packed in his rural persona, when it was apparent the public was no longer interested in a bucolic vision of rural America. He successfully transformed himself into a sociopathic killer in such films as Don Siegel's *Baby Face Nelson* (1957), Charles Haas's *The Big Operator* and Howard W. Koch's *The Last Mile* (both 1959).

Ironically, Koch also directed Rooney in the last of the Andy Hardy films, *Andy Hardy Comes Home* (1958), in which Andy, now a middle-aged businessman with a wife and children, returns to his mythical home-town of Carvel (the state was always unspecified, but it was generally agreed that Carvel was located somewhere in the Midwest) and becomes embroiled in a local political upheaval. An air of undeniable sadness permeates the film, even though most of the original cast members returned for the finale, with the exception of Lewis Stone as Judge Hardy, Andrew's father, who had died in 1953. But *Andy Hardy Comes Home*'s failure to recapture the supposed charm of small-town American life is testimony to the fact that society, for better or worse, had moved on. The series had won a special Academy Award in 1942 'for its achievement in representing the American Way of Life' (Maltin 2002: 43); now, it was clear to all that if such a 'way of life' had ever existed, it was now a thing of the past.

The noir ethos was everywhere, destroying everything in its path. Marilyn Monroe got her first big break as a psychotic babysitter in Roy Ward Baker's *Don't Bother to Knock* (1952), and then was brutally murdered by jealous husband Joseph Cotten in Henry Hathaway's Technicolor noir *Niagara* (1953); the fabled honeymoon site had become instead the locus of death. In the same year that she made *Niagara*, Monroe

Figure 3.7   Marilyn Monroe is a psychotic babysitter in Roy Ward Baker's *Don't Bother to Knock* (1952).

also starred in the frothy Technicolor entertainments *Gentlemen Prefer Blondes*, under the direction of genre specialist Howard Hawks, and Jean Negulesco's *How to Marry a Millionaire*, but her sexuality was seen as almost a threat to 1950s morality, and she was pushed into a variety of films that did not exploit her undeniably sexual energy, despite her strenuous protests.

Thus, as the decade moved on, Marilyn started a downward spiral in her career, which would end with her last film, John Huston's *The Misfits*, in 1961, and her premature death in 1962. Sexuality in the 1950s had to be contained; clearly, Marilyn was a threat to conventional mores. Always nervous before the camera (Hathaway actually used the 'rehearsal' takes of *Niagara*, which he shot surreptitiously, for the final film, noting Monroe's tendency to freeze up with repeated retakes), Monroe became even more agitated when it was clear that her career was slipping away from her. Her last project was to have been yet another assembly-line sex comedy co-starring Dean Martin, George Cukor's *Something's Got to Give*, but when Monroe repeatedly failed to appear for filming, she was summarily fired. A month later, she was dead. The penalty for ignoring society's demands in the 1950s was sharp, and exacting.

Figure 3.8 Intern Alex Nicol and detective Richard Conte are up to their ears in the dope trade in George Sherman's *The Sleeping City* (1950).

In George Sherman's *The Sleeping City* (1950), Bellevue Hospital is the site of drug pushing, gambling, and murder, as seemingly affable janitor 'Pop' Ware (Richard Taba) masterminds a morphine smuggling ring that steals from patients' daily doses of anesthetics, and resells the drugs on the black market. When rumors reach the police, undercover detective Fred Rowan (Richard Conte) is sent in to investigate. To his shock, he finds that nearly everyone is in on the racket; doctors, interns, and nurses alike share in the profits, and many are addicts themselves. When one young intern tries to blow the whistle on 'Pop,' the janitor trails him to a bleak waterfront park and shoots him dead at point blank range, literally sticking the gun in his victim's face. Seldom has a hospital been portrayed in a more depressing light. Even idealistic young intern Dr Steve Anderson (Alex Nicol) is sucked into this maelstrom of greed and depredation, ruining his once-promising career.

Amazingly, the film was actually shot on location at Bellevue, and presents such an unrelentingly bleak picture of 1950s medical care that the hospital threatened to sue Universal International, the film's production company, unless they tacked on an opening speech by Conte, extolling the many virtues of Bellevue and the American healthcare system in general, and declaring the film's plot to be 'entirely fictitious in all respects.' But the spectacle of wards full of patients writhing in pain under leather restraint straps when they have been slipped a placebo rather than the prescribed narcotic, to single out just one of *The Sleeping City*'s many disturbing sequences, lingers long in the memory after Conte's opening encomium has been forgotten.

If noirs of the 1940s seem subdued and somber, with the protagonists accepting their lot with an air of fatalistic resignation, the noirs of the 1950s are often more violent, even hysterical. In the wake of the House Un-American Activities Committee (HUAC) hearings, a series of overheated and preposterous anti-Communist films streamed forth from the studios, especially from RKO Radio, which was then owned by the eccentric billionaire Howard Hughes, an avowed anti-Communist. Sensing the shift in public sentiment, the other studios quickly joined suit, afraid to be labeled as being 'soft' on communism, or worse, 'pinkos.'

Robert Stevenson's *I Married a Communist* (aka *The Woman on Pier 13*, 1949) was one of the first films of this cycle, and one of the most notorious. *I Married a Communist* tells the story of former Communist Frank Johnson (a tense Robert Ryan), who has forsaken his old life with the party, assumed a new identity as labor leader Bradley Collins, and married all-American girl Nan (Laraine Day). But the party, in the persons of local cell leader Nixon Vanning (Thomas Gomez) and loyal acolyte Christine Norman (Janis Carter), who once dated Brad during his party days, has never forgotten Brad. They were 'young Communists in love' then, as Christine ironically puts it, and soon she is engaged in forcing Brad to jeopardize his union work with a series of wildcat strikes at the shipping yard he manages.

In the film's climax, Brad plunges to his death while skewering Nixon with a grappling hook. Ultra-paranoid by any standard, *I Married a Communist* conflates 1940s noir gangsterism with 1950s 'Red' fear mongering, resulting in an uncertain blend of melodrama and sheer sadism. At one point in the film, Brad is forced to witness the drowning execution of a party underling suspected of disloyalty in excruciating detail; Stevenson's camera lingers on the body of the bound, hapless victim as it sinks into the murk of the waterfront backwash.

That fixture of 1940s noir, the femme fatale, is prominently featured in *I Married a Communist*; Janis Carter's predatory image dominates not only the film itself, but also all the publicity materials for the project. 'Nameless, shameless Woman!' the poster screams, 'Trained in an art as old as time . . . trading her love . . . yielding kisses that invite disaster, destroy . . . then – KILL!,' superimposed over the image of Carter spilling out of a low-cut evening gown, her hair swept back in a platinum blonde hairdo, as her teeth glisten with almost vampiric urgency.

It is interesting, too, that the key Communist party official's first name is Nixon; a clear irony, in that Richard Nixon was at the time making a name for himself as an ardent anti-Communist, aligning himself with Senator Joe McCarthy and his attorney, Roy Cohn, in a smear campaign that would destroy the careers, and in some cases, the lives of many of Hollywood's most talented actors, writers and directors (see Vaughn 1972 for a detailed account of the Hollywood blacklist).

Noir anti-Communist propaganda was a peculiar staple of the early 1950s, and Hughes attacked the production of the film with 'patriotic' zeal; indeed, he had the entire studio, dressing rooms, sound stages, telephones, and all, secretly bugged so that he could keep tabs on his employees (Dixon and Foster 2008: 182). In such an atmosphere of hypersurveillance, the most preposterous scenarios were suddenly plausible, so long as they could be enlisted in the fight against the supposed Communist infiltration of Hollywood.

In William Cameron Menzies's equally bizarre *The Whip Hand* (1951), another Howard Hughes/RKO effort, ex-Nazi and now Communist conspirators plan to spike the nation's water supply with a deadly chemical that will decimate the country's population, leaving the country open to a sweeping Soviet invasion. *The Whip Hand*'s original scenario, in fact, was even more outré; in the first draft of the screenplay, Hitler himself (as played by Bobby Watson) has somehow escaped death in his Berlin bunker at the end of World War II, and is personally supervising the entire operation as a path to return the Reich to its former 'glory.'

This version of the film was actually shot, but at the last minute, Hughes, who often poured hundreds of thousands of dollars into retakes of nearly completed films, scrapped the Nazi angle, and called the cast back for several more weeks of filming to pump up the Communist theme instead; it was suddenly more topical. Directed with Menzies's customary visual brio, replete with threatening extreme close-ups and brutal, high-key lighting, *The Whip Hand* compels the viewer's attention through the sheer visual frenzy of its violent, aggressive camera work, coupled with its nightmarish, forced-perspective sets, which seem to overpower both the viewer and the film's protagonists.

Yet the film, like *I Married a Communist*, was a failure at the box office, perhaps because of Hughes's cost overruns during production; he would eventually sell the entire RKO studio in 1955 to a fledgling television company, General Teleradio, which in turn sold the entire production complex to Desi Arnaz and Lucille Ball in 1957 as the physical plant for

Arnaz and Ball's Desilu Productions (see Jewell and Harbin 1982: 15, 290). Thus, the 'house of noir' became the home of *I Love Lucy*, and Hughes effectively passed out of the motion picture industry.

But other production companies rushed into the breach, eager to prove their loyalty to the government, no matter how extreme their cinematic iterations proved. In Harry Horner's *Red Planet Mars* (1952), an independent production released through United Artists, scientist Peter Graves picks up radio messages that prove that God is alive and well, and living on Mars, where His Morse-code messages of hope and guidance eventually bring about a Christian revival in the Soviet Union, and precipitate the fall of the Stalinist regime, and communism as a whole.

In Edward Ludwig's *Big Jim McLain* (1952), John Wayne and James Arness are FBI agents on the trail of Communists in Hawaii, who are led by a dapper Alan Napier (later Alfred, the butler, on the 1960s television series *Batman*, and an alumnus of the Val Lewton stock company at RKO in the early 1940s). *Red Snow* (1952) is an even stranger project, 'an unusual documentary/spy thriller [created] from a combination of studio shots and stock footage [left over from producer/director Boris Petroff's] 1949 release *Arctic Fury*,' as well as footage from Ewing Scott's 1932 documentary *Igloo*, co-directed by Petroff and Scott, and patched together for 'less than $100,000' (Fienup-Riordan 1995: 92). Starring Guy Madison as Lieutenant Johnson and Ray Mala, an Alaskan native actor, as Sergeant Koovuk, Lt Johnson's generic 'sidekick,' *Red Snow*

> opens with heroic music and a dedication to 'loyal American Eskimos.' The story tells how the US Air Force, alarmed over strange lights and sounds from the Russian side of the Bering Strait, sends Eskimo soldiers back to their tribes to investigate. Working with Eskimo troops, the Air Force saves an important base from enemy destruction . . . Although the words 'Russia' and 'communism' did not appear in the script, the dialogue included 'Siberia,' 'Uncle Joe's borscht,' 'political commissar,' and 'die for the party.' (Fienup-Riordan 1995: 92)

Released through Columbia Pictures, the film did modest business, but tragically was Mala's last work as an actor; he died of a heart attack at the age of forty-six, shortly after production wrapped. Ironically, Mala's first starring role, in *Igloo*, was intercut with newer footage shot for *Red Snow*, so that his first and last roles meld together in an uncomfortable conflation of the past and present.

Alfred E. Green's equally threadbare *Invasion USA* (1953) takes place in a Manhattan bar, where the sinister and enigmatic Mr Ohman (Dan O'Herlihy) hypnotizes the bar's patrons into believing that the United

States has been attacked by the Soviet Union in an all-out nuclear war. Using footage shot during World War II bombing raids, the film intercuts library material with scenes shot on a few hastily constructed sets, as unconvincing miniatures of skyscrapers crumble, and nominal protagonist Gerald Mohr (usually a noir heavy, and here cast against type) strolls through the wreckage with tough-guy aplomb, pursuing a romance with leading lady Peggie Castle.

Despite the fact that the film was made in seven days on a minimal budget ($127,000 cash and $60,000 deferred), it adroitly tapped into the fears of the American populace, earning net profits of nearly $1,000,000 for the film's producer, exploitation veteran Albert Zugsmith (McCarthy and Flynn 1975: 413). The trailer for the film resolutely pushed the project's most sensationalist angles; 'SEE! New York Disappear! SEE! Seattle Blasted! SEE! San Francisco in Flames!' Nuclear armageddon was never so profitable, or so nakedly proffered as mass entertainment. At the film's end, of course, the entire scenario is revealed as merely a 'prediction' of things to come, unless America prepares for the worst.

Other 'Red Scare' noir films appeared in droves; Samuel Fuller's *Pickup on South Street* (1953), in which patriotic pickpocket Richard Widmark makes the 'right choice' between personal self-interest and the good of the nation when confronted by a Soviet spy ring and a roll of stolen microfilm; Josef von Sternberg's *Jet Pilot* (1950–7), another Howard Hughes fetishist fantasy, in which John Wayne becomes embroiled in the clutches of ravishing Soviet spy and jet fighter pilot Janet Leigh (Hughes shot the first 'draft' of the film in 1950, and then reworked it with writer/director Jules Furthman for an astounding seven years before releasing it in 1957); Russell Birdwell's *The Girl in the Kremlin* (1957), in which Zsa Zsa Gabor plays a dual role, as twins enmeshed in Soviet intrigue, one of whom is Stalin's secret mistress; and George Waggner's *Red Nightmare* (1962), narrated by Jack Webb, in which a small American town is transformed into a Soviet slave state in another fantasy scenario replete with barbed wire fences, machine gun nests, and forced indoctrination classes.

This last film, running only thirty minutes, and made 'under the personal supervision of Jack L. Warner' for use in schools, churches, and civic organizations, is particularly interesting because it demonstrates that rather than evaporating, as one might expect in the late 1950s, the Red Scare mentality persisted well into the next decade, informing the consciousness of American popular culture. That these films, by their very design, were noir projects is hardly in dispute; their visual and aural structure alone (an extreme use of shadows, constant rain, paranoid voice-overs, threatening camera angles, and jarring close-ups, all designed to create an atmosphere of perpetual dread and unease) is incontestable proof of the noir origins.

Fear was now part of American life on an institutionalized basis; the advent of the atomic, and then the hydrogen bomb, plus the added threat of a Communist invasion, made for an uneasy climate. Although any number of mainstream films continued to insist that all was well in postwar America, at the margins, the 1950s in the United States were informed by fear.

In 1957, a young producer named Herman Cohen produced a prototypical 1950s noir, Gerd Oswald's *Crime of Passion*, with Barbara Stanwyck cast as a bored and ambitious suburban housewife who sleeps with her husband's boss so that he can 'earn' a promotion. It's a brutal vision of the banality and conformity of middle American life, and of course, it ends disastrously. But it also ended disastrously for Cohen, when the film, despite excellent reviews and a solid cast (Stanwyck was supported by Sterling Hayden as her husband, and Raymond Burr as his slimy boss) stiffed at the box office. For the thinly capitalized Cohen, this spelled disaster. Why had the film, with well-known stars, solid direction, and a taut script, failed to attract paying customers? He decided to take a trip across the country to see what audiences were watching, and who the audiences were. He got a shock:

> I got out of Hollywood and saw what was happening, and that it was the teenagers who were buying the records. It's the teenagers that were leaving the home, getting away from the TV box in the living room. The teenagers wanted to get away from home. They wanted to get away from their parents, and they went to the cinema. (as quoted in Rhodes 2003: 54)

The 'teenagers,' in short, had become the main market for films, now that mom and dad were content to sit at home and watch Milton Berle on television for free. Cohen realized why *Crime of Passion* had failed; it was aimed at adults. He immediately plunged into production with two of the most iconic hits of the 1950s, which would shape not only his future career, but the future of American-International Pictures, and a whole new cycle of films; teen horror noir.

Hiring director Fritz Lang's former editor, Gene Fowler, Jr, to helm the project, Cohen produced *I Was a Teenage Werewolf* (1957), starring Michael Landon in the title role, followed by Herbert L. Strock's *I Was a Teenage Frankenstein* (1957) in short order. Booked heavily on the drive-in circuit and in downtown urban theatres, the films were an immediate sensation. In *Teenage Werewolf*, Landon persuasively plays Tony Rivers, a moody, troubled teen who falls under the sway of an unscrupulous psychiatrist, Dr Alfred Brandon (veteran character actor Whit Bissell). Pretending to help the young man, Brandon uses a regimen of drugs and hypnotherapy to transform him into a snarling werewolf, who then goes on a killing spree. His bloodlust satiated, Tony reverts to human form, but any loud noise (a school recess bell, for example) or moment of stress causes him to revert to his hidden animal nature, and more mayhem ensues.

The film was carefully designed by Cohen to trigger a number of emotional responses from his youthful audience. Firstly, all the adult figures in the film are either powerless, clueless, or corrupt; in Cohen's cinematic universe, teenagers are alone in an uncaring, corrupt world. Adults are never to be trusted. Secondly, the film mixed liberal doses of sex and violence, as in the sequence in which Tony turns into a werewolf while watching a young woman in a skimpy leotard work out on a jungle gym in the school gymnasium. His passions aroused, Tony attacks and kills her, fleeing before he can be discovered. In *Teenage Frankenstein*, the monster (played by Gary Conway) becomes so obsessed with his newly constructed body that he spends most of his time simply gazing into a mirror at his newly acquired face, lost in a narcissistic dream world. When Professor Frankenstein (Whit Bissell again) attempts to 'disassemble' the monster to throw the police off his trail, the teenager understandably rebels, triggering an apocalyptic laboratory fire that abruptly ends the film.

Thirdly, Cohen created a great deal of sympathy for both of his teenage protagonists; in both cases, what transpired could never be construed as their fault. In *Teenage Werewolf*, a trusting, naive teenager turns to a supposed healing figure for help and guidance, and is transformed into a savage outsider. In *Teenage Frankenstein*, the monster is constructed from stolen or butchered body parts by adults, who view the resulting creation as nothing more than an interesting experiment, devoid of a soul or free will. Finally, Cohen depicts a world in which only violence rules; the monsters kill because they can't help themselves, or because adults order them to do so. When the teenage werewolf is apprehended by the police, he is cut down in a firestorm of bullets, with no chance of survival. In similar fashion, the teenage Frankenstein is destroyed in a massive electrical short circuit that triggers the film's ultimate lab fire.

To all these ingredients, Cohen added several final touches. Both films know exactly what they are, and pretend to be nothing else. They are efficient killing machines that depict a brutal, harsh, and unforgiving world, and then offer no comfort. Like the world they depict, they are cheap and mercenary. Shot quickly and cheaply, the films are nevertheless at base absolutely serious, and never burlesque the often improbable situations in which they traffic. Lastly, Cohen's posters and promotional materials centered on the most violent and sensational angles, and although *Teenage Frankenstein* was a black and white film, it featured a brief color sequence at the end, so that the film's poster could 'truthfully' trumpet, 'See the monster destroyed in flaming color!' 'Body of a boy! Mind of a Monster! Soul of an unearthly thing!' the publicity materials screamed, and teenage audiences, distrustful and bored, came in droves, absorbing Cohen's dystopian message, identifying with his tortured, doomed protagonists.

By the time Cohen graduated to full color films, with director Arthur Crabtree's remarkably sadistic *Horrors of the Black Museum* (1959), Cohen's formula had become a rigid series of rules that formed a cheerless, utterly desolate moral universe. It's violence all the way through, from beginning to end, with cruelty and greed the only emotions on display. In *Horrors of the Black Museum*'s justly infamous opening, a bright red delivery van pulls up to the apartment house of an attractive young woman, who is surprised to receive an expensive pair of binoculars from the van's driver, as a gift from an anonymous admirer. As she puts the binoculars over her eyes, and tries to focus them, a sharp spike pops out of each lens, killing her instantly.

The culprit is almost immediately revealed to the audience (but not the police) as crime reporter Edmond Bancroft (Michael Gough), who realizes that his readers are hungry for the gory details of violent crimes, and consequently arranges incidents like these to keep his public satisfied. In addition to writing a daily column for one of the sleazier London tabloids, Bancroft also writes books on brutal sex crimes, including a bestseller entitled *The Poetry of Murder*, which is devoured by his fans. Bancroft also keeps his own private 'black museum' showcasing the savage crimes he's committed, and is a thoroughgoing misogynist; at one point, he blurts out that 'no woman can hold her tongue. They're a vicious, unreliable breed!' In short, Bancroft's world is one of hate, brutality and death incarnate.

Not content with this level of violence, Bancroft hypnotizes his teenage assistant Rick (Graham Curnow), and sends him out to murder and decapitate a young prostitute, after injecting Rick with drugs that destroy the young man's free will. When Rick falls in love with pretty Angela Banks (Shirley Ann Field), Bancroft flies into a jealous, obviously homosexual rage, and orders Rick to kill Angela. Rick does so at an amusement park 'tunnel of love,' but then turns on Bancroft, and after scaling a Ferris wheel, Rick jumps to his death, stabbing Bancroft fatally as he falls to earth before a group of startled onlookers.

Working for Cohen, director Arthur Crabtree, who earlier in his career had specialized in romance films, shot *Horrors of the Black Museum* in

England in lurid color and CinemaScope to take advantage of the then-cheaper production facilities available in the UK, just one year before the much more famous, and now generally respected, *Peeping Tom* (1960), directed by another British veteran, Michael Powell. *Peeping Tom* chronicles the daily existence of Mark Lewis (Karl Boehm), a young man who works as a film cameraman, but whose real passion is murdering young women with a spiked tripod while photographing their death agonies. Greeted with critical outrage and disappointing box-office returns when first released, *Peeping Tom* has since become something of a cult classic, and the template for many slasher films to follow. It's odd to me that *Peeping Tom* has now achieved a level of critical acclaim that *Horrors of the Black Museum* will never enjoy; both films are spectacles of unrelieved carnage, but at least one can argue that *Horrors of the Black Museum* is more forthright about its intent.

All of Cohen's films, then, have high levels of violence, all feature teenage protagonists, and all depict a world in which cruelty and brutality are undetected until a violent social rupture brings the criminal to light. The adults are the real monsters, using teenagers as their tools of murder and mayhem; in Powell's film, it is Karl's sadistic psychiatrist father, A. N. Lewis (played, astonishingly, by Powell himself) whose experiments in fear have marked Karl for life. These films are usually classed as horror films, but are they? Or are they films about the horror of everyday existence, the uncertainty of life, the mendacity of authority, the failure of hope and the inevitability of corruption? What better words could one use to describe a film noir?

With the Korean War looming, and the Cold War well underway, noir films began to reference themselves, and their auteurs. When the Red Scare films of the early 1950s started popping up, Bogart was one of the first who spoke out against the new blacklist, but was forced to recant to save his career; others, such as 1940s noir specialist Edward Dmytryk, were sentenced to jail for refusing to cooperate with the authorities, and resumed their former careers only after appearing before the HUAC and informing on their former associates.

In Dmytryk's case, his 'testimony' resulted in his immediate return to the director's chair, where he created one of his most vicious and despairing films, *The Sniper* (1952), starring Arthur Franz as Eddie Miller, a psychopath who kills women at random with a high-powered rifle. *The Sniper*'s vision of American life is vicious, cold, and clinical; people exist in the film only to be destroyed, and the police are seemingly powerless to stop the killer until the film's final moments. Ironically, veteran actor Adolphe Menjou is cast in the film as Police Lt Frank Kafka; a nice touch, and almost certainly intended, since Menjou was one of the most ardent supporters of the blacklist, and among the first to give 'friendly' testimony in this most 'Kafkaesque' of investigations, where one was guilty until 'proven' innocent. As a document of big-city random violence, *The Sniper* remains absolutely up to date today, as recent sniper killings in the Washington, DC and Baltimore area attest.

Significantly, Franz's Eddie Miller repeatedly seeks help from the authorities, realizing that he is about to go over the edge, but no aid is forth-coming. Eddie is left to fall through the cracks, until he re-emerges as a figure of violent death. In the 1950s, our fear of the Other in our backyard was replaced by the fear of foreign invasion, and even atomic attack, from an entirely new and unanticipated antagonist. After all, weren't the Russians our allies in World War II? The basic precepts of noir – to trust no one, to believe nothing as truth, to expect the worst in all possible situations, to realize that deception was an integral feature of social discourse – were all coming true.

Fifties noir films thus directly contradicted the split-level dream that was being consumed by most of American society, which nevertheless had begun to collapse from the inside out, revealing the rot behind the placid exterior of suburban society. As always, it is the cheapest films of this era that most authentically mirror its desperations and hidden crises. While the major studios tried to ignore the changing mores of the era with a series of escapist comedies, it was left to the minors to accurately document the Cold War era, replete with newsreels that promised 'the beginning of World War III' on a weekly basis, and an administration that remained polarized by the global power struggle between the Soviet Union and the United States.

The 1950s were a site of profound cultural disease; on the one hand, the threat of nuclear annihilation was continually stressed in American culture, with such films as the animated cartoon short *Duck and Cover* (1950), in which children are falsely told that by simply ducking under their school desks, they can escape the fatal impact of a nuclear attack; on the other hand, Delmer Daves's *A Summer Place* (1959) offered a world of teenage escape from the problems of the adult milieu, even if it, too, was compromised by the social unrest of the era.

CHAPTER 4

The Flip Side of the 1960s

Peter Collinson's *The Penthouse* (1967), a key British noir film of the 1960s, followed in the tradition of Joseph Losey's more restrained dramas of claustrophobic domesticity gone horribly wrong in *The Servant* (1963) and *Accident* (1967). London in the early 1960s was typically depicted as a zone of carefree abandon in such films as Richard Lester's *Help!* (1965), *A Hard Day's Night* (1964) and his sex comedy *The Knack . . . and How to Get It* (1965), a surprise winner at the Cannes Film Festival that year.

Other pop films, such as John Boorman's *Catch Us If You Can* (aka *Having a Wild Weekend*, 1965) with pop stars The Dave Clark Five, also exploited the image of 'Swinging London,' as did Desmond Davis's *Smashing Time* (1967), in which Rita Tushingham and Lynn Redgrave come to London for a whirlwind shot at pop celebrity. But as always, beneath the gloss and the electricity of the era, an undercurrent was readily detectable. Pop stardom proved to be utterly transient, and as drugs and disillusion set in, the mood became more somber. Life wasn't always a party. Sometimes, it was quite brutal.

The Penthouse was Peter Collinson's first film as a director, and was based on a play, *The Meter Man*, by C. Scott Farber. The film's, and the play's, premise is simple; an adulterous couple spend a stolen evening in a vacant luxury flat. Bruce Victor (Terence Morgan) is a real–estate broker stuck in an unhappy marriage, and finds momentary solace in the arms of Barbara Willamson (Suzy Kendall). Bruce tells Barbara that he intends to leave his wife for her, but this is merely a ploy to keep her content for the moment. Bruce's real interests, of course, are only in himself.

They've had these illicit liaisons before, but this night will be different. Drifting off to sleep in each other's arms, they imagine a rosy future. But morning dawns, and suddenly the doorbell rings. Tom (Tony Beckley) and Dick (Norman Rodway) appear, passing themselves off as meter readers. But they're nothing of the sort; Tom and Dick are here to terrorize the

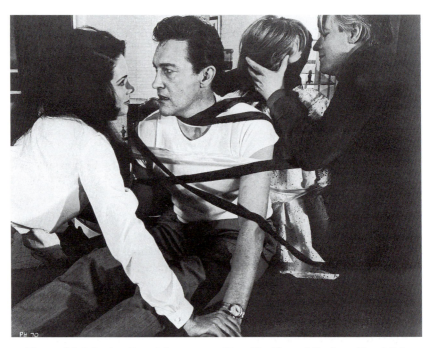

Figure 4.1 Martine Beswick torments Tony Beckley, while Suzy Kendall is molested by Norman Rodway in Peter Collinson's *The Penthouse* (1967).

complacent lovers with an ever more dangerous series of 'funny games' to cite Michael Haneke's 1997 film which operates on much the same premise (and which Haneke remade in 2007).

Tom and Dick are nothing less than agents of destruction, destined to create social disruption wherever they go. Tying Bruce to a chair, the pair ply Barbara with alcohol and smoke marijuana, and then take turns repeatedly raping her, while Victor looks on, helpless. Tiring of their 'games,' Tom and Dick discuss how they'll dispose of Barbara and Bruce to avoid being arrested by the police, as Bruce begs the pair to untie him, and leave them in peace. The pair laugh at Bruce's pleas, but then, as suddenly as they arrived, they vanish from the flat, leaving Barbara in a state of shock, and Bruce still tied to a chair.

Bruce's cringing behavior during the entire episode has killed whatever feelings Barbara may have had for him, and she loosens his bonds reluctantly, seeing him for the first time as the fraud he is. Nevertheless, their ordeal seems over, until the doorbell rings again, and Harry (Martine Beswick, in a role originally intended for a male actor) appears, announcing that she is Tom and Dick's parole officer, and that she has brought them back to apologize.

Naturally, Harry is nothing of the sort, and soon the 'games' start up again, with even more violent and despairing consequences, until Tom, Dick, and Harry finally vanish from the penthouse forever, having completely destroyed any sense of safety and/or security Bruce and Barbara may once have had. There's no real explanation for their actions; they simply destroy people's lives, and then move on. It's what they do. And they'll be back again, to visit another penthouse, and terrorize more 'innocent' and defenseless victims . . . perhaps even you.

The film has a total of five characters, and was shot by Collinson when he was just twenty-eight years old, on a single set, for a budget of roughly $100,000, in a brief three-week shoot. The cinematography by veteran Arthur Lavis seeks out as many unsettling angles as possible, and the cool color scheme of the vacant flat foregrounds the characters in the sordid drama in sharp relief. While the film was a solid commercial success when first released, most critics despised it as a gratuitous exercise in sadism and violence, although it now looks tame by twenty-first-century standards. Yet Roger Ebert, writing in the *Chicago Sun Times*, got the point of the film immediately.

Ebert described *The Penthouse* as a 'pretty good shocker . . . successful ones are rare. It's a relief to find one that's made with skill and a certain amount of intelligence.' He continued, 'this isn't an evil movie, and it's not an example of the pornography of violence . . . When I interviewed [Collinson] a couple of months ago, he said he was trying, purely and simply, to tell an exciting story. He did not believe in "message" movies, he said.' Perhaps, and yet *The Penthouse* stands out as a prescient thriller with a disquieting message, whether Collinson intended it or not (and I very much think he did). The home is no longer a place of safety, but rather a zone where 'push in' robbers can rape and pillage with impunity.

Explaining their motivations to Barbara and Bruce, Tom delivers a long, hypnotic monologue, likening the psychotic pair to miniature, pet alligators (a brief fad, believe it or not, during the period) that have been flushed into London's vast, dark sewage system when their owners can no longer control them. Stuck in the sewers, these alligators never see light, grow to enormous proportions, become blind and albino from lack of sun, and only occasionally emerge to wreak havoc on an unsuspecting city dweller who chances to cross their paths. 'We're like those poor little tiny alligators,' Tom tells the imprisoned couple. 'We didn't want to be flushed into the sewers, but we were. And we can't help it if we're alligators.'

And yet social rupture was happening at all class levels. Sidney J. Furie's long forgotten *The Leather Boys* (1964) chronicles the outlaw lifestyle of a group of bikers who operate at the margins of society, with little education or hope for the future. They live for the moment, and are only dimly conscious of what may lie over the horizon. Reggie (Colin Campbell) and Dot (Rita Tushingham) fall in love, or so they think, on a 'run' with their fellow gang members, while Pete (Dudley Sutton), a closeted gay biker, hovers in the background. Rapidly married, Reggie and Dot find that they have little in common; Dot spends her money on hairdressers, chips, and pop magazines, while Reggie prefers to work on his bike.

Pete, enamored of Reggie, waits for an opportunity to declare his passion, while Reggie, completely in the dark about Pete's sexuality, watches his marriage to Dot collapse. Shot on location at grimy cafes and garages, including the Ace Cafe, a popular biker hangout on the North Circular Road in London, Furie's film uses black and white CinemaScope to create an atmosphere of desperation and longing – all of the film's protagonists are in a rush to get away, but where? A bike race to Edinburgh and back is beautifully staged, as the bikers take over the road in an act of social defiance, but at the race's end, Reggie and his mates are back right where they started from, in a working-class world, with no hope of escape.

The film's final moments are heartbreaking; Pete convinces Reggie to go away with him, and leave London behind, but at the last minute, Reggie finally realizes that Pete is in love with him, when Pete arranges a meeting in a gay bar. Shocked and surprised, Reggie backs out of their planned 'escape,' and goes back to Dot; it is the only life he knows, no matter how dissatisfying it may be. As with all noirs, there is no escape for the protagonists of *The Leather Boys*; for all their energy and movement, they are essentially going nowhere, stuck in an endless cycle of flight and inevitable return, repeating the same patterns day after day, their dream of freedom a momentary illusion.

Perhaps the most nihilist film of the 1960s British new wave is Michelangelo Antonioni's *Blowup*, centering on a narcissistic fashion photographer, Thomas (David Hemmings), who accidentally photographs a murder in progress while shooting snapshots one afternoon in a London park. As with most of Antonioni's films, *Blowup* is an essay in loneliness, isolation, and emptiness; Thomas is at the top of his profession, but takes little joy in his work, and spends his free time buying worthless knick-knacks at antique shops – an enormous airplane propeller, in one case – while pursuing an empty lifestyle of casual sex, drinking, and drug use, with a group of disposable 'friends.'

Jane (Vanessa Redgrave), complicit in the murders, visits Thomas and tries to get the photos from him, offering sex in exchange for their return. When Thomas realizes what he has actually 'seen' through the lens of his camera, he begins an arduous process of rephotographing the images he's shot, blowing them up again and again, until the outline of the corpse of a man is clearly visible beneath a shade tree. Alarmed, he revisits the location, and finds the corpse still there, undiscovered by anyone else. He goes to a party where his stoned friends have no interest in his discovery; he drifts into a performance by the Yardbirds, as Jimmy Page smashes his guitar to bits before a frenzied audience.

It's a long night's journey into day, and as the dawn breaks, Thomas again finds himself in the park, but the body is no longer there. Nearby, a group of traveling mimes pretend to play tennis with a phantom ball and racquets. In a dazzling tracking shot, the invisible 'ball' goes out of bounds, and comes to rest on the grass. Thomas hesitantly 'picks it up', and mimes throwing it back into play; moments later, Thomas himself has vanished from the playing field, as phantasmal as the corpse he photographed the day before. Or did the body ever exist at all?

Antonioni's film is ultimately an interrogation of the unreality of everyday existence. Everything is unreal and transitory, and despite all of his worldly success, Thomas still feels trapped by the trappings of celebrity status as a photographer. Much like Reggie and Dot in *The Leather Boys*, he just wants to get away – anywhere, it doesn't matter. 'I wish I had tons of money,' he muses. 'Then I'd be free.' But of course, he will never be free; as shallow as he is, he barely exists at any real level. Thomas's world is as disposable as he is; no one will miss him, or his works, when he's gone.

Roman Polanski's contribution to the British 1960s noir tradition, *Repulsion* (1965), is a straightforward study of personal disintegration, as a young woman, Carole Ledoux (Catherine Deneuve), slowly goes insane in her sister's flat, imagining hands thrusting through the walls of the apartment to grab her and sexually violate her. When the greasy landlord (Patrick Wymark) comes calling for the rent, and leeringly suggests an afternoon liaison, Carole reacts with unexpected violence, slashing him to death, and then leaving the corpse to rot in the living room.

Joseph Losey's enigmatic film *The Servant* (1963), with a script by Harold Pinter from Robin Maugham's novel, is another tale of interior claustrophobia, as the weak aristocrat Tony (James Fox) takes on the seemingly humble Hugo Barrett (Dirk Bogarde) as his general factotum, only to slowly discover that he is no longer the dominant force in the household, for Barrett is soon taking liberties with Tony's person and possessions. When Tony's fiancée Susan (Wendy Craig) tries to intervene, Barrett forces her out of the household, and strengthens his grip on Tony through drugs and debauchery, adding the mysteriously vixenish Vera (Sarah Miles) to the mix for added sexual adventure.

Figure 4.2 Dirk Bogarde and James Fox offer a new definition of housekeeping in Joseph Losey's *The Servant* (1963).

The Servant was shot in a vacant luxury two-level flat, recalling Peter Collinson's *The Penthouse*; filming took place in the dead of winter on a minuscule budget, and when director Losey was hospitalized for several weeks with pneumonia, Dirk Bogarde personally took over the direction of the film, relying on Losey's telephoned instructions to complete the required setups for each day's work. Had the executive producers known of this situation, no doubt they would have shut the film down; but

Losey soon returned to work, albeit at first on a stretcher, and then in a wheelchair, smothered in blankets, and drinking copious amounts of strong tea to keep warm.

As Barrett, Bogarde effectively shrugs off the light romantic persona that made him 'The Idol of the Odeons' in such films as Ralph Thomas's *Doctor in the House* (1954), and emerges as a sinister, sensual force of corruption and temptation, utterly implacable in his quest for power and control. James Fox, a newcomer to films at the time, is perfectly cast as the spineless Tony, all pretense and foppery, and an attractive target for Barrett's machinations. Immaculately photographed in crisp black and white, with John Dankworth's melancholic jazz score supporting Losey's austere images, *The Servant* is one of the key films of the British new wave. It paved the way for what would prove to be the quintessential domestic noir of the decade, Nicolas Roeg and Donald Cammel's *Performance* (1970), which would expand on many of the themes of *The Servant* in a far more explicit manner. Indeed, there seems to be a strong tradition in British noirs towards narratives of class conflict and societal control, usually set in hermetically sealed surroundings. *The Servant* is emblematic of this school of claustrophobic introspection, and remains today a compelling, dangerous piece of bravura filmmaking.

In America, things were proceeding in a far more brutal fashion. The maverick director Al Adamson, who was ultimately murdered in real life by his own handyman, and walled up in the concrete foundation of a luxurious bathtub in his home, created a series of dystopian narratives in the mid to late 1960s, working for the ultra low-budget production company Independent International. *Satan's Sadists* was Al Adamson's 'breakthrough' film, and a logical conclusion to the biker trend started by director Laszlo Benedek with the Marlon Brando vehicle *The Wild One* (1954), which depicted the activities of a motorcycle gang terrorizing a small California town until the state police step in.

In *The Wild One*, social disruption is easily contained once the outside forces of the law step in; the problem is the permissiveness of the local people, who let things get out of hand. By the time of Roger Corman's *The Wild Angels* (1966), the situation had become more sophisticated and more complicated, and yet, in the end, the threat posed by the bikers was finally dealt with by law enforcement, effectively putting a stop to a rampage of lawless mayhem. No such happy ending exists in *Satan's Sadists*, shot in 1969 and released in 1970, which reflected the growing nihilism of the end of the 1960s dream.

As Gary Kent, an actor in the film, summarized it, *Satan's Sadists* 'reflected a rampant anti-establishment feeling . . . it wasn't a peace and love attitude. There was a lot of anger when things went bad at the end of the 60s' (as quoted in Konow 1998: 43). Sam Sherman, the film's producer, agreed, noting that '*Satan's Sadists* is a story of anger and hostility, but the real anger was not the bikers against society . . . it was Al and myself fighting against the film industry. That film contained our seething anger bubbling to the surface' (as quoted in Konow 1998: 51).

In *Satan's Sadists*, star Russ Tamblyn plays Anchor, the leader of an impossibly evil band of biker renegades who ride through the film leaving violence and death in their wake. The film opens with a young couple parked in a car, making out. The gang surprise the pair, and repeatedly rape the young woman, while drugging the young man into stupefaction. Not content with this, the Satans then drag the couple back into their car, and push it off a cliff, killing them both. There's no reason for any of this; it just happens. And there's no real narrative connection to the rest of the story; this framing scene simply establishes that the Satans are seemingly beyond the control of any authority whatsoever.

The film then cuts to the lone figure of Johnny (Gary Kent), a Vietnam veteran hitching down the road, who is picked up by a passing policeman (noir veteran Scott Brady) and his wife; they make the fatal mistake of pulling into a diner for a bite to eat as the Satans also arrive. The owner (another noir veteran, Kent Taylor) tries to pacify the gang, but the atmosphere of violence and tension explodes and a fight breaks out. The gang ties up the policeman, his wife, and the diner's owner, while Anchor rapes the policeman's wife, and then kills all three in cold blood. Johnny witnesses all this, unable to help his erstwhile friends, but finally springs into action with assistance from Tracy (Jackie Taylor), a young waitress who works at the restaurant. Johnny and Tracy kill two of the Satans in suitably grisly fashion, and escape into the desert, with Anchor and his gang in hot pursuit.

But soon, everything falls apart for the outlaws. One kills himself playing Russian roulette; another drives off a cliff; yet another dies of snakebite. After more murder and mayhem, Johnny and Anchor are left for a climactic showdown. In the film's one concession to conventional narrative closure, Anchor dies, while Johnny and Tracy manage to survive the Satans' onslaught.

Anchor's motivation, if one can call it that, for his murderous rampage is best summed up in a speech that he delivers to the helpless policeman, his wife, and the restaurant owner just before he shoots them to death in the restaurant, as the trio are tied up like hogs ready for slaughter. As Anchor rapes the policeman's wife, the cop calls Anchor a 'rotten bastard,' and swears vengeance, shouting at the top of his lungs, 'I'll get ya! I'll get ya if it's the last thing I do!' Anchor considers this for a moment, and then replies

> You're right, cop. I am a rotten bastard, I admit it. But I tell ya somethin'. Even though I got a lot of hate inside, I got some friends who ain't got hate inside. They're filled with nothin' but love. Their only crime is growin' their hair a little long, smokin' a little grass under the stars at night and writin' poetry in the sand. And what do you do? You bust down their doors! Dumbass cop! You bust down their doors and you bust down their heads! You throw 'em behind bars! And ya wanna know somethin' funny? They forgive ya!' (as quoted in Konow 1998: 45)

Then, without another word, he shoots all three in the head methodically, then steps back to admire the carnage. Satisfied, he adds two words to his tirade; 'I don't.' This, in microcosm, is the world of Al Adamson, a desperate filmmaker with a passion to succeed against all odds, who spent his lifetime working on the margins of the industry on projects scorned by mainstream audiences. There is no forgiveness in Adamson's work, and no future either. All Adamson offers is the embrace of death and mindless, motiveless nihilism. The Satans kill, plunder, and rape simply because they've got nothing better to do. They don't need a motive, or a reason, or even a catalyst. They simply exist to destroy everything, and everyone else.

A noir auteur to the end, Adamson depicts in his films a universe of desperation and loneliness, violence and revenge, of hatred without motivation and unremitting fear of the future. His films are brutal, uncompromising, and shoddy, but, as David Will memorably noted in a different context, discussing the films of Roger Corman, 'there is no better medium than a cheap movie to convey a cheap rotten universe' (Will 1970: 74). Of his shooting methods, Adamson noted that he had learned the cardinal rule of low-budget filmmaking from his father, and he never forgot it: 'When you ran out of money, whatever you got was done. You could use it' (as quoted in Konow 1998: 23). In Adamson's world, he used the tools he had to create the films he could; films that, as he admitted, spoke to his own sense of furious despair and nihilism.

The American dream was collapsing; that much was certain, and many wished they could live their lives over again, recapturing the pleasures of their lost youth. In particular, the light sex comedies of the 1950s had long since passed out of vogue. John Frankenheimer's dark *Seconds* (1966) allowed Rock Hudson, for once, to step out of his stereotypical leading-man image, in the story of a man who is literally given a second chance at life, through the services of a mysterious corporation that offers him a new face, a younger body, and a chance to escape the boring circumstances of his nine-to-five existence.

Arthur Hamilton (John Randolph) is a bored, graying businessman whose life has ground to a halt; discontented with his work and his home life, no longer attracted to his devoted wife Emily (Frances Reid), Arthur is desperately seeking a way out. An old wartime buddy, Charlie Evans (Murray Hamilton), approaches him, and suggests that perhaps there might be a solution to his problem; Arthur can be 'reborn' and leave his past behind. Intrigued, Arthur sets up a meeting with the corporation's sinister boss, never named in the film, played by the blacklisted character actor Will Geer, later a regular as 'Grandpa' on the ur-domestic family television series, *The Waltons*. Geer explains that the corporation will fake Arthur's death, and provide him with a new face, body, and identity – as an artist, something that Arthur has always aspired to. With all this comes a beach house, and a new girlfriend, Nora Marcus (Salome Jens). The price: everything he owns. To make sure that Arthur won't back out, now that he is cognizant of the corporation's existence, Geer drugs Arthur and stages a 'rape,' photographed by concealed cameras, to frame him into agreeing to the scheme.

With little choice Arthur acquiesces, and after a marathon round of plastic surgery is reborn as Tony Wilson (Rock Hudson), a sixty-year-old man in the body of a thirty-year-old bachelor. At first, life is exactly as promised. At his new beach house, Arthur paints abstract expressionist canvases for the adoring Nora, and takes long walks on the beach, finally out of the rat race. The corporation has even provided Tony with new 'friends,' who show up for barbecues and parties, and a butler, John (Wesley Addy), who attends to Tony's every need.

But the adjustment proves impossible to make. Tony longs for his wife, and his old existence, and realizes too late that 'you can't repeat the past' in life. Tony visits his old house in his new persona, where his wife Emily no longer recognizes him, and mourns the passing of her husband. In an almost unbearably poignant scene, Arthur/Tony realizes what he has given up, and tries to opt out of his new, bought existence. But the corporation has other ideas; when Tony asks to be 'reassigned' to a different existence, they harvest his body for another client, this time killing him for real.

As the surgeon's saw cuts into his skull, Tony's last mental image is of walking on the beach, free from care, with his wife. Arthur Hamilton's life and his 'second' life have now been terminated – there will be no chance for 'seconds' again. Shot in bleak black and white, *Seconds* was a commercial failure when first released, and it is easy to see why. Can't you buy happiness? Can't you always get a fresh start? Isn't youth available for sale, through pills, diets, exercise, plastic surgery, and the like? Can't you transform yourself into your own ideal, with money being the only obstacle? Of course you can't, but this dream of eternal renewal is one of the most persistent myths of our contemporary culture, and in the twenty-first century, much of what *Seconds* prophesied has sadly come to pass. A new face, a new home, a new wife, a new job in a different town; this will make everything new again, won't it? You can start again; isn't that true? Frankenheimer's uncompromising film suggests that this myth of an 'Extreme Makeover' is not only a lie; it is dangerous to even pursue.

Arthur Dreifuss, another refugee from the Nazis in the early 1930s who landed in Hollywood, had been a precocious pianist and conductor when still a youth in his native land, and later switched to producing and choreographing stage musicals (Katz 2005: 405). But when he fled Germany, he was only able to find work in the United States as dance director on low-budget Hollywood musicals; and although he finally broke into direction with *Mystery in Swing* (1940), again, it was a modest film, with no real artistic ambition.

Dreifuss thus labored in Hollywood through the 1940s, 1950s, and 1960s with no real direction, unable to get a foothold on a major project, consigned to directing such films as *Melody Parade* (1943), the series noirs *Boston Blackie Booked On Suspicion* and *Boston Blackie's Rendezvous* (both 1945), *Two Blondes and a Redhead* (1947), *Juke Box Rhythm* (1959), and other forgettable projects. But in 1967, the ultra cost-conscious producer Sam Katzman teamed with Dreifuss to make two dystopian youth culture films that attracted a great deal of attention when first released, and still resonate today: *The Love-Ins* and *Riot on Sunset Strip* (both 1967).

Both films were shot in color as part of a production program to create low-cost films for theatres starved for product; each took a mere six days to shoot, with budgets hovering in the $350,000 range; certainly not luxurious by any standards. Yet, in their own perverse way, both films have much to tell us of the true tenor of the late 1960s in America, when young people without direction, and disenchanted by existing authority figures, sought any way to escape from their increasingly regimented lives.

The Love-Ins, which came first, chronicles the rise and violent fall of Dr Jonathan Barnett, a Timothy Leary stand-in played with a good deal of skill and subtlety by Richard Todd, a British actor who had fallen on lean times. Barnett is a free-thinking English professor who quits his job in protest when two of his students, Larry Osborne (James MacArthur) and Patricia Cross (Susan Oliver), are expelled from university for publishing an 'underground newspaper' entitled *Tomorrow's Times*.

Hailed as a hero by his students and their peers for this act of self-sacrifice, Barnett follows them to the Haight Ashbury district where Larry

Figure 4.3 Richard Todd takes too easily to the role of acid guru, as acolyte
Susan Oliver looks on in Arthur Dreifuss's *The Love-Ins* (1967).

and Patricia share a crash pad with dozens of others, and publish
Tomorrow's Times in their basement office. Turned on to LSD by his students, the initially self-effacing Barnett rapidly becomes a self-promoting
egomaniac, and falls under the malign influence of Elliott (Mark Goddard),
a smooth-talking hustler who rightly senses that all the 'peace, love, and
harmony' can be profitable for the right person.

Barnett now styles himself the leader of a growing cult, and makes 'Be
More, Sense More, Love More' (a direct lift from Leary's directive to

'Tune in, Turn on, Drop out') the group's slogan. Holding mass rallies in Golden Gate park, Barnett effectively lures thousands to his cause, with Elliott directing merchandising efforts that make both men a fortune. At the same time, Barnett has replaced Larry in Patricia's affections and, in short order, Patricia discovers that she is pregnant with Barnett's child. Patricia is ecstatic, but Barnett is less than thrilled, telling her directly to 'get rid of it,' and confessing that he thinks of her only as a sexual plaything, and has no time for any responsibilities.

Distraught, Patricia realizes that she and her compatriots have been duped by Barnett's false promise of freedom. Larry, furious with Barnett for his betrayal of both Patricia and 'the movement,' buys a gun and trails Barnett to the cult's largest rally yet, held in a massive outdoor stadium. Walking right to the front of the assembled throng, Larry pulls out his gun and shoots Barnett dead, then immediately surrenders to the police. Elliott grabs the microphone, assuring the stunned crowd that 'Dr Barnett's work will go on without him,' but people start to drift away. It won't be so easy to replace Barnett, and so, for the moment at least, the 'movement' splinters into nothingness.

The narrative of the film is odd because on one level, it is entirely fraudulent; and yet on another, it's all too accurate. Leary was, indeed, an insanely egotistical self-promoter, whose influence in the 1960s accomplished, in the end, more harm than good, as Robert Greenfield's recent biography makes abundantly clear (see Greenfield 2006 for more details on Leary's long and complicated life). On the other hand, much of *The Love-Ins* is flatly ridiculous, both in its depiction of the late 1960s alternative lifestyle, and its obvious 'back lot' look. Then, too, the film dismisses all countercultural activity, any act of insurrection, as inherently destructive, which overlooks the wealth of cultural, artistic, and personal insights (the birth of the women's movement, for example) that flowered in the late 1960s era.

And yet the film ultimately emerges as a compellingly 'fake' yet authentic document, projecting the fears of 'normative' society onto a new generation, dismissing antiwar protests as anti-American, and portraying an entire generation of adolescents as gullible, impressionable naïfs. Much of what *The Love-Ins* depicted was all too true; the exploitation of the young for personal gain, marketing 'youth leaders' to create a cult of personalities, and the exploitation of innocence for monetary profit. Shortly after the release of *The Love-Ins*, in fact, the entire 'hippie' movement collapsed, as the events of 1968 – the assassinations of Robert F. Kennedy and Martin Luther King, Jr, the escalation of the Vietnam War, and the disastrous Democratic presidential convention in Chicago, during which protesters were clubbed and maced by unsympathetic police – caused many to move further left, and embrace violence as the only effective tool of social change.

Equally unsettling, although in a less ambitious fashion, is Dreifuss's *Riot on Sunset Strip*, which was written in a matter of days to capitalize on the real-life 1966 Sunset Strip curfew riots (see Dixon 2005: 52). Aldo Ray plays Lieutenant Walt Lorimer of the LAPD, whose daughter Andy (Mimsy Farmer) embraces the counterculture with disastrous results. As a divorced father, Lorimer has to try to balance parental concern with his duty as a cop, while also trying to placate more traditional business owners on the Sunset Strip, who argue (as they did in real life) that hordes of teenagers are driving customers away from their restaurants and cocktail lounges.

Interestingly, Dreifuss seems to have little sympathy for the 'straight' bar and restaurant owners in the film, who are continually portrayed in an unflattering light as bigots, who would be just as happy if all the teens vanished from the face of the earth. On the other hand, many of Andy's 'friends' are predatory, vicious manipulators; in the film's most striking sequence, Andy's drink is spiked with acid, and as she dances blissfully to rock music in extreme slow motion for a number of minutes, her hair spilling over her shoulders in youthful abandon, five of her male 'friends' stare at her with naked lust and malevolence.

Predictably, Andy becomes the victim of a gang rape, and is left behind when the police raid the party (which, by the way, takes place in a deserted house the teens have broken into). Lt Lorimer's subsequent attempts to arrest the rapists are once again balanced with his desire to protect the other teenagers still on the Strip from his own officers, who want to club them into submission without any provocation, and the 'establishment' business owners, who are indifferent to Lorimer's personal anguish over his daughter Andy's victimization. The film ends with the conflict unresolved; the kids 'have to go somewhere,' and for the moment, this is it. No solutions have been offered, no problems really solved; Dreifuss's narrative is without closure, uncertain as to where it stands in relation to the events it has presented to the audience.

Perhaps the most popular counterculture film of the late 1960s, Dennis Hopper's *Easy Rider* (1969), ends with a brutal murder of two cocaine-dealing bikers by a passing redneck in a pickup truck; the halcyon vision of swinging London and San Francisco as some sort of blissful Eden has long since vanished. Both *The Love-Ins* and *Riot on Sunset Strip* are, at a certain level, simplistic and naive, and yet each contains a certain level of auteurist integrity in the haste and unease of its execution that spills over into the finished work. What exactly is happening here? Can we understand it, or even hope to comprehend it? Are we wrong? Are they wrong? Are we all wrong? It is on this last point, I would ague, that both films ultimately rest; nothing is really 'knowable,' society is in flux, all value judgments are suspect. For the present, we will just have to do the best we can with the prejudices and desires we're confronted with; a noir sentiment, to say the least.

Barry Shear's *Wild in the Streets* (1968) is an even more extreme vision of this 'youth runs wild' thesis: Max Frost (Christopher Jones) is a twenty-four-year-old musician and self-styled activist whose band, The Troopers, includes fifteen-year-old legal whiz kid Billy Cage (Kevin Coughlin), Max's girlfriend Sally LeRoy (Diane Varsi), cultural anthropologist Stanley X (Richard Pryor, in a very early role) as the band's drummer, and Abraham Salteen (Larry Bishop) as the group's keyboard player. When seasoned politician Johnny Fergus (Hal Holbook) asks Max to sing at one of his rallies in support of a proposal to lower the legal voting age to eighteen, Max responds, on live television, that the voting age should be fourteen, not eighteen. Intense publicity for the televised event leads to mass demonstrations around the country, and eventually a counterproposal of a fifteen-year voting age is passed into law.

Through a complex series of events, Max is eventually elected president, and with his ascendancy to office, declares thirty as the mandatory retirement age. Max's parents (Shelley Winters and Bert Freed) are among those who are rounded up and thrown into detention camps, where they are dosed with massive amounts of LSD. Max institutes even more radical policies, dissolving the Secret Service and the FBI, and withdrawing US troops from their stations around the globe to supervise the imprisonment of the over-thirty generation, and then settles back for an extended run of sex, drugs, and rock and roll.

There's only one problem; at twenty-four, he has only six years left before he, too, will be carted away to the forced detention camps. And there's one more wrinkle; the under-ten set aren't all that happy with many of Max's policies, and in the film's final moments, a youngster suggests darkly that, soon, they will be in power, and Max will be an 'old man.' Peppered with cameos from Dick Clark, celebrity attorney Melvin Belli, *Variety* columnist Army Archerd, and veteran character actor Ed Begley, *Wild in the Streets* is a curious hybrid of youth and age, of raw talent (Jones and Pryor, who brings sullen conviction to his role) and calculated experience (Holbrook and Begley, particularly, lend credence to their roles, making the preposterous scenario seem, at times, almost likely). Yet Shear's direction of Robert Thom's apocalyptic script is so overblown, so extreme, that the film is hard to take seriously. Even so, at moments, *Wild in the*

Figure 4.4 Mick Jagger, Michèle Breton and Anita Pallenberg relax in the bath in Nicolas Roeg and Donald Cammel's justly notorious *Performance* (1970).

Streets offers a compelling vision of societal collision, in which the values of one age have completely erased that of another.

The film, however, that more effectively put paid to the dreams of the 1960s counterculture was the noir gangster film *Performance*, which, appropriately, appeared in 1970, just as the tumultuous decade was coming to a close. The film was one of the few genuinely successful co-direction efforts in screen history, helmed by writer Donald Cammel and cinematographer Nicolas Roeg, who had made a name for himself as a director of photography in the 1960s on a wide variety of projects, including Roger Corman's 1964 production of *Masque of the Red Death*. The plot of the film is deceptively simple; Mick Jagger plays Turner, 'old rubber lips,' as one character refers to him, a retired, jaded rock star who lives in squalid splendor in a London townhouse with Pherber (Anita Pallenberg) and Lucy (Michèle Breton), two young women who have sex with Turner and each other, take all sorts of drugs (from injected speed, to mushrooms, LSD, cocaine, STP, DMT, and anything else they can ingest), and generally waste time, with nothing to do for an unforeseeably endless future.

Into this decadent mélange comes Chas (James Fox), a violent gangster on the run from his former associates, who shakes up the whole household.

But as the film progresses, Turner gradually grinds Chas's personality down with drugs and bisexual experimentation, while Chas plans to flee the country for a new life in Morocco. Too late; Chas's criminal colleagues have discovered his hiding place, and arrive at Turner's house to reclaim him. As if coming out of a trance, Chas reverts to his former personality, and agrees to go with them, but only if he can have a moment with Turner first. Entering Turner's bedroom, Chas shoots Turner through the head, killing him with a single bullet, and then departs with his 'mates.' But as their car pulls away, we see that it is Turner in the back seat, not Chas. Have their identities been merged? What precisely has happened?

This, unfortunately (or fortunately), is something we will never know. Although the film was meticulously scripted, Jagger improvised a good bit of his dialogue, and James Fox, now light years away from his performance as the effete aristocrat in *The Servant*, brings a real and frightening authority to his role as Chas, the psychotic gangster. The first third of the film runs along two parallel but not intersecting tracks; we follow Chas through a typical day's work as a strong-arm man for his boss, Harry Flowers (Johnny Shannon) – 'he likes his work, that one,' one of Harry's minions comments, noting Chas's extreme sadism and love of violence – while Turner indulges in fooling around with his Moog synthesizer, and spray painting his flat.

The film opens with Chas engaged in some extremely violent sado-masochistic sex with a young woman, glimpsed in fragmented shots, reflected in mirrors, and enhanced by freeze frames and rapid intercutting. Chas's world is violence; Turner's is indolence. Together, like the Kray twins who dominated London's underworld during the 1960s, they make the ideally complementary couple, although neither would ever have admitted it before, or even after, their paths crossed.

Roeg and Cammell shoot the film in a highly stylized manner, intercutting the past and present with impunity, using all manner of optical effects to play with the image, even referencing Ingmar Bergman's 1966 film *Persona* in one scene, in which Chas and Turner's faces are superimposed on each other, as Turner solemnly intones on the soundtrack, 'it's time for a change.' Time for a change, yes, but from what, and to what? *Performance* offers no answers in this regard, and frequently references the writings and themes of Jorge Luis Borges, particularly his obsession with the mutability of identity, to amplify this intentional uncertainty. When Chas shoots Turner in the head in the last minutes of the film, the camera literally follows the path of the bullet through Turner's head, at one point encountering a portrait of Borges which instantaneously shatters, before the viewer is magically transported to the street outside Turner's townhouse.

Almost universally reviled upon its initial release, given an 'X' rating in the United States, and severely restricted elsewhere, *Performance* is a one-of-a-kind movie, a one-off collaboration that could never, and would never, be repeated. Donald Cammell went on to a variety of other films, including *The Demon Seed* (1977), a futuristic computer thriller that was only partially successful, but many of his other projects failed to come to fruition, and his career was cut short by an early death.

Nicolas Roeg went on to direct *Walkabout* (1971), a survivalist thriller set in the Australian outback; *Don't Look Now* (1973), a surprisingly effective thriller starring Donald Sutherland and Julie Christie; as well as *The Man Who Fell to Earth* (1976), with pop star David Bowie as an enigmatic alien. Jagger went right back to being a real-life pop star with his band The Rolling Stones (though he has acted in a few other films, with varying degrees of success), while James Fox was so unmoored by the experience that he left the industry altogether, becoming an evangelist for the Navigators, an obscure religious sect, before returning to the business in 1983 as an older, more dissolute version of his younger, colonialist self.

Performance is a film that left its mark on everyone who was associated with it, for better or ill; that it managed to survive the corporate culture that spawned it remains a virtual miracle. With *Performance*, the entire decade of 'free love' and swinging London came crashing down; it had all been a dream, marred by violence and excess almost from the beginning. We are a long way from the more cheerful precincts of *The Knack . . . and How to Get It*, which despite its theme of persistent sexual license remained a droll, sophisticated exercise in youthful abandon.

Curiously, both Lester's film and Roeg and Cammell's film are excessively stylized; Lester uses fast motion, freezes, intertitles, reverse motion, rapid lap dissolves, wipes, and every dizzy camera angle he can devise to transform Ann Jellicoe's stage play into a formalist film exercise, which constantly aggressively strives to entertain. The interiors of the townhouse where most of *The Knack . . .* takes place are painted bright white by one of the tenants, the Bohemian painter Tom (Donal Donnelly), who comes to the house to bring in light and change. Turner, in *Performance*, is busy painting the walls of his bedroom blood-red; an effect that is enhanced by Roeg and Cammell's intercutting Turner's decorating with one of Chas's more violent episodes of mayhem in the service of his employer Harry Flowers.

The world that once seemed so bright and promising has turned into a dark and ominous locale that one only seeks to escape from; there is no more living in the world, just avoiding it. The curtains to Turner's bedroom, living room, kitchen and sitting room are always drawn, no matter what the hour; it is late, and it's better that we don't look outside. The windows in *The Knack . . .* are always open, as if to invite passers-by in for a cup of tea, or a chat, or a romantic interlude. Indeed, both films center on a boarder who moves in and transforms the household. Nancy (Rita Tushingham) enters the world of womanizer Tolen (Ray Brooks) and meek schoolteacher Colin (a pre-*Phantom of the Opera* Michael Crawford) to bring life into the house, and break Tolen's malign spell over Tom's love life; Chas brings only death. *Performance* is thus in many ways the ultimate noir of the 1960s, announcing not only the end of a decade, but also the end of an entire era – an era of hope and possibility.

No consideration of noir in the 1960s would be complete without a few thoughts on Hammer Films, most famous for their color gothic horror films, many directed by Terence Fisher. Hammer's short series of psychological thrillers, the best of which were directed by Freddie Francis, include *Paranoiac* (1963), *Nightmare* (1964), and *Hysteria* (1965). In *Paranoiac*, the rich, demented scion of a wealthy British aristocratic family, Simon Ashby (Oliver Reed), drinks himself insensible, while engaging on a rampant campaign of murder, deception, and random violence, before succumbing to total madness in the film's final moments. *Nightmare* centers on a young woman (Jennie Linden) being driven mad for an inheritance. *Hysteria* concerns itself with an amnesiac who tries to piece together his past from tantalizing bits and fragments he can barely remember. In all of these films, Francis, and his scenarist Jimmy Sangster, paint a world of greed, manipulation, and sinister intent.

Paranoiac was one of Francis's first films as a director, after a long and distinguished career as a cinematographer; indeed, towards the end of his life, he returned to cinematography, shooting such films as Martin Scorsese's remake of *Cape Fear* (1991), David Lynch's *The Elephant Man* (1980), Edward Zwick's *Glory* (1989, for which he won his second Academy Award for cinematography), and Lynch's atypically humanist *The Straight Story* (1995), which was Francis's last work in the cinema; he died in 2008.

In *Paranoiac*, Francis staked out a new psychic terrain of perpetual uncertainty that permeates the entire fabric of the film. Cynical, dissolute Simon Ashby (Reed) is the only surviving son of John and Mary Ashby, who were killed in an airplane crash in 1952. Now, ten years later, Simon's Aunt Harriet (Sheila Burrell) still holds memorial services in the local church to mark each passing anniversary of their death, which both Simon and his sister Eleanor (Janette Scott) are required to attend. Eleanor is clearly mentally unbalanced, teetering on the edge of madness, obsessed with the death of Simon's brother Tony, who apparently committed

Figure 4.5 Oliver Reed drowns a troublesome co-conspirator in Freddie
Francis's *Paranoiac* (1963).

suicide by throwing himself into the sea, unable to deal with the loss of his
parents.

As the macabre ceremony progresses, however, 'Tony' (Alexander
Davion) suddenly appears in the doorway of the church. But is it really
Tony? Before his true identity can be ascertained, 'Tony' vanishes.
Distraught, Eleanor descends into hysterics, and is heavily drugged by her
'nurse,' Françoise (Liliane Brousse), actually Simon's lover and co-conspirator; together, they hope to drive Eleanor completely insane, have her
committed, and inherit her portion of the Ashby fortune. But 'Tony's'
sudden appearance has pushed Eleanor over the edge, and she, too, tries to
kill herself by jumping off a cliff into the sea, when 'Tony' appears from
the shadows, and comes to her rescue.

Taking her back to the Ashby family estate, 'Tony' establishes his bona
fides with the family lawyer, John Kossett (Maurice Denham), and is
accepted into the family by everyone except Harriet and Simon. Indeed,
Simon knows that it can't be Tony; for Simon actually murdered Tony
shortly after their parents' death, and stuffed his body into a hole in the
wall behind the organ in the family chapel, faking a suicide note in
Tony's handwriting. The false 'Tony' is actually an exact double hired by
Keith Kossett (John Bonney), son of John, the family's attorney; Keith

Figure 4.6 Sheila Burrell in a clown mask menaces the viewer in Freddie
Francis's *Paranoiac* (1963).

has been dipping into the Ashby family trust, and wants to use 'Tony' to
gain control of the Ashby fortune, and thus avoid embezzlement proceedings.

For the first half of the film, we aren't sure whether to accept 'Tony' or
not, but at the film's midpoint, we find Keith and 'Tony' in a pub, scheming to split the proceeds from their illicit venture, and we realize that he's
an impostor. But this is just the first act of *Paranoiac*; knowing that Tony
is actually dead, Simon embarks on an energetic campaign to kill both
Eleanor and 'Tony' in a variety of ways, such as cutting the brake-fluid
lines in the family car when Eleanor and 'Tony' go out for a picnic. Simon's
plan nearly works, and the car hurtles over a steep cliff, just as 'Tony' pulls
Eleanor to safety. Complicating matters further, Eleanor is soon romantically attracted to 'Tony' and passionately kisses him before recoiling in
horror, thinking herself guilty of incest.

In the meantime, Simon is becoming unbalanced, and regresses to his
childhood, imagining that the youthful Tony he murdered is still alive. To
keep him from being committed, Aunt Harriet dresses up in choir robes,
and wears a mask of Tony as a youth, while Simon, lost in a dream, accom-
panies this phantasmal apparition on the organ, playing along to a recording of Tony's youthful voice. Pacified to some degree by this bizarre ritual,

Simon still drinks himself insensible at the local pub, pours drinks over an old man whom he also takes to be 'Tony,' and finally, in a fit of pique, murders Françoise when she threatens to expose his plans, drowning her in the large pond on the family estate.

In the film's denouement, Simon goes completely mad, yet Aunt Harriet still tries to protect him by starting a fire in the family chapel, where the false 'Tony' has discovered the real Tony's decaying skeleton. With 'Tony' bound to a chair, Harriet sets fire to the sacristy. Displaying some sense of independent thought for perhaps the first time in the film, Eleanor helps the false 'Tony' to escape, while Simon, utterly insane, embraces the corpse of his long-dead brother with feverish passion, and perishes in the flames.

A young, dashing, utterly demented Oliver Reed is the centerpiece of the film, which manages to look like a big-budget production despite the fast shooting schedule and the use of some rather obviously faked exterior shots. Francis gets excellent performances from Sheila Burrell, Maurice Denham, and Janette Scott in the lead. Only Alexander Davion, who looks and acts a bit like a youngish Cary Grant, is less than ideal for his role as the false 'Tony.' *Paranoiac* manages to be quite unguessable almost until the end of its running time, and still packs quite a wallop for contemporary audiences, although the violence used in the film is actually quite restrained.

The key visual set pieces in the film are handled with flair and panache: the car crashing over a cliff, nearly killing Davion and Scott, featuring some nifty back-screen process work; Burrell's nocturnal 'choir practice' sessions with Reed in the deserted family chapel, in which she attempts to convince the 'paranoiac' Reed that she is the brother whom he murdered long ago; and Reed drunk in a bar, regaling his 'friends' with tales of the inheritance he will soon come into. Everyone in the film is corrupt, or hiding something, with the exception of Maurice Denham's John Kossett; as Keith Kossett, John Kossett's son, John Bonney is cheerfully despicable, the mastermind of the film's convoluted narrative.

What remains powerful in *Paranoiac* is the film's ability to surprise, shock, and entertain even the cleverest audiences. Francis's tracking shots, his darkly atmospheric lighting, and the over-the-top performances by the cast combine to make *Paranoiac* a compelling and hypnotic noir, inhabiting a world that is luxuriously seductive, but fraught with menace and the constant threat of personal and physical destruction.

Nightmare, which followed *Paranoiac* in 1964, is perhaps the most beautiful and fully accomplished of all of Francis's psychological noirs. Photographed in black and white CinemaScope, as noir thrillers often are, the film is, like *Paranoiac*, a dark comedy masquerading as a horror film. In his aggressive use of rock music, adolescent stuffed dolls, knives, birthday cakes, transistor radios, and other pop culture paraphernalia, Francis structures a system of visual shorthand here which he will recycle in some of his later noir thrillers, such as Margaret Johnston's inordinately large doll collection in Francis's later *The Psychopath* (1966), and the use of the spectral Clytie Jessop as the woman holding the 'Shears of Fate' in Francis's omnibus film *Torture Garden* (1967).

Nightmare opens with an exterior miniature shot of the gloomy asylum where Janet's mother (Isla Cameron) is being held as a violently homicidal patient. (Years earlier, on Janet's eleventh birthday, Janet's mother had suddenly 'gone insane,' stabbing her husband to death for no apparent reason.) The camera dollies in on the building, and then dissolves inside to a tracking shot down an equally cheerless hallway. Sounds of dogs barking are heard in the distance. Janet (Jennie Linden) wanders through the building, lured on by the sound of her mother's voice, whispering to Janet that she needs help.

At length, Janet discovers her mother piteously cringing in a firmly locked cell, begging to be released. Janet opens the door, but as she does so, it swings shut behind her, trapping her in the cell with her mother. Her mother's expression changes from fear to maniacal glee, as she repeatedly screams at Janet, 'Now they've got you, too! We're both mad! We're both mad!' Janet starts screaming uncontrollably, and Francis cuts to Janet waking up in her dormitory room at Hatcher's School for Young Ladies, where she had been left by her 'guardian,' Henry Baxter.

As the nightmare subsides, Mary Lewis (Brenda Bruce), a teacher who is quite understandably worried about Janet's sanity, decides that she must be taken out of school to avoid disrupting the normal routine of the other students. It isn't so much a matter of Miss Lewis's solicitousness; Hatcher's School must continue on without interruption, and Janet's recurring screaming fits have to be dealt with privately.

Home life, however, is little better. The family mansion is huge, rambling, and constructed very much like the asylum of Janet's nightmares, with endless, poorly lit corridors through which Janet must walk every day. We immediately suspect that the absent Henry Baxter (David Knight) is up to no good, and we are right; he is conspiring with Grace (Moira Redmond) to drive Janet round the twist. No sooner has Janet arrived home than she is subjected to all manner of sleeping pills, round-the-clock medical attention, and the underhanded attentions of Grace, who, masquerading as Henry's wife (Clytie Jessop, whom Henry wishes to dispose of at the earliest possible opportunity), chases Janet around the mansion when the servants aren't about.

Figure 4.7 Jennie Linden confronts the phantasmal corpse of Clytie Jessop in
Freddie Francis's *Nightmare* (1964).

Eventually driven to desperation, Janet's mind cracks under the
repeated appearances of the phantasmal Clytie's double. During a birthday
party thrown in her honor, Janet grabs the cake knife and stabs Henry
Baxter's wife to death. As a consequence of her actions, Janet is condemned
to the same asylum where her mother resides, and must spend her days in
the cheerless cell she had so often conjured up in her dreams. Just as she is
taken away from the huge mansion where she has spent so much of her life,
Janet catches a glimpse of 'Grace as Clytie' at the window of her bedroom.
Francis cuts inside to show Grace peeling off the mask and throwing it on
the fireplace, where it is consumed by the flames.

It is at this juncture that Sangster's narrative neatly cuts itself in two; the
second half of the film is devoted to the servants' efforts, aided by Mary
Lewis, to bring Grace and Henry Baxter to justice. This section of the film
is perhaps slightly less successful than the first, if only because we know
that Grace and Henry inevitably must be punished. The servants con-
trive to make it appear to Grace that Henry is having an affair with
another woman. Faked circumstantial evidence in fact leads Grace to
believe Henry is unfaithful, and she becomes more and more irrational as
a result.

Finally, Grace is led to believe that a dangerously homicidal Janet has escaped from the asylum, and will attempt to kill her on the orders of Henry. Grace sequesters herself in the mansion, where manufactured apparitions begin to haunt her, just as she had tormented Janet. Janet's radio mysteriously appears in Grace's bedroom, blasting rock music; Janet's doll is found repeatedly in different corners of the house, grinning in cheerful mockery. Henry is oblivious to Grace's distress, which eventually proves his downfall. Now quite mad herself, Grace goes berserk and stabs Henry to death, thinking that she will pin the crime on the 'escaped' Janet. A final phone call revels that Janet is still in the asylum, where she is making 'splendid' progress and will soon be released; Grace will go on trial for the murder.

Nightmare is above all things a visual tour de force, a black and white noir thriller. Francis's camera prowls the hallways of the mansion with assurance, and a fine sense of the inherent menace of the piece. Like Seth Holt's *Scream of Fear* (1961), Francis's *Nightmare* has a firm sense of the seriousness of its construction throughout its running time, and this keeps the film simultaneously entertaining and true to its generic origins. It is a world of complete deception on all sides; nothing is what it seems, and everyone has a deeply hidden agenda.

Hysteria was the third and final film of the series; though lacking the polish and flair of its predecessors, the film continues thematic preoccupations evident in the earlier works, and has a fine sense of pacing throughout its running time. *Hysteria*'s plot line is simplicity itself; the amnesiac 'Christopher Smith' (Robert Webber) finds himself adrift in London, without a clue to his past life or true identity. He is given the keys to a luxury flat, but soon finds that, as in the preceding two films in the cycle, someone is trying to drive him mad. But why?

As in *Nightmare* and *Paranoiac*, the protagonists of *Hysteria* live in a world devoid of a past (particularly Webber's Smith), a world that can be concretized only through consumption, impersonation, and sadomasochistic power play. As in *Paranoiac*, Sangster and Francis here once again find cold comfort in wealth, lack of responsibility, and the sort of life that most film fantasies usually hold out as ideal. For Francis and Sangster, this dream of a life beyond daily care is immediately suspect, as if it is work which anchors us morally, as well as practically, in existence.

It is perhaps not accidental that Hemmings (Maurice Denham), a private detective who tries to help 'Smith' unravel the mystery of his past, and who is the only character in the film who really works at his trade (following leads, getting beaten up occasionally in the line of duty, working in a shabby office which is obviously all he can afford), is the one who restores

Smith to Gina (Jennifer Jayne), a nurse whose devotion to Smith is seen within the film as being his only hope for a constructive life.

Dr Keller (Anthony Newlands), Smith's psychiatrist, mouths platitudes with little conviction or care, and relies instead upon pills in his treatment of Smith; Marcus Allan (Peter Woodthorpe), an advertising/fashion photographer who grudgingly agrees to help Smith, not only depends upon his models to help him sell products, but also is assisted in his work by a large coterie of anonymous assistants who clearly do most of the heavy work (placing lights, setting up props, positioning subjects). In short, his work is done for him.

There is also in *Hysteria* the very real suggestion that one must ultimately bear the responsibility for one's own existence, and take one's own counsel above that of all others. Psychiatry, never a discipline viewed favorably in suspense films since the Hollywood noir cycle of the 1940s (for one immediate example, Edmund Goulding's circus-themed noir *Nightmare Alley* [1947]), is seen here as both inexact and ultimately duplicitous. Keller thus joins the long line of doctors, attorneys, nurses, and teachers whose own motives fail to withstand extended scrutiny in this cycle of films.

In this film, as with the others in the Hammer 'psychological' group, it often seems as if Francis is more interested in the details of the lavish apartment Smith is given by a mysterious benefactor than he is in the characters who inhabit it. The camera lovingly tracks through the apartment from the balcony looking in, or from the inside looking skyward, and the sequence in which Smith first takes possession of the flat, underscored by one of Don Banks's best jazz music scores, is a wish dream of material consumption which rapidly segues into nightmare.

In any discussion of these three films, one should also mention Michael Carreras's 1963 companion film *Maniac*, which carries on many of these same themes in another Sangster script starring Donald Houston, Nadia Gray, and Kerwin Matthews in a tale of a young drifter, Paul Farrell (Matthews), who meets and fall in love with hotel owner Eve Beynat (Nadia Gray) in a deserted seaside resort town. Infatuated with her, Paul agrees to help her insane former husband, Paul, break out of an asylum where he has been confined for committing a particularly hideous murder with an acetylene blowtorch. Of course, nothing is precisely what it seems in all of this, and soon Paul is thrown into a whirlpool of intrigue, double-crosses, and murderous impersonation.

Joseph Losey's *Accident* (1967) also moves in a world that is privileged, stillborn, insular, and sodden with alcohol; it is also a world of great beauty and sudden death, power and weakness, splendor and decay. Above all, the world of *Accident* is a world of light and the absence of light, of nights redo-

Figure 4.8 Dirk Bogarde and Jacqueline Sassard have a brief and
fateful affair in Joseph Losey's *Accident* (1967)

lent with heat and torpor, and days of interminable beauty. Picnicking on
the lawn, boating on the river, or ensconced in his rooms at Oxford,
Stephen (Dirk Bogarde) is the sun-blessed intellectual who prefers to
squander his days, and his talents, in pursuit of the ineffable – the dream
of the eternal and immutable present. The world of *Accident* is summer,
and the summer of *Accident* is the world entire for Stephen, Charley
(Stanley Baker), Anna (Jacqueline Sassard), William (Michael York),
Rosalind (Vivien Merchant), and Francesca (Delphine Seyrig). One
cannot imagine them existing in another universe. Like inverted vampires,
they must live in the sun in order to exist. When they venture out at
night, the results (as seen in the opening moments of the film) are usually
disastrous.

Accident is also about celebrity, the creation of images to support the
myth of celebrity, and the jettisoning of outmoded visual constructs that
no longer appeal to the public or serve to propagate the myth of interchangeable celebrity. Charley is a television 'intellectual.' He discusses
books, cultural trends, and social mores on television, wears the proper
glasses to give him a more forbiddingly 'intelligent' look, and holds
Stephen in contempt because Stephen is unable to command a similar
position. Still, when Stephen tells Charley that he has 'a meeting with your

producer' during a particularly alcoholic and nasty supper at home, Charley is unnerved.

Stephen and Charley have hit the glass ceiling of academe; they are afraid of scandal, afraid of reproof from the aging but implacable provost, afraid of their aging bodies, afraid of their inner vacuity. Their relationships are lies or competitions. Stephen is unfaithful to his wife Rosalind in the most casual manner, as if infidelity within marriage is both inevitable and hopelessly boring. When Stephen meets Francesca in a shabby London restaurant and then returns to her flat, their thoughts are heard on the film's soundtrack, but they have no need to actually speak to each other. Whatever they might say would be utterly banal (as indeed it is), so why bother? Stephen and Charley both inhabit a world they no longer believe in. They simply go through the motions and repeat the required phrases, cite the appropriate texts.

Within the world of *Accident*, all is a contest. Manners merely cover up the savagery that lurks underneath the manicured surface. Within the context of this world of endless trials and rematches, William's death comes almost as a relief, because only death can take him out of play, out of jeopardy. By the conclusion of the film, in which Anna dumps Charley after their brief relationship (much to Stephen's ill-concealed delight), we have come to feel as trapped within Losey and Pinter's world as the protagonists of *Accident*.

At the very end of the film, as Stephen gathers up his children, Ted and Clarissa, and takes them back into the house under a dazzling sun, there is no sound at all except for a replay of the car crash that opened the film (Pinter 1978: 284), directly indicating that the only escape from this hell of class privilege is death, and an ignominious death at that. All of Pinter and Losey's characters will continue to play out their parts, silhouetted against a serene, bucolic landscape, a landscape of surface beauty and internal, ceaseless corruption.

The sexual ethics of the 1960s are everywhere apparent in *Accident*: blatant infidelity is routinely condoned, no one seems to use any sort of contraceptives, and the issue of sexually transmitted diseases is never broached (at the time, of course, AIDS did not exist). The endless days of leisure at Oxford must naturally give way to a harsher reality in time, but in the static world of *Accident*, that day of reckoning exists in the dim and distant future, if at all. There is the sense throughout the film that one can play a seemingly endless series of highly dangerous games and still get away with it because the safety nets of wealth, tenure, and class are firmly in place and will scoop up anyone unlucky enough to make a potentially fatal misstep.

If the world of *Accident* is alluring and romantic in a decadent, excessive fashion, something like a fantasy of Lautréamont or Rimbaud, it is also a domain of endless, circular pain (witness the repeated car crash) and disappointment. Losey and Pinter have contrived to make this world real and immediate to us, but even as we are seduced by the luxurious aimlessness of *Accident*, the film's final frames serve as a warning. This picture-perfect world is a gigantic and alluring deception, and we would be well advised not to be taken in. *Accident*, that most British of noirs, holds a mirror up to life, but the reflection is not flattering; it is the unvarnished truth. As J. A. Place and L. S. Peterson note,

> the 'dark mirror' of film noir creates a visually unstable environment in which no character has a firm moral base from which he can confidently operate. All attempts to find safety or security are undercut by the antitraditional cinematography and mise-en-scène. Right and wrong become relative, subject to the same distortions and disruptions created in the lighting and camera work. Moral values, like identities that pass in and out of shadow, are constantly shifting and must be redefined at every turn. And in the most notable examples of film noir, as the narratives drift headlong into confusion and irrelevance, each character's precarious relationship to the world, the people who inhabit it, and to himself and his own emotions, becomes a function of visual style. (1976: 338)

John Boorman's *Point Blank* (1967) is another superb example of this tendency towards narrative confusion and excessive stylization, with the Orphic figure of Walker (Lee Marvin) literally returning from a watery grave after a botched robbery to wreak vengeance on his former colleagues, who betrayed him during the heist. As Walker, Lee Marvin strides through the film with an air of implacable confidence, beating up a variety of underworld figures in a quest for his share of the loot. His wife Lynne (Sharon Acker) has become a hopeless drug addict; his former partner Mal Reese (John Vernon) has risen to the top of the rackets using Walker's share of the take, but lives in constant fear of Walker's seemingly inevitable retribution.

Mob figures move in and out of the film with disconcerting vagueness; it seems there is no 'top man' to confront. All Walker wants is his $93,000, but no one is willing to give it to him, or even believe that this is all he wants; even the underworld has become a giant corporation, with various figureheads, run like a business, with no one really accountable. Cash never changes hands. One mob kingpin, Brewster (Carroll O'Connor), tries to explain to Walker that his quest for vengeance simply isn't practical, shouting at him that 'you threaten a financial structure like this for $93,000? No, Walker, I don't believe you. What do you really want?'

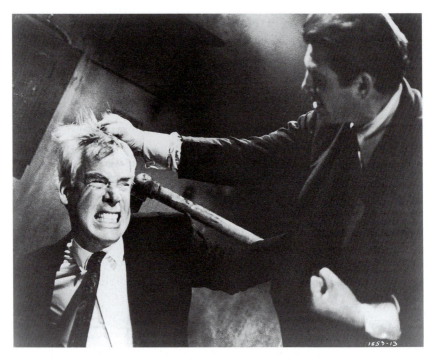

Figure 4.9 Lee Marvin gets beaten up by a rival mobster in John Boorman's
violent revenge thriller *Point Blank* (1967).

But the $93,000 *is* all Walker wants, and no one is able to stop him – not
a nameless hit man (James Sikking), nor smooth corporate heavy Frederick
Carter (the exquisitely corrupt Lloyd Bochner), nor the sleazy used car
dealer Stegman (Michael Strong), who works as a bagman for the mob. In
his campaign of retribution, Walker is helped by the shadowy figure Yost
(Keenan Wynn), an informant who may or may not be part of the organization, but seems intent on using Walker to destroy it for his own personal
ends. Walker's sometime girlfriend Chris (Angie Dickinson) also helps
Walker penetrate mob headquarters, offering herself to the detestable Mal
Reese as a sexual plaything, so that Walker can sneak into Reese's bachelor
penthouse, and shove a gun in Reese's face, demanding his money.

'Kill me, Walker,' the now-naked Reese perversely pleads, hoping
Marvin will shoot him and be done with it. But Walker still just wants his
money, and plans to brutalize Reese until he comes across with the $93,000.
But nothing works out as planned; in a final confrontation on the penthouse balcony, Reese plummets to his death, leaving only an empty bed
sheet behind; a fatal souvenir of his abortive tryst with Chris. Walker
stares dumbly at the sheet, wondering what to do next. It wasn't supposed

to turn out this way, and now his key bargaining chip has been taken from him.

At the end of the film, Yost, satisfied that Walker has smashed the organization, offers to pay him the $93,000 out of a cash drop at the now defunct Alcatraz Prison – where the original robbery took place – a location which is used on a weekly basis as part of a gambling operation. But when a helicopter arrives with the money, Walker senses a trap, and fades back into the shadows, this time permanently. Yost is furious, and screams into the darkness, 'come and get your money, then! I pay my debts!' Yost's hired gun, lurking in the dark, comes forward; he had been ready to shoot Walker, if he'd been foolish enough to take the bait. The hit man reaches for the money, but Yost waves him off. 'Leave it,' he intones wearily; it doesn't really matter to him. And, somehow, it no longer matters to Walker, whose long quest has ended in emptiness.

Shot in a jagged, impressionistic style reminiscent of the work of Alain Resnais and other practitioners of the French New Wave, flashing backward and forward in time with impunity, intercutting the past and present into an artfully coherent Möbius loop, *Point Blank* is at once an art film and a genre film; a personal statement from director Boorman on the futility and meaninglessness of violence, and a meditation on the facelessness of modern criminal enterprise. Walker's return from the dead avails him nothing in the end of the film; he has no one to go after, no real adversary, just flitting, shapeless non-persons who are as replaceable as pegs in a board, or prefab houses in a postwar landscape. *Point Blank*'s vision is one of pure nihilism, laced with a sense of death and desperation, and shot through with the scent of personal betrayal. No one will help Walker, no matter how self-defiant he seems to be; no one can stop him, either. But nothing is to be gained. The quest is finally useless, and the energy expended is equally wasted. Walker is a ghost chasing ghosts, sleepwalking in a dream from which he will never awaken.

Richard C. Sarafian's *Vanishing Point* (1971) is a similarly nihilistic narrative, another meaningless quest that ends in death and destruction, but this time, the stakes are merely bragging rights. Jimmy Kowalski (Barry Newman) makes his living driving cars to various destinations for delivery to customers, and prides himself on knocking out transcontinental runs from the East to the West in three days or less. Fueled by drugs, Kowalski attempts to beat his own record from Denver to San Francisco in fifteen hours, racing against himself and the clock in a battle against time and death; as long as Kowalski keeps moving, always one step ahead of the police dragnet that keeps closing in on him, he is alive. If he stops to rest, he dies, both figuratively and literally.

A blind, psychic DJ in a small desert town, Super Soul (Cleavon Little), gets news reports on Kowalski's progress from the Teletype in his radio station's newsroom, and begins hyping Kowalski on the air as 'the last American hero, fighting against the system.' In the car, Kowalski picks up Super Soul's broadcast, and begins using the DJ's advice to elude the authorities. Using a police scanner, Super Soul guides Kowalski around police roadblocks, issuing warnings and encouragement as Kowalski pushes his Dodge Challenger faster, faster, faster. The state police pursue him from one jurisdiction to another, trading off at the state line as Kowalski gets ever closer to his goal, but as he continues to accelerate, he loses track of time, of himself, and of his psychic connection to Super Soul.

The police devise a gigantic roadblock composed of two enormous bulldozers, blocking the road entirely. Kowalski is now so caught up in his dream of speed and power that he is completely out of it. Switching off the radio, he pushes the car even faster, and fails to see the roadblock until it's too late. But, paradoxically, it seems as if his death will be his real victory and he embraces it; he seems oblivious to his imminent destruction, lost in a trance of freedom and velocity. The car hits the two bulldozers head on and explodes in a fireball, killing Kowalski, and ending the film. Super Soul switches off his microphone, and sits back in his chair; Kowalski's run is over.

The entire film is structured, as are many noirs, as a flashback. The first thing we see is the police putting the bulldozers in place, confident that this time, Kowalski won't be able to get past them. Kowalski seemingly accepts his death as the logical conclusion to his journey, which was doomed from the start. As the film progresses, Sarafian shows us Kowalski's life in a series of flashbacks within the framing flashback; a Vietnam veteran, Kowalski lost his job as a cop when he stopped his partner from raping a young girl during an arrest.

Framed by his colleagues for a narcotics offense, Kowalski is busted out of the force, and works as a racecar driver and a motorcycle racer, but his racing career is marred by a series of accidents. Car delivery – a common gig for restless teens and twentysomethings in the 1960s (I once rode along on a two-and-three-quarter-day run from Philadelphia to Los Angeles as part of such an arrangement in 1969, after responding to an ad in the *Village Voice*) – seems to be Jimmy Kowalski's last chance before the bottom falls out entirely.

Shunned by the military and the police, Kowalski drifts towards the counterculture, which embraces him, and Kowalski's outsider status is confirmed. Indeed, the film celebrates the outlaw lifestyle as the only way that one can be an individual in contemporary society and stay true to one's

Figure 4.10 Anthony James and Arthur Malet are homicidal hitchkikers
threatening driver Barry Newman in Richard C. Sarafian's *Vanishing Point*
(1971).

ideals; society is utterly corrupt, and only those who live on the margins
are free.

As Kowalski drives through the country, moving from Colorado into
Utah, then Nevada and finally California, guided by Super Soul's disembodied voice on the car radio, he runs into a variety of similarly disenfran-
chised loners. An old man (Dean Jagger) who lives in the desert and catches
snakes for a living offers him aid and encouragement; two hitchhikers
(Anthony James and Arthur Malet) Kowalski picks up in a gesture of com-
radeship try to rob him, but he manages to shake them off. Meanwhile,
Super Soul's anti-establishment rants have attracted unwanted attention
from the police and some members of a white supremacist organization,
who bust into the radio station and beat up Super Soul and his engineer.
Still Kowalski races on, aiming for an existential deadline of importance to
no one but himself.

Death is Kowalski's ultimate rendezvous, from the first frame of the film
to the last. For all the speed with which Kowalski rockets through the film,
he is actually going nowhere. As the film's tag line suggests, 'it's the
maximum trip . . . at the maximum speed.' But that 'maximum' experience
can only end in death, and in the reckless manner with which Kowalski

continually downs large quantities of Benzedrine tablets throughout the film, one quickly becomes aware that he will only sleep when he's dead. This is a trip no one will ever return from.

Far more despairing than Roger Corman's *The Wild Angels* or *The Trip*, *Vanishing Point* suggests that life is a meaningless, high-velocity chase sequence, punctuated by brief idylls when Kowalski stops the car and walks though the desert, trying to calculate his next move. But no matter how much he ponders his fate, Kowalski's destiny is to return to the Challenger, floor the gas pedal, and head out on to the highway to oblivion, with the police in constant pursuit.

The film's final sequence, too, is a noirish epitaph. Kowalski can't escape from the faces of authority, and his momentary freedom and media celebrity only assure that his demise will come that much sooner. Someone has to be made into an example, to show that the outlaw culture will inevitably be crushed by the mainstream. *Vanishing Point* is one of the most compelling noir visions of the 1960s; a philosophical tract masquerading as an action film, preaching the ultimate futility of revolt and dissidence. Society, corrupt and bigoted, has jettisoned Kowalski because he won't play along. Now, because of the circular narrative structure of the film, he is condemned to repeat his endless runs through the desert over and over again, every time the film is unspooled for a new audience, with the same final result: violent death.

Targets is another 1960s noir of peculiar provenance; the directorial debut of wunderkind film critic Peter Bogdanovich, who co-wrote, directed, starred in, and edited the film, *Targets* was the result of Roger Corman's typical enterprise and cost cutting. Boris Karloff, who appeared in numerous Corman-Poe films in the 1960s, owed Corman two days' work. Corman told Bogdanovich to use Karloff's two days, and also required that Bogdanovich use at least twenty minutes of material from Corman's film *The Terror* (1963), a film that *itself* was shot on leftover sets from Corman's *The Raven* (1963), when that film also finished ahead of schedule. Corman told Bogdanovich that he could do anything he wanted with the material, just so long as the film ran to ninety minutes, and that if it was any good he'd sell it to Paramount as a negative pick-up deal; if not, he'd unload it though AIP.

Working with his then-wife Polly Platt, who also served as the film's production designer, Bogdanovich whipped up a script in eleven days, centering on aging horror star Byron Orlok (Karloff) who wants to quit the business, tired of making one predicable film after another. Sammy Michaels (Bogdanovich), a young director on the rise, desperately wants Orlok to commit to one more film, as it will be the project that finally puts

Figure 4.11 Tim O'Kelly, a clean-cut American boy, lines up another
victim in Peter Bogdanovich's *Targets* (1968).

Sammy on the map. Intercut with this is the parallel story of all-American
boy Bobby Thompson (Tim O'Kelly), obsessed with guns, who goes on a
shooting rampage killing his young wife, his mother, and an errand boy for
no apparent reason, and subsequently sequesters himself atop a giant fuel
tank, picking off drivers on the nearby freeway at random.

As night falls, Orlok attends the premiere of his latest, and supposedly
final film, *The Terror*, at a local drive-in. Bobby has hidden behind the huge
drive-in screen, and while *The Terror* plays before an audience of young
lovers and families in parked cars, Bobby begins methodically shooting
them one by one. Orlok, suddenly aware of the real horror that has
intruded upon his fantasy world of the macabre, summons all his remaining strength, and storms up to the front of the screen, striking down Bobby
with his heavy cane, even as Orlok's image on the drive-in screen seems to
threaten Bobby, as well. Bobby is reduced to a gibbering wreck; as the
police take him away, Orlok looks down at the young killer and asks, won-
deringly, 'Is that what I was afraid of?'

Bogdanovich, a film buff and aficionado of such maverick directors as
Fritz Lang, Allan Dwan, and Samuel Fuller, worked with Fuller on the
script. It was Fuller who came up with the idea for the final drive-in

confrontation, with the 'doubled image' of the real Orlok (or Karloff) and the screen image both converging on Bobby for the climax of the film. Deftly juxtaposing reality and fiction, Bogdanovich's film is at once a social commentary on the increasing violence of the 1960s, and also on passing trends within the film industry. Watching one of his old films on television within the film, Howard Hawks's *The Criminal Code* (1931), Karloff, as Orlok, sighs that 'they don't make films like that anymore,' and indeed they don't. Like it or not, the blank violence of Bobby Thompson, psychotic sniper, is the face of our future; a serial killer without motive, or remorse.

Bogdanovich took his inspiration for the film from the real-life shooting spree of Charles Whitman from the top of a clock tower at the University of Texas at Austin in 1966; at the time, Whitman's random web of violence seemed indecipherable to American society. Whitman was a clean-cut, solidly grounded youth of no particular distinction, just a nice, eversmiling ex-Marine who suddenly snapped, killing his wife and mother, before climbing the tower stairs with an arsenal of assault weapons, then calmly killing sixteen people and wounding thirty more, before the police managed to storm the tower and kill him.

Whitman's violent spree was a national media sensation, even before the days of 24/7 cable news networks, and Bogdanovich seized upon it as the perfect framing story for his comparison between the almost fairy-tale quality of classic horror films, and the savage brutality of the present. Karloff adored the script for *Targets*, sensing that Bogdanovich was really on to something, and that the film would be – as it is – exceptional. As Bogdanovich told Karloff's wife, Evie, and her friend, film critic Cynthia Lindsay, after the film was shot,

> two days before we shot the film [in 1967], Boris and I had never met. I had never directed a picture – just some second-unit stuff - and yet he demonstrated faith in me from the start. The first thing he said after reading the script was, 'I believe in this picture, but you can't do [my part] in two days.' I said that regrettably nobody was coming up with more salary for him, so I'd have to. He simply answered, 'Take as long as you like.' He worked five days. (Lindsay 1995: 168–9)

The finished film was shot in a total of twenty-five days, for a budget of only $130,000, which included Karloff's salary (Lindsay 1995: 168). Corman took one look at the film, recognized that Bogdanovich had done something extraordinary with almost nothing at his disposal, and sold the distribution rights to Paramount Pictures for a tidy profit. As Lindsay notes,

Bogdanovich's integration of ideas and steady pursuit of the story – which is a frightening observation of the American way of life, and death – are successful because he explains nothing and shows everything. Laszlo Kovacs's photography and Polly Platt's art direction are equal to the quality of the direction. The filming, despite the speed at which it was done, the terrible hours, and the themes of freeway shooting and mass murder, [was] a rich experience and a labor of love for all concerned . . . (1995: 171)

The finished film hit a nerve with the public, and was an immediate critical and commercial success; it effectively captured the transitional nature of the times. As Raymond Durgnat presciently observed in 1970, when the 1960s were still a relatively recent memory,

The '60s obsession with violent death in all forms and genres may be seen as marking the admission of the film noir into the mainstream of Western pop art, encouraged by (a) the comforts of relative affluence, (b) moral disillusionment, in outcome variously radical, liberal, reactionary or nihilist, (c) a post-Hiroshima sense of man as his own executioner, rather than nature, God or fate, and (d) an enhanced awareness of social conflict. The cinema is in its Jacobean period, and the stress on gratuitous torment [. . .] emphasize[s] [. . .] crimes less than the rottenness of [. . .] society, or, perhaps, man himself. (1996: 98)

And yet the 1960s were just a curtain raiser to even more harrowing visions yet to come, that seem to be without end, and become ever more explicit, brutal, and devoid of hope or compassion. Noir beyond the 1960s is a deadly serious business, as it always was, but now the representational stakes have been significantly increased. We have not yet reached the end of this new cycle of noir, and in a post-9/11 social economy, it seems that it will only proliferate, and continue to inform our collective cinematic consciousness.

Targets is Karloff's last work of any real distinction, although he soldiered on afterwards for several years in a variety of formulaic horror films. Karloff's physical condition during the filming of *Targets* was very poor; with only half of one lung left, braces on both legs, and an oxygen tank at the ready, it was a struggle for Karloff simply to perform, and yet he worked several days until three in the morning to keep the production on schedule. As Bogdanovich recounted,

One of the most extraordinary scenes I've ever witnessed before or since [as a director] was the one in which Boris, as Byron Orlok, is wondering what to do to entertain the audience at his last appearance. 'I think I'll tell them a story,' he says, and he reads from an ancient fable about death [the one used by John O'Hara in his novel *Appointment in Samarra*]. The speech is two pages long and I was going to break it up by panning around the room while he was speaking. Boris said, 'I want to do this without a script.' I asked him if he wanted cue cards instead. He said, 'No.' We rehearsed the mechanics of the scene – he was letter-perfect. I realized I was an idiot not to stay on him. The camera was at the end of a long table. I said to the cameraman, 'Stay on him. Start with a long shot, we'll sneak the table away as you dolly in.' It was electrifying. (Lindsay 1975: 172)

This is the epitome of the noir aesthetic; no time, no money, a skeleton crew, unholy hours on the set, and yet the end result is more compelling because of all the privation and cost-cutting; the intensity shows on the screen. *Targets* is both a farewell to the past, and a gesture towards the future of now. Bogdanovich knew, and Karloff as well, that we no longer need to manufacture horror. It's all around us, in the news, in politics, in the economy, and in the unfathomable depths of the next-door neighbors we will never really know. We live with horror, now, every day.

CHAPTER 5

The Failure of Culture

Walter Hill's *The Driver* (1978) typifies the noir films of the 1970s in America; aimless, rootless, devoid of hope or compassion. The driver in question, never named, is Ryan O'Neal as a top 'wheel man' for hire, specializing in driving getaway cars for bank robberies and other criminal enterprises. He's a loner and a perfectionist; if he doesn't like the way a job is being handled, he walks. Tailing him is 'The Detective,' Bruce Dern, obsessed with catching him in the act. The whole film, like *Vanishing Point*, is one long chase sequence.

Hill's other films, such as *48 Hours* (1982), *Johnny Handsome* (1989), and *Another 48 Hours* (1990), often descended into near parody, and by 2004, Hill was content to serve as producer of Paul W. S. Anderson's execrable *Alien vs Predator*, thus forfeiting whatever claim he might have had to any artistic legitimacy. But Hill's early films pack a solid punch. After working as a scenarist on Robert Culp's violent noir cop drama, *Hickey and Boggs*, and Sam Peckinpah's ultra-violent heist thriller *The Getaway*, based on ultra-noir author Jim Thompson's original novel (both made in 1972), Hill graduated to the director's chair with *Hard Times* (1975), a boxing drama set in the Depression starring James Coburn and Charles Bronson. *The Driver* was only his second film as a director, but already the signature elements of Hill's vision are in place; speed, violence, and ruthless sadism.

No one in *The Driver* has a name; they are known simply by their roles within the narrative. Hence, we have not only 'The Driver' and 'The Detective' but also 'The Player,' 'The Connection', and so on down the cast roster. As 'The Driver,' O'Neal is taciturn and more than a little shopworn; he works the shady side of the street, and he knows it. In the entire film, O'Neal's character says only 350 words of dialogue; for the rest of the film, he drives, or waits, or ponders his next move. Violence in *The Driver* is both sadistic and misogynistic; as 'The Connection,' Ronee Blakley is forced into giving up information by performing fellatio on a gun, and then shot to death through a pillow.

Hill's disturbing penchant for such sadistic scenes marks the point at which scenes of such extreme violence could now routinely expect to get only an 'R' rating, not an 'X.' Explicit sex scenes, no matter how normative or heterotopic, were still proscribed by the MPAA Production Code, but an increasing tolerance for violence was creeping in. Hill's other major work of the period, the teen noir *The Warriors* (1979), follows a group of youthful gang members as they cross through the wasteland of Coney Island at night through rival gangs' 'turf' in a search for their home base. Like *The Driver*, *The Warriors* revels in its violent action sequences, and keeps the plot to a minimum; life in *The Warriors* is constant gang warfare, a continual struggle to survive.

Arthur Penn, who had scored with the noirish gangster film *Bonnie and Clyde* in 1967, went the full mile in his much more restrained *Night Moves* (1975), starring Gene Hackman as Harry Moseby, a rundown private detective investigator in what appears to be the simple case of a missing person, one Delly Grastner (played by a very young Melanie Griffith). But the more Moseby becomes involved in the case, the more he realizes that nothing is as it seems, and that his own powers of deduction are often severely lacking; indeed, many parts of the case are solved almost by accident.

With a solid cast of noirish figures, including James Woods, the smarmy Harris Yulin, Ed Binns, and Susan Clark, *Night Moves* is an atypically dark film for Penn, one which centers most on the frailty of its protagonist. As in Robert Culp's aforementioned *Hickey and Boggs* (1972), which featured Culp and Bill Cosby (both then best known as a team on the 1960s American television series *I Spy*), Moseby is a tired, beaten man, at the end of his rope. Al Hickey (Cosby) and Frank Boggs (Culp) are, as the film's tag line notes, not 'cool, slick heroes. They're worn, tough men, and that's why they're so dangerous.'

Hickey and Boggs was Culp's only film as a director, and marked a distinct departure from the banter and light sophistication of the globe-trotting spy series the two men had previously appeared in. Alan Sharp's script is marvelously complex, and insistently violent; Culp never flinches when delivering the film's somber, brutal message; everyone is on the take. The tone of menace is more insistent now than it was in the 1940s and 1950s, and there's little time for wisecracking as the two men plunge into a maelstrom of deceit and decay, ripping the slick veneer off the 1970s like so much rotten, peeling wallpaper.

Ted Post, a reliable television director for many years, created one of the most vicious crime films of the early 1970s in *Magnum Force* (1973), the second film in the 'Dirty Harry' series, starring Clint Eastwood. As Harry Callahan, the detective forced to pick up the pieces on the cases no one else wants to touch, Eastwood is his usual laconic self, as he deals with a gang of vigilante policemen, working within the department as a secret 'Death Squad,' under the direct control of Callahan's superior, Lt Neil Briggs (Hal Holbrook). The bad cops are portrayed as clean-cut, all-American killers, calmly dispatching pimps, drug dealers, and corrupt politicians with deadly efficiency.

As the body count rises, with each murder or 'execution' more grisly than the last, Callahan is finally brought face to face with the members of the death squad (including a young David Soul), and, in a climactic shoot out, restores some semblance of normalcy to the LAPD. But from what we've seen, we know nothing will ever be 'normal' again. Post's obvious relish in directing this violent action thriller again signaled that the boundaries of explicit violence had been pushed back yet again; what could possibly come next?

As if in answer to this question, Martin Scorsese directed perhaps his finest film, *Taxi Driver*, in 1976. Working from a script by future director Paul Schrader, Scorsese shot *Taxi Driver* on the streets of New York in the summer of 1975 on the Lower East Side of Manhattan, near the notorious Variety Photoplays theatre, once a regular movie house, but by the early 1970s a hangout for hookers, johns, drug addicts, and pimps. The story is well known; Travis Bickle (Robert De Niro) is a psychotic Vietnam veteran who works the night shift as a cab driver in the most dangerous sections of Manhattan, gradually descending into homicidal mania as he watches the city self-destruct around him.

Travis takes an interest in teenage prostitute Iris (Jodie Foster, just graduating from lighthearted Disney musicals) and goes on a rampage, dressed in camouflage fatigues and armed to the teeth, saving Iris from her pimp, Sport (Harvey Keitel), in the film's final bloodbath. The end of *Taxi Driver* is something of a shocker in a different way; Travis somehow manages to explain away his psychotic, murderous escapade as an act of self-defense, and at the end of the film still drives the streets at night, as a 'hero' who rescued Iris from the streets.

Of all of Scorsese's films, this is the rawest, with Scorsese himself appearing in a cameo as one of Travis's fares, obsessed with killing his unfaithful wife, spilling out a torrent of violent threats in the back of Travis's cab. The film was shot on a minimal budget, and looks like it; while the corrupt sheen of the city comes through intensely, it's obvious from the production design of the film that very little money was available. Jodie Foster patterned her character after a real-life teenage streetwalker whom Schrader and Scorsese met on the streets while scouting locations; she appears in the film as Iris's confidante, wordlessly pulling her out of traffic when Travis's cab almost runs her over. Most of Iris's dialogue in the film came from 'workshopping' her scenes with De Niro, after watching how real-life hookers survived in the early 1970s on New York's Lower East Side.

The neighborhood itself was so dangerous that gunfights were a fairly common occurrence, while drugs were dealt openly on street corners, and prostitutes lined Second Avenue as soon as the sun went down. The world of *Taxi Driver* was real. This was New York City in the mid 1970s, a churning, violent hotbed of creative activity, with a seedy underbelly so pervasive as to defy description. Even in his superb biography of the brutish boxer Jake LaMotta, *Raging Bull* (1980), Scorsese never again came close to matching the power of *Taxi Driver*, nor did Schrader, despite the many projects both men were subsequently involved in.

An insomniac of epic proportions because of his experience in the war, Travis simply doesn't know what to do with himself in this decaying metropolis. He tries to date the impossibly beautiful Betsy (Cybill Shepherd at her most luminous), a campaign worker for Senator Charles Palantine (Leonard Harris), but Travis has no idea how to relate to anyone, even his fellow cabbies, and takes Betsy to a porn film in Times Square on their first date. She reacts with disgust, and walks out, leaving Travis more alone than ever.

Travis begins to spiral utterly out of control, attempting to assassinate Palantine as a form of reprisal, and when that fails, turning his sights to Iris's pimp, Sport. What is Travis to do in New York, since he can't sleep, can't connect with other human beings, and has no friends, no direction, no hope, nothing to live for? Travis drives a cab because it's the only occupation he can aspire to. As he tells the dispatcher in the taxi garage during his initial employment interview, he simply needs something to fill up his empty time. Asked why he wants to drive a cab, Travis replies simply, 'I can't sleep ni ghts . . . I ride around most nights – subways, buses – but you know, if I'm gonna do that, I might as well get paid for it.'

No other film of the 1970s captures the sense of urban despair and rootlessness as well as *Taxi Driver*; no other film is such an authentic talisman of its time and era. Thankfully, there never was a *Taxi Driver II*, although rumors persist to this day that De Niro and Scorsese might pick up Travis's story some thirty years later for a sequel. What would Travis Bickle make of post-9/11 New York, with the very rich and the very poor more stratified than ever? What would he be doing now? Does one really want to know?

Wes Craven's *The Last House on the Left* (1972) is an even more extreme version of the nightmarish 1970s, an exploitational remake of Ingmar

Bergman's *The Virgin Spring* (1960) involving rape, murder, and revenge. The film is shot on an even more limited budget than *Taxi Driver*, in hand-held, home movie style, without any of the polish and professionalism of Scorsese's film. Indeed, *The Last House on the Left* plays like a documen-tary of a particularly vicious crime, in which the viewer is forced to either submit to the spectacle, or leave the theatre.

Tobe Hooper's equally nihilistic *The Texas Chainsaw Massacre* (1974), advertised with the tag line 'who will survive, and what will be left of them?,' was shot in 16mm on a similarly threadbare budget, but also manages to convey the immediacy of events, as a group of teens are butchered, one by one, by a reclusive band of renegades, seemingly for the sport of it. When he made *The Texas Chainsaw Massacre*, Hooper was working as a film professor at the University of Texas, and the film's visual sophistication – both in camera set-ups and editing strategies – is clearly the result of a great deal of thought before shooting. No matter what one might think of *The Texas Chainsaw Massacre* as a social statement, it is an accomplished piece of work, and was eventually honored with a screening at the Museum of Modern Art as one of the most influential and inventive independent films of the early 1970s.

The cast are all unknowns, which makes the film that much more 'real'; as Leatherface, the crazed, chainsaw-wielding butcher of the clan, Gunnar Hansen, with his immense bulk, conveys both the menace and the crudity of his character. Despite the film's title, *The Texas Chainsaw Massacre* actu-ally contains relatively few scenes of intense violence, and manages to build most of its tension through a measured unfolding of the plot, and by the extensive use of off-screen violence. I first saw the film on a double bill in Newark, NJ with Lee Frost's equally violent *The Black Gestapo* (1975) – 'the new master race!' – which featured castrations, rapes, and murders graphically depicted, and yet Frost's film has none of the impact of Hooper's, his first feature film as a director.

Since then, in the best (or worst) tradition of noir filmmakers, Hooper has wandered in the cinematic wilderness, making only one really main-stream film, *Poltergeist* (1982), produced by Steven Spielberg, who also had a hand in the film's screenplay. Predictably, the two directors soon clashed. Hooper held out for a darker vision of the film, while Spielberg, as pro-ducer, wanted to make it more accessible to audiences. Spielberg won, and the film became a substantial hit, spawning several sequels, but Hooper never really regained his initial stride.

Hooper's *Lifeforce* (1985), a British-made science fiction thriller based on Colin Wilson's novel *The Space Vampires*, failed to click with audiences or critics despite a lavish budget. Hooper then directed a dismal remake of

William Cameron Menzies's nightmarish *Invaders From Mars* (1953), in 1986, which was an even more pronounced misfire. As the creator of the *Texas Chainsaw Massacre* franchise, Hooper sees his first film being remade again and again, with predictably uneven results, but he stunned even his most ardent adherents by directing an ultra-violent remake of Dennis Donnelly's splatter film *The Toolbox Murders* (1978) in 2003; the film was never designed for mainstream sensibilities, and seemed in every sense an unsuccessful return to the past. The finished film received only limited distribution, and although Hooper keeps busy with episodic television work, his career has been mostly on the margins, and has never lived up to its initial, if brutal, promise.

The 1980s, indeed, gave rise to a wave of splatter films, in which victims are impaled, stabbed, raped, strangled, shot, or bludgeoned to death, beginning with Sean S. Cunningham's *Friday the 13th* (1980), which has spawned almost too many sequels to count. Devoid of any real plot, these films dispense brutal murders at regular intervals, in the case of this series at the hands of one Jason Voorhees (Ari Lehman), a psychopathic, disfigured killer who wears a hockey mask to cover his hideous visage. Indulged and aided by his mother Pamela (Betsy Palmer, who had been an ingénue in the early 1950s), Jason goes on a homicidal rampage, slaughtering anyone who dares to set foot on his home turf, Camp Crystal Lake. As with the other films discussed here, *Friday the 13th* was shot on a modest budget, but immediately clicked with the public, and began a long line of sequels which became even more preposterous, and decidedly less inspired. The original *Friday the 13th*, however, does have one small distinction; it contains one of Kevin Bacon's first screen roles, as yet another victim of the emotionless, mute engine of destruction that is Jason Voorhees.

John Carpenter's *Assault on Precinct 13* (1976) is another matter altogether. Carpenter had one feature film to his credit when he shot *Precinct 13*, the science fiction cult film *Dark Star* (1974), which he made while a student at USC with fellow classmate Dan O'Bannon, who five years later would score decisively as the screenwriter for director Ridley Scott's noir science fiction classic *Alien* (1979). *Precinct 13* was made on a bare-bones budget of $100,000, with a cast of unknowns, forcing Carpenter not only to write and direct the film, but also to edit it under the pseudonym of 'John T. Chance' (after John Wayne's character in Howard Hawks's *Rio Bravo* (1959), a film that bears more than a slight resemblance to Carpenter's film), and also compose the film's music score.

Assault on Precinct 13's plot is simple, as is that of *Rio Bravo*; in Carpenter's film, a group of people are trapped in a police station, and must fight off a gang of attackers intent on their destruction. In *Rio Bravo*, the invading marauders want to break one of their own out of jail; in Carpenter's version, a group of prisoners and guards must band together in an abandoned police station to combat a gang of youths seeking a man who has killed one of the gang members, whom the police are sheltering.

Assault on Precinct 13 had so little money that, on one particular day, the cast and crew had to keep working for twenty-four hours straight to keep on schedule – shades of PRC and *Detour* – but Carpenter's assured direction wrings every last ounce of paranoia and menace out of the situation. Ethan Bishop (Austin Stoker) is an African-American cop assigned to hold down the precinct during its final day; Precinct 13 is soon to be abandoned, and only a skeleton crew remains. He's not pleased with the assignment, but, as a superior tells him, 'there are no heroes anymore, Bishop. Just men who follow orders.'

At the station, he meets Leigh (Laurie Zimmer), a female police officer with a sharp attitude, and Julie (Nancy Kyes), the switchboard operator, who spends all her time complaining. Into the crumbling building come several disparate people, brought together by fate and circumstance. Napoleon Wilson (Darwin Joston) is a criminal psychopath whose various crimes are so vicious that no one ever specifies precisely what they are; some things are better left to the imagination. On his way to the Death House, Wilson is deposited in a cell at the deserted station house when one of his fellow prisoners falls ill, along with another prisoner, Wells (Tony Burton).

At the same time in another part of Los Angeles, a father watches in horror as a young punk (Frank Doubleday) guns down his daughter Kathy (Kim Richards) in cold blood, while the child is buying an ice-cream cone from a passing vendor. In a rage, the father shoots his daughter's killer, and flees to the derelict station house. When it becomes clear that the surviving gang members will do anything, and risk any number of casualties, to abduct the now-catatonic father, the lawmen and the lawless band together to stave off the assault.

Carpenter begins the film with panning shots of a desolate Los Angeles landscape, beautifully photographed in CinemaScope by the gifted Douglas Knapp, as derelict housing projects dot the horizon. On the film's soundtrack, we hear a radio announcer telling us of the recent theft of a cache of assault weapons, adding that the 'gang problem is completely out of control.' Carpenter cuts to the interior of a boarded-up building, as the camera pans past several crates of the stolen weapons, and comes to rest on a group of gang members, white, Chicano, and Asian, who swear a blood oath of vengeance against the forces of law.

Frank Doubleday, in particular, gives a mesmerizing performance as the young punk and child killer, never named in the film, who plays his part without uttering a single word. As Napoleon Wilson, Darwin Joston, who spent much of his career on the other side of the camera as a grip and technician, gives a stunning performance, cocky and assured, fully capable of violence when the situation demands it, but also capable of feelings for Leigh, who clearly reciprocates his affection.

The visual highpoint of the film is the gang assault on the station in the dead of night, as dozens of gang members break in through the boarded-up windows only to be cut down in a barrage of gunfire, edited by Carpenter with the assured precision of an Eisenstein or Hitchcock. Indeed, if one looks at the film carefully, one can see that Carpenter is compressing time by making imperceptible edits in the negative to create a more compelling rhythmic pattern for the fusillade of bullets. The film really has only one set, the police station itself, and for most of the film, it is obscured in darkness, but Carpenter's lighting and music cues work together so skillfully that our confinement within the station never seems oppressive; indeed, we fully identify with Carpenter's motley group of misfits, and cheer them on in their fight against the gang members.

The conclusion of the film is surprisingly downbeat; at last alerted to the gravity of the situation, other officers converge on the station and rescue the group. During the battle, Wilson, in particular, has behaved with exceptional resourcefulness and daring, and so, in deference to his new-found status within the group, Bishop walks Wilson out of the station, back into formal police custody. Though Napoleon Wilson has survived the night, he is now on his way to Death Row again, and will soon be executed. His bravery and courage under fire will never be remembered, nor will it help his case; whatever his crimes are, their enormity assures that society will put him to death. Why fight to stay alive? You will only die another day, by another hand, not of natural causes or even your own choice, but as a criminal, executed by the state. As he tells Leigh, 'in my situation, days are like women – each one's so damn precious, but they all end up leaving you.' Or, as he sums it up even more succinctly, 'It's an old story with me. I was born out of time.'

Carpenter went on to make the slasher noir *Halloween* just two years later, in 1978, for a mere $300,000; the film eventually grossed more than $60,000,000 worldwide, and established Carpenter as a major figure within the industry. But, as with all who document the dark side of human endeavor, his success was short-lived. In 1982, Carpenter created arguably the most compelling film of his career, a remake of Howard Hawks and Christian Nyby's *The Thing From Another World* (1951). The film was lavishly budgeted at nearly $10,000,000, and used a wide array of astonishing prosthetic effects by Rob Bottin and Stan Winston to bring the loathsome, shape-changing thing to life, but its nihilist vision of human isolation, lone-liness, and distrust alienated viewers, who flocked instead to Steven Spielberg's *E. T. – The Extra Terrestrial* (1982), which was released within a month of Carpenter's film.

As with Tobe Hooper, Edgar G. Ulmer, Fritz Lang, and other noir cineastes, Carpenter's films are above all personal statements, designed for their maker alone. The end of Carpenter's *The Thing*, in which the only two survivors of a polar expedition (one of whom may be the Thing in human form) are shown freezing to death while sharing a bottle of whisky, was so unremittingly bleak that Universal, the film's production company, soon dropped all advertising for the film, and audiences dwindled into nonexistence.

To a certain extent, Carpenter's career has never recovered from *The Thing*, although he continues to make films such as *Starman* (1984), *Prince of Darkness* (1987), *In the Mouth of Madness* (1995), and *Ghosts of Mars* (2001). Carpenter's vision, dark and forbidding, came into full flower with his versions of *The Thing*, and Hollywood wouldn't have minded that it was so fatalistic, if it only had made a profit. But as with all works that are ahead of their time, Carpenter's version of *The Thing* is now acknowledged as a classic noir science fiction film, one of the few film remakes that is as good, in its own way, as Hawks's more positive original.

As much as Carpenter admires Hawks, there is an essential difference in their visions that assured Hawks's long and multi-varied career as a genre artist, and just as surely sealed Carpenter's outsider, outlaw status. In Hawks's version of *The Thing*, the monster is destroyed, and the group sur-vives. In Carpenter's film, the group is destroyed, and the Thing, in all probability, has emerged triumphant, although we will never be sure, inas-much as Carpenter refuses to give us the generic comfort of narrative closure, in favor of an unresolved conclusion to the film. Hawks could never imagine such a thing; he works to please an audience. Carpenter can't imagine anything else; he works, as always, to please himself.

In the early 1990s, John Dahl emerged as one of the foremost propo-nents of neo-noir; noir for a new, even more jaded generation of viewers. For Dahl, neo-noir is a reaction to a new set of social values, or more accu-rately a lack of them, in which the film reflects 'the inversion of values, the alienation and pessimism, the violence, and the disorientation of the spec-tator' (Conard 2006: 2). Two complex films consolidated his reputation: *Red Rock West* (1992), and *The Last Seduction* (1994), boasting widely dis-parate casts that epitomize this new aesthetic.

Nicolas Cage, something of a shape-shifter in his many recent films (action hero, family man, comedy foil), plays Michael Williams, who is

Figure 5.1 Bill Pullman is part of a complex scheme of greed and betrayal in John Dahl's *The Last Seduction* (1994).

mistaken for a hit man hired by Wayne (J. T. Walsh) to murder his cheating wife. From there, the double-crosses pile up with lighting speed and frightening complexity. Dennis Hopper, a real 1960s survivor, has a solid role as an aging real-life hit man, Lyle, who suffers from a poor self-image because of his chosen line of work. Part black comedy, part thriller, and always ingenuously plotted, *Red Rock West* seemed to signal the start of a promising career for director Dahl, who also co-wrote the film's script.

The Last Seduction pairs Bill Pullman and Linda Fiorentino as an unlikely criminal duo, engaged, once again, in a complicated tale of greed, intrigue, and sexual passion. Clay Gregory (Pullman) has pulled off a scam that nets him $700,000, which his wife Wendy (Fiorentino) promptly absconds with, after a violent argument. Wendy moves to a small town, changes her name to Wendy Kroy, and hooks up with Mike Swale (Peter Berg), who is more than willing to help her spend the loot. But Pullman, a figure of almost comically dogged desperation, continues his pursuit of Wendy through a trail of twists and turns, until nothing is as it seems, and allegiances seem to shift with each new scene. What makes the film endearing, in a perverse sort of way, is that both Pullman and Berg play exceptionally dense characters, and, as Wendy, Linda Fiorentino is always five steps ahead of their rather clumsy machinations.

Alan Parker's modern Faust tale, *Angel Heart* (1987), stars the reliably downtrodden Mickey Rourke as 1950s private investigator Harvey Angel, on the trail of one Johnny Favorite. His employer, Louis Cyphre (Robert De Niro), is an obviously Satanic figure, and plunges Harry Angel into a world of violence and voodoo that takes him from his native New York to the Louisiana bayou country, where he falls under the spell of the exotic Epiphany Proudfoot (Lisa Bonet), a voodoo priestess. Angel, of course, is simply a pawn in the entire affair, while De Niro as Cyphre spends little time onscreen, content to manipulate the principals from the edges of the film's narrative. At once overheated and curiously unsatisfying in the end, *Angel Heart* benefits from Rourke's intensity, but finds its true gravity in De Niro's restrained, controlled performance.

Stephen Frears, director of *The Grifters* (1990), broke through to international acclaim with his low-budgeted British Channel 4 production of *My Beautiful Laundrette* (1985), after a long period as an assistant director for Lindsay Anderson at the Royal Court Theatre, and then on Anderson's films *If*. . . (1968) and *O Lucky Man!* (1973). In the early 1980s, imported films could still command at least some share of the American box office, and *My Beautiful Laundrette* was a surprise hit for Frears, allowing him to pursue larger projects.

As a result, given his penchant for downbeat material, Frears chose to direct *The Grifters* (1990) after the success of his lavishly appointed period noir, *Dangerous Liaisons* (1988), and neatly tapped into the mood of early 1990s fatalism in America without missing a beat. But more than anything, *The Grifters* remains the truest vision of noir at the juncture of neo–noir on the screen, in large measure because of the source material for the film, the novel of the same name by Jim Thompson, arguably the ur-noir novelist of the twentieth century.

Thompson, born on 27 September 1906, above the town jail in Anadarko, Caddo County, in the Territory of Oklahoma, wanted to be a writer from the start. But his vision of the world was one of an unremitting hell, in which each person is merely a pawn of fate. Thompson's early jobs included being an errand boy at a local burlesque house, and later a bellboy on the night shift at the Texas Hotel. As part of this lifestyle, Jim began to drink heavily while still in his teens, smoking up to sixty cigarettes a day, both habits that he kept for the rest of his life. Jim also became 'popular' with guests at the Texas Hotel for his ability to locate bootleg liquor and/or prostitutes at a moment's notice. Jim worked all night at the hotel, and attended high school all day, while Jim's father professed disgust at what his son had become; a pimp and a bootlegger.

Despite his unusual extracurricular activities, Jim graduated from Polytechnic High School in Fort Worth in June 1925. Less than an hour after the ceremony, he collapsed at home from a combination of tuberculosis, nervous exhaustion, and an advanced case of delirium tremens. As Jim recovered, he became even more withdrawn and bitter. Only eighteen, he had already seen too much of life, and noted that 'I hoped for the best, but expected the worst' (as quoted in McCauley 1991: 26). To regain his health, Thompson went to work in the oil fields, where he saw violent death, despair, and poverty – the poor being worked to death by the rich to bring in more oil, more wealth. Typically, Thompson sided with his co-workers rather than his bosses, and by the time of his departure, he had developed a lifelong hatred and suspicion of the machinations of big business (McCauley1991: 31). But more than that, Jim had been writing all the time he had been working on the oil pipeline, and he returned with some short stories that were published in *Texas Monthly* in 1929.

It was also during this period that Thompson wrote the short story 'Sympathy,' which remained unpublished until the literary magazine *Bomb* finally printed it in 2000, almost seventy years after Thompson crafted it. Drawing on his experiences as a collections agent for the Kay Bee Clothing Company, Thompson created a brutal 'short short' about the efforts of agents of the 'Planet Credit Stores' to collect on the credit purchase of a nightgown by one Oscar Bordes, an unemployed father whose children have died in a fire caused by the same nightgown, which had burst into flame, killing them instantly. Bordes commits suicide in response to a 'sympathy' letter cooked up by Planet Credit's agents, which expresses grief at the loss of Bordes's children, but still demands payment for the nightgown. The denouement is typically nihilistic for those familiar with Thompson's work; Bordes has willed his body to the Medical College of the State University to repay the loan. Thompson later used similar themes in his 1954 novel, *A Hell of a Woman* (Polito 1995: 173).

In 1942, after a checkered decade that saw him working as director of the Federal Writers' Project in Oklahoma, and then throwing that job over to try his luck in New York, Thompson wrote *Now and On Earth*, his first novel. In the early 1950s, Thompson entered his most prolific and successful period as a writer, working for Lion Books, whose editor in chief, Arnold Hano, recognized in Thompson a talent that needed only the surety of a reliable outlet.

Between 1952 and 1955, Jim Thompson published thirteen novels, including the classic hard-boiled thrillers *The Killer Inside Me* (1953), *A Hell of a Woman*, (1954), *Savage Night* (1953), *After Dark, My Sweet* (1955), *The Golden Gizmo* (1954), *A Swell Looking Babe* (1954), *Recoil*

(1953), *The Kill Off* (1957), and my own personal favorite of Thompson's work, *The Alcoholics* (1953), in which, in typically sardonic Thompson fashion, a man seeking a cure for his alcoholism enters a sanitarium run by an alcoholic, who seeks only to drain his 'patients' of their cash while keeping them drunk, kicking them out on the street when their funds are exhausted (see McCauley 1991: 136). Thompson also wrote (or co-wrote; there is much dissension on this point) two early films for director Stanley Kubrick, *The Killing* (1956), and *Paths of Glory* (1957); some of Thompson's novels, such as *The Getaway* (1959, were made into noir classics, although Thompson, still alive when Sam Peckinpah directed *The Getaway* in 1972, profited little from the project when his proposed screenplay for the film was rejected by the studio, and redrafted by other hands.

In his last years, Jim Thompson kept writing at a furious pace, and also appeared as an actor in *Farewell, My Lovely* (1975, directed by Dick Richards) portraying Judge Baxter Wilson Grayle, the cuckolded but politically powerful husband of the much younger Helen Grayle (Charlotte Rampling), in the third screen adaptation of Raymond Chandler's novel of the same name. This brief role was arranged as a favor by director Richards and the film's star, Robert Mitchum, so that Thompson would be eligible for medical care at the famed Motion Picture Country Home. Thompson also kept a file of projected novels in his desk, with thirty pages written for each new work; when presented with a contract, Thompson would finish the project. He wrote novelizations and other potboilers to keep the bill collectors at bay, but finally, worn down by illness and alcohol, Jim Thompson died on 7 April 1977 in Los Angeles.

Thompson's intensely bleak vision was deeply attractive to Frears, whose rise in the world of film had been anything but meteoric, and who now wanted to make a film entirely on his own terms. Hiring noir specialist Donald E. Westlake to write the film's screenplay from Thompson's novel, Frears tells the tale of a shady con man, Roy Dillon (John Cusack), who works 'short cons' for smalltime scores. His estranged mother, Lilly (Anjelica Huston) is also a 'grifter,' or confidence person, although she works for a large gambling syndicate, while Roy is the quintessential loner.

Roy falls for Myra Langtry (Annette Bening), another con artist, who wants to go into partnership with Roy, who is understandably skeptical. Through a spectacular series of double-crosses, Lilly is 'outed' for skimming off the top of her take for the mob, and turns to Roy for help. Without the slightest compassion, Roy turns her down, refusing to loan her money to get out of town. As a desperate, last-ditch measure, Lilly appeals to Roy's incestuous desire for her (which has always been a factor in their relationship), and while flirting with him, accidentally cuts his throat with a broken whisky glass. The cut is deep in Roy's jugular vein, and he bleeds to death in a matter of seconds. Lilly regards him with only the merest hint of regret, scoops up his money, and vanishes into the night. The nihilism and fatalistic despair of such a scenario are breathtaking; although Thompson's work has been adapted to the screen many times, this remains the most effective and unadulterated cinematic vision of his dark world. *The Grifters* is easily the best translation of Thompson's work to the screen, and a key film in the world of neo-noir.

Mike Hodges has had a long career as a director of contemporary noir films, beginning with the violent revenge film *Get Carter* (1971), starring a young Michael Caine, and *Pulp* (1972), an affectionate homage to the pulp thriller novel. After a detour into more conventional fare, such as *Flash Gordon* (1980), Hodges re-surfaced in 1998 with *Croupier*, arguably his most effective film to date, and one that first brought public attention to the actor Clive Owen. As Jack Manfred, a croupier and part-time writer, Owen portrays a rootless character whose motto is 'hang on tightly – let go lightly,' neatly summing up his attitude towards life, and to his relationships with others.

Hired as a full-time croupier by a sleazy London casino (the interiors were actually shot in Germany for tax reasons), Jack is soon balancing his relationship with Marion Nell (Gina McKee), his girlfriend who wants him to go straight, and his own desire for instant fame and fortune. At the film's end, he achieves the latter, but avoids the former, by writing an anonymous autobiographical account of his shady lifestyle, titled simply *Croupier*, which exposes the inside of the world of casino gambling, and instantly becomes a bestseller. Layered with one level of deception after another, with everyone on the make, or take, *Croupier* is one of the more complex and engaging noirs of recent vintage, with a hard brittle surface that is both inviting and sinister.

Another director in the recent era who specializes in scenarios of unremitting violence is Stuart Gordon, who created *Re-Animator* (1985) and *From Beyond* (1988). Because of their intense violence and graphic special effects content, both films have been hailed or reviled; Pauline Kael, the late hard-to-please film critic for *The New Yorker*, surprised many when she came out unreservedly in favor of *Re-Animator*, precisely because of its over-the-top Grand Guignol violence. The film was based on H. P. Lovecraft's grisly serial 'Herbert West – Reanimator,' which is not generally considered one of the author's more accomplished efforts, but unreels with grisly assurance on the screen.

Set at the fictional Medical College of Miskatonic University, the film is dominated by the performance of Jeffrey Combs as Herbert West, a brash young medical student who is obsessed with the notion of returning the recently dead to life. This isn't exactly new territory, but Gordon's fascination with the flesh and bone mechanics of the process raises the film above the level of a Frankenstein retread into an area distinctly its own. *Re-Animator*, no matter what else one might say about it, is a film that stands entirely alone: there is nothing quite like it, which perhaps accounts for a good deal of the film's success. In essence, the film represents a genre 'hot wiring' feat of considerable proportions: it is part horror film, part gore film, part black comedy, and part love story. All these elements are pushed past the boundaries of parody into a zone of hyper-realism (aided by the unsparingly graphic visuals) that sweeps the viewer along with the narrative into a unique and disturbing world that is Gordon's and Lovecraft's alone.

Although the score for the film is obviously reminiscent of (if not absolutely derived from) Bernard Herrmann's score for *Psycho* (Richard Band is credited with the composition of this music), the film is unexpectedly lavish in its execution, with vivid color, a good deal of gallows humor, and special effects that, for once, do not disappoint. Indeed, it is only through the recent advances in special effects by such artists as Tom Savini and Ed French that a film like *Re-Animator* becomes at all possible: the special effects crew of Anthony Doublin and John Naulin deserve special credit in this area.

One of the more memorable scenes in the film involves West's attempts to subdue one of a number of unruly, revived corpses; when the efforts of one of his colleagues are to no avail, West drily pushes his cohort out of the way with a mild 'excuse me,' and plunges a whirring surgical saw into the entrails of the corpse, cutting a neat hole directly through the body's midsection. Combs's detached performance as West is directly complemented by the more theatrical work of Barbara Crampton as Megan Halsey and Robert Sampson as Dean Halsey, whom West reanimates from the dead with disastrous results.

Ultimately, what sets *Re-Animator* apart from the seemingly endless flow of tepid 'slasher' films which dominate the cinema screens, particularly during the summer months, is the reflexive humor and intense self-examination which seem to have gone into the construction of every plot element, every frame of the final film. *Re-Animator* is thus a genre film that is fully cognizant of its ancestry; it takes the conventions and rules of the horror genre and breaks them into wildly configured shards of thematic material, pushing the normal audience tolerance for gore, and for outrageous plot exposition, past the boundaries that still, even in 1985, were rigidly enforced by audience expectations.

As many critics have remarked, the final reels of the film contain a graphic sequence of explicitly sexual material that seems designated to alienate all but the most jaded or passive viewers, and yet there is a panache in the creation of the film that makes the entire enterprise seem the result of hard work, a dark sense of humor, and a great deal of skill and knowledge. Gordon's own background before the film was as the director and co-founder of an experimental theatrical group that specialized in 'genre-bending' exercises not unlike *Re-Animator*; Gordon and his company of actors were fortunate to find a sympathetic producer in Brian Yuzna, whose other films have, for the most part, been neither commercially nor aesthetically successful.

Gordon's next Lovecraft 'adaptation' was *From Beyond*, released in 1986. Although production values remained high, and many of the original team members returned to the project, the film emerges as both schematic and joyless, as if everyone is simply going through the motions this time around, without much enthusiasm or desire. Perhaps this is because *Re-Animator* so successfully demolished what remaining audience boundaries there were in the area of 'shock' filmmaking; perhaps it is because the film has a higher budget, and with more money comes more supervision, which does not always help the finished product. *From Beyond* seems sadistic and ill-humored, something that the earlier film never gave the impression of being. Indeed, the violence in this film is presented with unflinching relish, as if Gordon has stepped over the edge of parody and found himself on the other side of the sadomasochistic chasm, and is, to our chagrin, enjoying the new positioning.

Although the final reels of *Re-Animator* contain some rather problematic material dealing with the objectification of the female body (the notorious headless 'cunnilingus' sequence being the most obvious example), there was something – a rather indefinite, yet certainly palpable diffidence and self-reflexivity – in the handling and playing of the material that made it seem as if Gordon and company were after higher stakes; making a claim on our psychic hidden ground with conscious deliberation, rather than simply seeking to revolt us with an unrelenting, inexorable catalogue of violent imagery. *From Beyond* seems to be interested only in this; for all the 'in' humor, it is a film which, at base, is both deadly serious and uncomfortably linked to the image-making process of pornographic films, and their exploitation and representational processes.

The 1990s and even 2000s were rife with accomplished noirs; Howard Franklin's *The Public Eye* (1992), starring Joe Pesci as a New York crime photographer modeled after the famous Weegee; Bryan Singer's *The Usual Suspects* (1995), a remarkable, complex ensemble acting piece with a superb

Figure 5.2 Kevin Spacey is a corrupt cop on the take in Curtis Hanson's *L.A. Confidential* (1997).

twist ending; David Lynch's *Mulholland Drive* (2001), a typical dark meditation on fantasy and reality set in Hollywood, where nothing is as it seems, and nothing really matters; Curtis Hanson's *L.A. Confidential* (1997), an affectionate if gritty homage to the scandal-ridden 1950s, with a more jaundiced view of law enforcement than one usually sees on the screen in a mainstream film; and Christopher Nolan's *Memento* (2000), featuring Guy Pearce as the hapless Leonard Shelby, the victim of short-term memory loss, trying to piece together the links in a complex case of murder and deception.

As Leonard, Pearce is a tabula rasa, blankness personified, unable to remember from one moment to the next what has happened, whom he knows, who is a friend or an enemy, or how he happens to be in any place, at any time. Waking up in a motel room near the start of the film, Leonard muses on his complete absence of identity or self-knowledge, in a typically noirish voiceover.

So where are you? You're in some motel room. You just – you just wake up and you're in – in a motel room. There's the key. It feels like maybe it's just the first time you've been there, but perhaps you've been there for a week, three months. It's – it's kind of hard to say. I don't – I don't know. It's just an anonymous room.

Nolan's films, often co-written with his brother, Jonathan, are pure twenty-first-century noir, even when, as in *The Prestige* (2006), a tale of two dueling magicians at the dawn of the twentieth century, he indulges in a period piece. Cold, hard, calculating, and devoid of humanity or warmth, Nolan may be the ideal director of contemporary neo-noir – cold, clear, distilled, and absolutely deadly.

No one can trust anyone anymore. No one can count on anything, or believe anyone, no matter what their credentials or reputation may be. Your closest friends will betray you. Colleagues will abandon you. Disaster lurks around the next corner, and in true noir fashion, you won't see it coming. Indeed, you may have no future at all. Steve De Jarnatt's overlooked thriller *Miracle Mile* (1988) is, in many respects, way ahead of its time, a direct expression of this sentiment, and in many ways a harbinger of themes that would be pursued in films of the late 1990s and early twenty-first century.

A young man, Harry Washello (Anthony Edwards, later a star on the teleseries *E. R.*), picks up a pay phone in downtown Los Angeles, and accidentally overhears two top military officials – who think they are speaking on a 'secure' line – matter-of-factly discussing the news that both the US and the Soviet Union have accidentally launched nuclear missiles against each other, and that Armageddon is only seventy minutes away. Edwards desperately tries to flee Los Angeles with his girlfriend, Julie Peters (Mare Winningham), but despite heroic efforts, their final attempt at flying by helicopter to a remote location fails, and they both drown, trapped in the helicopter's sinking fuselage, victims unable to avoid their ineluctable fate. Made for a modest budget, and released in a spotty nationwide campaign, *Miracle Mile* has vanished into the mists of memory, and doesn't even have 'cult' status. It might as well never have existed. This, of course, is the essential noir dilemma: does anything ever exist? And if it does, will we remember it five, ten, twenty years from now? Will we remember it at all?

In the future, we won't need televisions or even cell phones to experience alternative realities; images and experiences will be wired directly into our brains, as Montgomery Tully posited in 1957 with his film *Escapement*. The paranoid visions of Kathryn Bigelow's *Strange Days* (1995), from a story and screenplay by her then-husband, James Cameron, are injected directly into the brains of a group of willing subjects – 'VR' (virtual reality) addicts who imbed memory chips directly into their brains to 'experience' dangerous or illegal situations; suicide, murder, scenes of extreme violence. Ralph Fiennes is suitably slimy as Lenny Nero, a black-market dealer in the 'VR films,' who is not only a dealer of the chips, but an addict himself. When one of his friends is murdered, and the experience winds up as a VR film, Lenny goes on a crusade to discover who is behind his friend's murder, and not incidentally to recapture the love of his erstwhile girlfriend, Faith Justin (Juliette Lewis), whom he fears may be the next victim.

Paul Verhoeven's paranoid vision of a future of constant war is on vivid display in *Starship Troopers* (1997), a saga of interplanetary war between 'citizen soldiers' and giant, lethal bugs (arachnids, for the most part) that serves not only as a showcase for Phil Tippett's dazzling computer-generated special effects, but also as a perverse 'homage' to the despicable work of the Nazis' foremost filmic propagandist, Leni Riefenstahl, whose *Triumph of the Will* (1934) Verhoeven slavishly copied in creating a Fascist world of the future. Verhoeven, of course, began the decade with one of the most influential neo-noirs of recent memory, *Basic Instinct* (1991), starring Sharon Stone as a writer of best-selling novels who may or may not be a serial killer. Dark, brooding, and dripping with menace and overt sexuality, *Basic Instinct* provided the template for much of the neo-noir that was to follow in its wake.

James McTeigue's *V for Vendetta* (2005) is one of the latest in this series of increasingly paranoid visions, with a screenplay by Larry and Andy Wachowski that forecasts a Fascist, future England, ruled by a maniacal despot, Adam Sutler (John Hurt). Against this totalitarian society, a small group of rebels fight back, led by the mysterious V (Hugo Weaving), who enlists Evey (Natalie Portman) to his cause. Effectively positing that only violence helps where violence rules, *V for Vendetta* was heavily censored when first released, inasmuch as it frankly endorses terrorist violence (much like Gillo Pontecorvo's *The Battle of Algiers* [1965]), and government authorities worldwide were alarmed at the film's direct message: if you don't like the system, blow it up. Part comic book, part revolutionary tract, *V for Vendetta* attracted a wide audience on initial release, and remains a popular cult film to this day.

Perhaps the most disturbing and despairing filmic trend of the new millennium is the use of 'torture porn,' as evidenced in the *Saw* films, and Eli Roth's *Hostel* (2005) and *Hostel Part II* (2007). Roth's films document the torture and murder of two groups of backpacking teenagers – male in the first film, female in the second – who check into an Eastern European hostel that promises to be a paradise of earthly delight, only to discover that they are being sold as torture victims to rich, perverted businessmen. Unrelenting in its graphic detail, *Hostel I* and *II*, and other films of their ilk, confront the audience with their worst fears, and then transcend them to create a new level of brutality and savage violence. Disembowelments, eye gougings, ritual throat slittings, and most of all, cruelty in unrelenting doses are the hallmark of these films, in which torture is very real. Perhaps the most unsettling aspect of this series is the fact that Wal-Mart – supposedly the 'family store' – sold massive quantities of the DVD of the first installment in special merchandising displays located near checkout counters around the US; sex, once again, is off limits, but torture – hey, let's go for it. It's so American. As critic Mark Kermode commented of *Hostel: Part II*,

> We're back to the Slovakian torture camp, this time in the company of three young woman [sic] who are due to be sliced and diced by loathsome, misogynist businessmen [. . .] Roth clearly thinks he's doing his bit for equal opportunities by having female sadists enjoying virgin bloodbaths and showing a chauvinist getting his [penis] hacked off on screen. Yet what he's really interested in is dressing Bijou Phillips in clichéd slut-wear and taking a circular saw to her tightly trussed face. Talented Heather Matarazzo gets mocked, stripped, bled and killed without ever being allowed to act (which she can do rather well), while *Cannibal Holocaust* director Ruggero Deodate eats someone's leg in a [. . .] cameo. Oh, do grow up.

For his part, Roth is unconcerned about the level of violence that permeates both *Hostel* and *Hostel II*; as he commented in an interview shortly before the release of the first installment of the series,

> We're at war and people are dying everyday. How can you possibly say that my movie is going to damage society? There's actually a real war happening and everyday, on the news. Americans are getting killed, bodies are being burned, and no one knows when it's going to end . . . like it's hard to say, you put my film up against that and it's like theatre, magic tricks. It's incredible, but the sex is what they are really tense about. I guess if there was like a giant orgy going on they would freak, but with a war going on, I guess they are a little less concerned with violence. (Gray, 'Eli Roth Interview')

So, as long as it sells, 'torture porn' will continue to proliferate, and while *Hostel Part II* did only a fraction of the business of the original film, the *Saw* franchise marches on with increasing box-office success, and no end in sight. As much as we might hate to admit it, *Hostel* and its brethren are the logical extensions of contemporary neo-noir, in which the self is all, and everyone else is just a prop, or a useful tool for advancement. Roth has made links between his *Hostel* films and the American torture dungeons in Guantanamo Bay, and the disturbing fact is that there's no doubt about it; as Bela Lugosi, as Dr Richard Vollin in Lew Landers's 1935 version of *The Raven*, exclaims with Satanic glee, we 'like to torture.' We think torture is useful, even patriotic under the right circumstances, and television series like *24* have made it a staple of our everyday consciousness, as Jack Bauer (Kiefer Sutherland) uses nearly similar methods on a weekly basis to coerce the 'truth' from a stereotypical assemblage of terrorists – almost always with effective results. But what's the next step after that? Do we even dare to guess?

One of the most compelling and disturbing films of 2006 was Alfonso Cuarón's *Children of Men*, a noirish dystopian vision that vanished from sight almost immediately after release, despite superb execution and an excellent cast. The film is overtly political, depicting England in the year 2027 surviving the effects of a global social breakdown, brought about by the fact that no woman has been able to conceive a child for the past eighteen years. England alone remains functional, although it has been transformed into a police state, and suicide pills are routinely handed out to the dwindling populace. There is nothing to live for, since each person knows that when they die, no one will replace them. As illegal immigrants flock to England seeking sanctuary from the worldwide meltdown, Theo Faron (Clive Owen) is pressed into service by a gang of revolutionaries, led by Julian Taylor (Julianne Moore), to spirit Kee (Clare-Hope Ashitey), a pregnant African refugee, out of the country, so that she can give birth in safety, and perhaps mark the beginning of a human renaissance.

The production design of the film is remarkable; London has never looked so shabby and rundown, even by Orwellian standards. Based on a novel by P. D. James, the film is considerably enhanced by the handheld Steadicam camera work of the gifted Emmanuel Lubezki, who shot many of the sequences, including the opening scene – in which Theo gets his morning coffee in a shop that explodes seconds later, just after his departure – in one long take. The color design of the film is washed out and flat, and Cuarón deliberately chose the most derelict sections of London in which to shoot, to heighten the desperate nature of the film.

The noir element of the production is unmistakable; in a word devoid of hope or the promise of new life, what reason is there for going forward? While millions commit suicide using 'Quietus' kits, band concerts continue, as if everything were normal, in the London parks, and only renegades like Jasper Palmer (Michael Caine, in a superb performance) see the whole situation for what it really is; hopeless. One of the film's most compelling yet understated sequences takes place in a former grade school, which is now overgrown with weeds, the windows shattered, as wild animals drift in and out of the abandoned classrooms. No more children, no more school, no more knowledge to be passed on to the next generation.

But the most telling aspect of *Children of Men* is the direct criticism it offers to the Bush regime, from the police state atmosphere of the British constabulary, to the explicit references to the war in Iraq (within the context of the film, relatively ancient history, but still very much an open wound; a conflict that accomplished nothing) and the counterfeit value of supposed authority figures. The bombing that Theo narrowly escapes in the first moments of the film has been staged, in fact, by the government, and not the terrorists (although they will be blamed for it), simply to ratchet up the climate of fear in which the government clearly thrives. However, the revolutionaries are an equally unsavory lot, given to macho posturing and useless diatribes, addicted to violence, and utterly unscrupulous in their dealings with each other. Theo, for example, is recruited to help them, but when it seems convenient to do so, they plan to kill him, and keep Kee as a trophy to attract others to their cause.

Bored workers, staring at monitors in their decrepit government buildings, go through the motions of their jobs, but nothing more. Everyone takes drugs; alcohol, cigarettes, tranquilizers, suicide pills; everything but marijuana, which is still illegal, but which Jasper and Theo both use as a means to escape the pain of everyday existence. Jasper tries to escape from the madness by living far out in the country, off the grid, in a completely 'green' house that looks something like a relic from the 1960s, but even this sanctuary eventually is unearthed by the police, who gun Jasper down in cold blood, even as he laughs in their faces. Unflinchingly depicting a world devoid of hope, pleasure, or the dream of a future, *Children of Men* is at once a damning political indictment of the Bush-era political system, dependent upon torture, greed, control of the media, and individual coercion to achieve its ends, and also a no-holds-barred science fiction noir.

If *Children of Men* is less celebrated than Ridley Scott's much more famous *Blade Runner* (1982), with its Los Angeles of 2019 as a living hell crawling with Replicants, dominated by a contest between the very rich and the very poor, it is perhaps for the direct manner of its political address. *Blade Runner* is a stylish science fiction noir, which has gone through several re-edits, the first and most important of which took place in 1992, when Scott, his directorial power now unchallenged, removed a noirish voiceover that ran throughout the film. The voiceover was put in at the insistence of studio executives who found *Blade Runner* confusing without it; this was exactly the same case with Francis Ford Coppola's *Apocalypse Now* (1979), perhaps the most noir of all war films, which originally was presented without a voiceover by Martin Sheen, as Captain Benjamin L. Willard, hunting down Colonel Walter E. Kurtz (Marlon Brando) in the jungles of Vietnam. Exhibitors protested, and Coppola capitulated, inserting a voiceover written by Michael Herr, but the film remains more effective without it.

In *Blade Runner*, Harrison Ford portrays Rick Deckard, a retired Blade Runner, or Replicant hunter, who is forced out of retirement by his corrupt boss, Bryant (the reliable noir standby M. Emmet Walsh). Four Replicants – part human, part machine – are on the loose and they're dangerous. Deckard is essentially a twenty-first-century version of the trench-coated antihero who dominated the screen in the 1940s, although the trappings of the future have considerably more allure than the shabby alleyways of the classic studio era. The film, typically for Scott, is a lavish spectacle on every possible level, vividly depicting a hyper-commercialized future in which everything costs a fortune, no one can be trusted, the police and government rule with an iron fist, and even parking meters promise 'instant death by electrocution' if tampered with.

Yet *Blade Runner* is in many ways a very safe commercial proposition; Scott edited the film again in 2007, resulting in what he termed his 'Final Cut,' which restores more material to the film, but doesn't really affect the end result all that much. For many, the film's special effects overwhelm the story, and Harrison Ford's characterization appears thin and lacking in internal motivation. Scott, a dictatorial presence on the set, often angered Ford, who wouldn't speak to him by the end of the film's production (see Shone 2004 for more details on this). But *Blade Runner*, for all its flash and atmosphere of corporate, big-government nightmare, is ultimately a spectacularly designed chase film, with a deliberately designed open ending that seems contrived. But the film has developed a cult following, and in most circles is widely respected.

The same could be said for the films of the Coen Brothers, who to many observers, along with David Lynch, represent the epitome of the neo-noir impulse in the twenty-first century. But for this observer, at least, there is less here than meets the eye. The brothers' critically acclaimed *No Country For Old Men* (2007) is more or less a remake of John Boorman's *Point Blank*, shot in a flat, predictable style that telegraphs its intent from the first frame forward; for clarity and the true instinct of noir, I much prefer *Blood Simple* (1984), their first effort, which again featured M. Emmet Walsh as Loren Visser, a down-at-heel private eye involved in a complex and visually stylish case of murder and betrayal.

As with many of the most interesting noirs, *Blood Simple* was shot for a relative pittance, and was the brothers' do-or-die effort to break into the film industry; subsequent films have been quirky and darkly comic, but again, to decidedly calculated effect. *Barton Fink* (1991) is the tale of a playwright who goes to Hollywood, but soon sells out to the system; his roommate in the shabby boarding house from hell where he lives is the homicidal Charlie Meadows (John Goodman), full of false bonhomie and empty promises. *Miller's Crossing* (1990) is a flat remake of Dashiell Hammett's 1931 noir novel *The Glass Key*, filmed twice before by Stuart Heisler (1942) and Frank Tuttle (1935); to my mind either of these versions is infinitely more authentic to Hammett's vision.

But what matters most here, and what seems to impress as well, is an excess of stylization in muted colors, deliberately monotonal camera set-ups, and flat, measured pacing throughout the film. This passes for ponderousness, but it strikes me as embracing the style, rather than the substance, of the piece, and seems labored and overly calculated. There's no real life in any of the Coen films, with the exception of *Blood Simple*, and perhaps that's the way they want it. Their remake of Alexander Mackendrick's classic noir comedy *The Ladykillers* (1955), which they shot in 2004 with a very uneasy Tom Hanks in the lead, suggests further to me that the Coens are content to repackage the past in appealing confections that don't have a center of their own; all is borrowed.

CHAPTER 6

Living in Fear

In the early twenty-first century, we live to consume. We live in fear, and so we buy things to fill up the empty spaces in our lives. It doesn't work, and it never worked, but we keep on consuming, as if the objects we purchase, our homes, our cars, will somehow protect us from mortality, debt, violence, disease, unhappiness. With the decline in cinema attendance in the early 2000s eerily mimicking the same pattern in the early 1950s (with the dawn of television, and the advent of the Cold War), television programming has become a new and potent source of noir. *CSI* unravels grisly mysteries on a weekly basis; *Law and Order: Special Victims Unit* deals in brutal sex crimes and murders with studied detachment, even nonchalance; Fox's utterly meretricious *Moment of Truth* hooks its contestants up to a lie detector, and then asks them increasingly invasive questions about their personal lives, for ever larger sums of cash.

This is the new millennium after all, an era of bank collapses, corporate mega-mergers, and personal isolation. Real communities have vanished, to be replaced by 'virtual' ones, in which people never meet, yet exchange the most intimate details with the click of a mouse. Group 'sharing' spaces on the web such as Facebook and MySpace offer only the illusion of community, when they are in fact primarily designed to harvest marketing information on their participants. Free 'wealth management' seminars dupe thousands out of their life savings; pension funds are raided; jobs are outsourced overseas to take advantage of cheap labor; healthcare plans leave millions uninsured.

This is the true 'reality' of life in the twenty-first century; rapacious greed, fear, violence, endless war, terrorism, and the continual droning of either threats or assurances from impotent authority figures, interested only in their own acquisition of power. For those lacking wealth, power, or influence, there is always the narcotic effect of television to dull the pain. Surely others are worse off than we are; famine in Darfur, riots in Baghdad, terrorist bombings in Gaza. But suppose that we could make ourselves over, and attain the seemingly unattainable. We could start a new life, build a new house, make ourselves over with plastic surgery, eliminate fear and want from our lives, and finally realize all our dreams – couldn't we?

The new breed of television reality shows, such as *Extreme Makeover: Home Edition*, *I Want a Famous Face*, and *The Swan*, to name just a few, all specialize in 'converting' their subjects' lives through a shock attack of new televisions, instant luxury mansions, completely overhauled bodies, and other artefacts of American consumer culture, to create the impression that one can 'buy' whatever one wants; a new life, a new future, an entirely new 'self,' which, of course, is impossible.

But were this illusion to collapse, not only those television series, but also their numerous progeny, such as *The Apprentice*, *Survivor*, *Wife Swap*, and many other 'extreme makeover' shows would vanish, leaving a gaping hole in the four networks' programming schedules (ABC, NBC, CBS, and Fox, no longer a 'mini-network' but a major player in the business, and a leader in the creation of reality programming). On *Extreme Makeover: Home Edition*, an Endemol production, the concept is simple, as detailed on the show's website:

> Put together one very run-down house, a deserving family, several opinion-ated designers, seven days and what do you get? The answer is *Extreme Makeover: Home Edition* [. . .] The lives of the lucky families are forever changed when they learn that they have been selected to have their home walls moved, their floors replaced and even their façades radically changed. The result should be a decorator's delight [. . .] if it can be done in time [. . .] Then viewers witness not only the unbelievable transformation of the house, but during the final and emotional reveal, they see how the home makeover has impacted the lives of the deserving families. (*Extreme Makeover: Home Edition* website)

As might be expected, the *Extreme Makeover: Home Edition* crews are not interested in projects where only a little preventive maintenance is required, or perhaps a new room is added to the family homestead. No, nothing else will suffice to satiate the viewer's appetite for spectacle than to completely destroy the existing home, and then 'magically' replace it with a Trump-esque McMansion created in a mere seven days, constructed by a veritable army of contractors, carpenters, plumbers, electricians, land-scape artists, interior decorators, and the like, all using high-end luxury carpeting, kitchen appliances, flat-screen plasma TVs, custom-designed beds, and sunken Jacuzzis to create not so much a new home, but rather a visually exaggerated suggestion of one – in short, a movie set.

This is the core of the show's appeal. Take a family in extreme distress, offer them a brand-new luxury house, and watch all their problems disappear, at least for the moment. The show's visual style perfectly mirrors its 'wham bam, thank you ma'am' approach to each new project. The team leader, Ty Pennington, arrives at the target house with massive amounts of energy and a large bullhorn, and hustles the family into a waiting limo for a trip to Disney World (or some equally phantasmal location), and then recruits a staggering team of carpenters to raze and then reconstruct the house in seven days.

To capture the manic speed of the construction, time-compression techniques are used with extravagant abandon (time-lapse photography, speeded-up motion, rapid, MTV-style editing), as Pennington runs around the site screaming at his co-workers that 'time is running out.' In most episodes, the houses are completed literally minutes before the family returns, and then the visual tone of the show shifts dramatically, in favor of slow-motion shots, lingering dissolves, and tearful hugs between crew members and the family of the week. In nearly every case, the sequences of the family touring their new house provoke shrieks of delight, tears of joy, and stunned expressions of amazement. If a family member's death has precipitated a visit by the *Extreme Makeover* team, a photo of the missing person is usually framed and hung in a prominent space in the new house, as mute testimony to the person's role in facilitating the makeover. Finally, goodbyes are tearfully exchanged, and the *Extreme Makeover* crew hits the road, on their way to transform another family's life, for better or worse.

Isn't the essence of noir a result of a constant media barrage of televised advertisements of idealized existence, print ads depicting an idyllic couple in luxurious surroundings, automobile ads that equate a new car with power, youth, and sex appeal, and a culture that values image over substance at the expense of the self? In light of this new wave of reality shows, such pioneers of the genre as *Queer Eye for the Straight Guy* seem positively quaint: a new wardrobe, a redecorated apartment or house, some 'consumer art' on the wall, and you're supposedly ready to reinvent your existence. It's no longer sufficient.

The new wave of reality shows insists that self-transformation begins externally, and then seeps inside. Your old body simply isn't good enough; scrap it, and begin anew. Your existing house, though comfortable, isn't a showplace; what are neighbors for, if not to envy your exterior success? As the makeover regimes grow more extreme, it seems that inconsequential items such as books and the arts matter less and less, and the performance of your own life, in which you appear as a star of your own design, assumes paramount importance.

In the twenty-first century, we are told, beauty comes from without – assisted by a phalanx of coaches, surgeons, cosmeticians, dentists, trainers, designers, and assorted personal advisors. The future of commercial social intercourse thus belongs to those who strive for, and conform to, an increasingly rigid series of specifications, dictated by a universe of images whose existence is justified only by their effectiveness as a medium of commerce. In short, we have become the product, to be marketed and exploited by the same advertisers who extol the virtues of Xanax, Zoloft, Viagra, Cialis, Nexium, and a host of other panaceas as essential elements of our existence. The future looks tranquilized and very uniform, and we seem to be embracing it with fearful enthusiasm. But what are we afraid of?

In the post-9/11 world, the romance of Armageddon is being replaced by the specter of inevitable destruction, albeit on a smaller scale. Piece by piece, city by city, landmark by landmark, the delicate balance of post-World War II nuclear politics has given way to a new war, in which atomic bombs, capable of decimating an entire metropolis in just one blast, fit in suitcases. The global apocalypse depicted by Stanley Kubrick in 1964's *Dr Strangelove* now seems simultaneously remote and infinitely more tangible. The twenty-first century will be defined not by wars, but by terrorist incursions. The current US administration seems intent on upping the ante with each new pronouncement, as tension spots in India and Pakistan, the Middle East, Africa, and Northern Ireland continue to simmer, even after decades of conflict. We cannot say what will happen in the future, but so much damage has been done that it will take decades – if it is at all possible – to resolve any sense of equity to our existing social system.

In a speech at the US Military Academy at West Point (USMA) on 1 June 2002, George W. Bush declared that 'preemptive' military strikes may be necessary to 'confront the worst threats before they emerge,' thereby creating a scenario in which attack becomes defense (Dixon 2003: 128). This policy of perpetual alarmism, it seems to me, creates a self-fulfilling prophecy, just as violent action thrillers and video games inspire those who become addicted to them to take the 'games' to the next step: real weapons, real victims. Even a casual glance at the social landscape of contemporary America reveals that we have become a nation marked by outbursts of senseless violence. One of the latest examples is the series of random shootings at US colleges and universities, most recently at Northern Illinois University on St Valentine's Day, 14 February 2008, in which five students were killed and several more injured before the gunman, one Steven Kazmierczak, committed suicide at the scene of the crime (Heher and Rousseau 2008).

The culture of noir, of death, of 'kill or be killed' must inevitably lead to violence; is that not its message? Thus, in a post-9/11 cinematic landscape, we must fight to find a path towards reason and understanding of a new cinematic landscape in which violence and catastrophe are viewed as constants. It is an entirely new world we live in after 9/11; the stages of representation have been irrevocably altered. How will we view, and be affected by, these new scenarios of imminent destruction? The idea of nuclear terrorism is hardly new. E. B. White, in his 1949 study *Here is New York*, after celebrating the city's multicultural heritage and magnificent urban sprawl, sounded a note of warning:

> the city, for the first time in its long history, is destructible. A single flight of planes no bigger than a wedge of geese can quickly end this island fantasy, burn the towers, crumble the bridges, turn the underground passages into lethal chambers, cremate the millions. The intimation of mortality is part of New York now; in the sound of jets overhead, in the black headlines of the latest edition. Of all targets, New York has a certain clear priority. In the mind of whatever perverted dreamer might loose the lightning, New York must hold a steady, irresistible charm. (quoted in Dixon 2003: 17)

Thus, long before the prophets of disaster turned Armageddon into a pop culture pastime, the author of *Charlotte's Web* and *Stuart Little* had a perfect fix on precisely what makes Manhattan so alluring: its vulnerability. Today, such a scenario would be even easier. One suitcase, left in the right location, would spell the end of centuries of cultural work, and the lives of potentially millions of people. Is it no wonder that this nightmarish vision haunts us, and continues to play out in the popular media with ever-increasing frequency? For it seems that the day that White prophesied is coming closer all the time. The twenty-first-century cinema is primarily a vehicle for special effects, violence, and scenes of mass destruction.

Indeed, our fundamental notion of what a movie is has changed dramatically over the past ten years; no longer do we require narrative so much as excessive spectacle and sound, to suture the gaps between audience and object viewed, and create an artificial aural/visual bridge between film and audience. Such films as Matt Reeves's *Cloverfield* (2008), Brett Ratner's *X-Men: The Last Stand (2006)*, Andy Wachowski and Larry Wachowski's *Speed Racer* (2008), and other recent projects testify to the fact that what enthralls audiences now is the manufactured image made possible by computer generated imagery (CGI) and other methods of image manipulation, rather than any supposedly humanist narrative structure.

What sort of distribution and production strategies will be embraced by Hollywood in the twenty-first century? At the turn of the century, in

Manhattan, an entire multiplex of twenty-five theatres was converted solely to digital projection for the premiere of Don Roos's film *Bounce* (2000), an event that the stars of the film and several of the production executives celebrated with the ceremonial act of throwing conventional 35mm prints of the film into an oversize wastebasket marked 'Obsolete.' The consequences of this shift, both aesthetically and commercially, will be enormous.

When the first 'talking' film, Alan Crosland's *The Jazz Singer* (1927), opened in New York, it was a one-theatre phenomenon, but within five years, the industry had converted completely to sound, and theatres coast-to-coast were wired to accommodate the new technology. Earlier experiments in sound and film had come and gone, but finally, the emerging Vitaphone technology allowed a workable, practical way to synchronize image and sound. Given the enormous cost savings involved for studios and distributors using the new digital image distribution technology, what sort of changes can we expect in production, distribution, and exhibition as the new digital model takes hold? And what sorts of films will be made? My answer is that they will be films that project a landscape of fear and violence, such as Jon Avnet's *88 Minutes* (2008), a flimsy, exploitational serial killer film with a dispirited Al Pacino in the lead, during which audiences can suspend taste, morality, and judgment. They have only to react.

Even the news has become noir, dealing in paranoia, fear, and obsessive speculation. On the *CBS Evening News* of 13 June 2007, reporter Bob Orr, in a piece entitled simply 'Nuclear Terror,' described the now routine practice in which:

> New York cops, armed with Geiger counters, pull over trucks for random inspections. Robotic underwater cameras troll along the hulls of cruise ships, looking for explosives and traces of radioactivity. And from the air, sensors snoop for radiation hot spots. It is the last line of defense against an unthinkable threat [. . .] terrorists would like nothing better than to hit the US with nuclear weapons [which would produce] devastation far, far beyond what we saw on September 11th.

To drive home his point, Orr delivers a stand-up in front of the White House, noting that with current technology, 'a small nuclear device in the back of a van here in the heart of Washington would take out the White House and everything else within a square mile.' He then segues into a mock 'preparedness' exercise involving military personnel from twenty-eight countries 'working together to detect and disrupt terrorists seeking nuclear materials,' while arguing that weapons-grade nuclear material 'would not be easy' for terrorists to get, despite the fact that 'thousands of

Cold War [nuclear] weapons remain in Russian stockpiles,' and the further knowledge that there have been, to date, 'eighteen cases of illegal trafficking of weapons-grade uranium,' a figure that seems, when one considers the ubiquity of the worldwide market in nuclear material, probably only a fraction of such transactions. As Orr's piece wraps up, he asks FBI director Robert Mueller how much of the threat of nuclear terrorism is 'hype' and how much of it is 'real.' Mueller replies that the possibility is 'not hype,' and further insists that whatever the cost, 'we just cannot let that happen' (Orr 2007).

Illustrated with clips from Phil Alden Robinson's *The Sum of All Fears* (2002) in which Baltimore is reduced to rubble, and with dreamy slow-motion inserts of Osama Bin Laden ominously superimposed over a map of possible international nuclear co-conspirators, including Iran, Pakistan, and North Korea, Orr's piece, in the end, depicts little more than a desperate game of catch-up, in which the authorities seemingly chase down cold leads and shadowy figures with free-form abandon, all in an attempt to forestall what many see as an inevitable possibility. This is noir in real life.

Cinema, as we knew it in the twentieth century, is undergoing a radical transformation. Even now, it is interfacing with the next generation of imagistic recording and reproduction (the net, the web, digital tape and discs, the availability of films via cable and satellite, not to mention video-tape, laser discs, and new systems not yet known but certain to be invented, not least of which may be a simple chip encoding all the information necessary to reconstruct the sounds (and images of a 'feature film'). When more recent 'art-house' low-budget films are made, their makers hope to graduate immediately to large-scale Hollywood films, thus rendering the independent cinema nothing more than a potential proving ground for future masters of the dominant cinema.

The model of theatrical feature filmmaking foregrounding the director as auteur is similarly obsolete, as directors now serve merely as 'traffic cops' (no matter how stylish their technique) for producers whose interests are solely directed to the bottom line. The films of the past are dependably profitable; current releases are another matter. As one media analyst recently noted, 'the television divisions make money, the film library makes money, but current releases lose money. It's worse than it has been for the past couple of years' (Weinraub and Fabrikant 1999: 1). Adds Hollywood producer Ron Meyer, 'in today's climate, with risks so great, it's just much easier for a studio to say no to anything they believe is not very commercial.' David O'Connor of Creative Artists Agency agrees, noting that 'if a movie doesn't fit a studio's financial model, they can do without making it' (Weinraub and Fabrikant 1999: 15).

And yet a plethora of cheap programming dominates the marketplace. With every person having access to a camcorder or video surveillance device, we are now offered *Taxicab Confessions*, *America's Funniest Home Videos*, and the beleaguered cast of the television 'reality' shows *Survivor* and *Big Brother* as the televisual spectacle of choice. But the terminal nature of the theatrical cinema experience is best exemplified by the opening of a multiplex theatre in Valley Stream, Long Island, where the patrons must pass through metal detectors and body searches to get to their assigned seats, and are repeatedly warned by a recorded tape played through the public address system that they are under surveillance at all times.

The shared communality of the theatrical cinema experience is thus rendered an obsolete social contract, as movies on video encourage us to stay within the social sphere of our own home. Cinema, as Godard predicted in *Le Mépris*, is 'dead.' It remains only to bury the corpse in an avalanche of $95 million genre thrillers, where even the most compliant and creative directors are hard pressed to create an individual signature in the face of ever-tightening narratological requirements.

Cinema, once the most contemporary of the arts, has been eclipsed by nascent technologies. The past can be profitably recycled, as Robert Daly of Warner Brothers comments: 'DVD, pay per view, video on demand – these are the critical areas of the movie business over the next few years. And the good thing about DVD is it's going to bring in revenues in the area that doesn't push up costs: the library.' Herman Allen, head of the investment banking firm of Allen and Company, offers an even grimmer prognosis: 'there has been an explosion of industries with a visual orientation, with the computer and the Internet, and for the moment, these are far more interesting . . . the Internet businesses make everyone else look small, boring, and pale in comparison' (Weinraub and Fabrikant 1999: 15). And producer Ted Hope, whose credits include Todd Haynes's *Safe* (1995), Ang Lee's *The Wedding Banquet* (1993), and other thoughtful films, claims that

> The marketplace is nasty and brutal, remembering only the latest successes and never forgetting its failures. It allows no room for taste beyond the mainstream. Truly unique films cannot get screens, let alone hold them for more than a week or two. There is virtually no American audience for art films, political films, or non-narrative films. The specialized distributors have morphed into mass marketers, not niche market suppliers. Monopolistic business practices drive most corporate strategies. (1995: 18)

Thus, under Hope's model, although the mainstream cinema continues to proliferate, and blockbuster films capture huge theatrical audiences, the cinema itself is going through a period of radical change at the end of its first century, coexisting with CD-ROM interactive 'movies,' videocassette and laserdisc distribution, cable television, satellite television, video games, and a host of competing sound/image constructs. The exponentially rising cost of film production (not to mention distribution and publicity) helps to ensure the hegemony of the dominant industrial vision in the middle-American marketplace, and the super conglomeration of existing production, distribution, and exhibition entities further assures the primacy of the readily marketable, pre-sold film, as opposed to a more quirky, individualistic vision.

The few foreign films that attain moderately wide release in the US are lavish costume spectacles. In the twenty-first century, it is apparent that audiences go to the movies not to think, not to be challenged, but rather to be tranquilized and coddled. Sequels are safe bets for exploitation, provided that the original film performs well at the box office; it is for this reason alone that nearly every mainstream film today is designed with an 'open' ending, allowing the film to be franchised if the parent of the series captures the public's fancy. Television has become a wilderness of talk shows and infomercials, with time so precious that even the end credits of series episodes are shown on a split-screen with teasers from the upcoming program, to dissuade viewers from channel surfing, which is nevertheless rampant.

Psychic hotlines offer spurious counsel at $3.99 a minute, shopping channels commodify the images we see into discrete, marketable units, 'no money down' real-estate brokers hope to dazzle us with their varying formulae for success; we've seen how *that* last scheme turned out. The cable movie channels run only current fare, or thoroughly canonical classics, avoiding subtitling and black and white imagery (with rare exceptions) at all costs. Revival houses screen films in only a few major cities, particularly Paris and New York, and even these are closing with stunning regularity. In view of this, it seems very much as if the first century of cinema will now be left to the ministrations of museum curators and home video/laserdisc collectors, rather than remaining a part of our shared cultural heritage.

With mainstream contemporary films so banal, is it any wonder that more adventurous viewers/auditors are turning to the Internet, e-mail, the nascent world of cyberspace, in search not only of a cheap medium of expression, but also human contact? For this last is what the cinema inherently denies us; sealed in a can, protected on a screen, we watch it, and it surveils us, but the connection between viewer and viewed is gossamer thin. Video games, such as *Grand Theft Auto IV* (2008), seemingly offer a more concrete, though still synthetic connection to the spectacle witnessed by the viewer/participant – an illusion, in fact, of control and interactivity.

The limits of this insular spectacle are striking, and the technology at present is clumsy and expensive. But the experiential horizon is there, and the strip of film that runs through a conventional 35mm projector is an archaic *aide-mémoire* of an era of puppet shows and magic lanterns. To satisfy us, the spectacle must engulf us, threaten us, sweep us up from the first. The 'plots' of most interactive games are primarily simple – kill or be killed. These games achieve (at home and in the arcade) a wide currency among viewers bored by the lack of verisimilitude offered by the conventional cinema. And because of this lack, the cinema, many argue, is dying. Laura Mulvey asserted that the Hollywood studio system film

> is really a thing of the past – I mean, it's like studying the Renaissance. But at the same time I think perhaps, like the Renaissance, it's something that doesn't go away and still stays a source of imagery and myths and motifs . . . although we could say that the studio system is dead and buried, and that Hollywood cinema, however very powerful it is today, works from very different economic and production structures, at the same time, our culture – MTV images, advertising images, or to take a big obvious example, Madonna – all recycle the images of the old Hollywood cinema, all of which have become points of reference, almost as though they've become myths in their own right, which are then taken over, absorbed, and recycled every day in the different media. (Súarez and Manglis 1995: 7)

In a *New York Times* op-ed piece on 12 June 2007, William J. Perry, Secretary of Defense in the Clinton administration, Ashton B. Carter, then Assistant Secretary of Defense, and Michael M. May, a former director of the Lawrence Livermore National Laboratory, state flatly that 'we are still woefully unprepared for a nuclear attack,' adding that in 2005, former US Senator Sam Nunn asked

> On the day after a nuclear weapon goes off in an American city, [we will ask] 'what would we wish we had done to prevent it?' But in view of the increased risk we now face, it is time to add a second question to Mr Nunn's: What will we actually do on the day after? That is, what actions should our government take? (Perry, Carter, and May 2007: A23)

For Perry, Carter, and May, the prognosis is decidedly downbeat. In addition to the initial devastation of one nuclear blast, they argue that one must face

> the unpleasant fact that the first nuclear bomb may well not be the last. If terrorists manage to obtain a weapon, or the fissile material to make one (which

fits into a small suitcase), who's to say they wouldn't have two or three more? (2007: A23)

Who indeed? As the authors postulate,

terrorism has surged into a mass global movement and seems to gather strength daily as extremism spills out of Iraq into the rest of the Middle East, Asia, Europe and even the Americas. More nuclear materials that can be lost or stolen plus more terrorists aspiring to mass destruction equals a greater chance of nuclear terrorism. (2007: A23)

Can anything contain this? I would argue that while, with the severe curtailment of personal rights, and massive surveillance camera presence (London, Amsterdam, New York, and other major cities now exist under literally continual televisual surveillance, exceeding Orwell's most noir visions of paranoid intrusiveness), one might postpone this day of unimaginable destruction, there seems to be no definitive method of preventing it. Thus, we live in fear – fear that can be marketed, packaged, and sold. This opens up a host of opportunities for new products that may protect us from terrorist attacks, or then again, may not.

Researchers at the Technion-Israel Institute of Technology have developed 'a hand held scanner that detects [the] explosive [. . .] triacetone triperoxide (TATP).' It's easy to make TATP, according to Technion's advertisement:

three simple ingredients available in any grocery or hardware store, plus instructions accessible on the Internet. That's all the London terrorists needed to build triacetone triperoxide (TATP) explosives. This new explosive looks like sugar and can be molded to resemble the most innocuous of objects, such as a scented candle or a rubber duckie, making its detection virtually impossible. (American Technion Society 2007: A12)

But in addition to the scanner that detects this explosive, Technion has also developed

nano-sized parachutes that scatter in the wind like dandelion seeds to detect airborne toxins; ultra strong concrete for shelters and personal armor; a face recognition system so effective it distinguishes between identical twins; [and] software that identified computer users by each person's unique typing patterns. [. . .] (2007: A12)

It seems to me that we've made a jump here, from a product that directly addresses a specific explosive, to technology that is certainly intrusive, and seeks to strip away what little privacy we have left in the digital age. And yet, who is to say that these measures will not be necessary to combat the threat of nuclear terrorism? And conversely, who is to assure us that once exploded, these methods will not be used by totalitarian regimes against citizens who simply dissent from their government's policies?

As one indicator of how far technology has progressed in its search for an alternative synthetic reality, the film *Final Fantasy* (2001) provides some clues, although the techniques it utilized are now seriously outmoded. Using the voices of actors Donald Sutherland, James Woods, Alec Baldwin, Ving Rhames, and Ming-Na, *Final Fantasy* boasts a completely computer-generated cast of characters in a film based on a series of PlayStation games, budgeted at $70 million. Produced by Columbia Pictures, the film was virtually 'created' in an office building in Honolulu, where hundreds of computer technicians labored for years to bring to the finished product a disturbing air of humanoid reality.

The director of *Final Fantasy*, Hironobu Sakaguchi, notes that 'we've created characters that no longer feel blatantly computer generated. If we press on, we can achieve the reality level of a live-action film . . . it's something people have never seen before' (Taylor 2000: 56). *Final Fantasy* was not only an experiment, but also a harbinger of things to come; an entire wave of films can be produced with computer generated 'stars' who won't go on strike, demand pay raises, or refuse a script. Such complete corporate control of moving image production may well prove irresistible to the visual multinational conglomerates of the twenty-first century; if such a shift does occur, it will fundamentally alter the way we think of a film, and of those who create it. No more actors, no more sets; just an endless series of computer stations, with anonymous technicians plotting points in the day.

But today's genre films have pretty much done away with acting anyway; performers are reduced to tailor's dummies reciting genre-motivated dialogue, which does nothing more than advance the plot; characterization and depth have been abandoned for much of commercial mainstream cinema. We've abandoned the human aspect in the most of the current wave of Hollywood films: Jon Favreau's *Iron Man*, Andrew Adamson's *The Chronicles of Narnia: Prince Caspian*, Steven Spielberg's *Indiana Jones and the Kingdom of the Crystal Skull*, Louis Leterrier's *The Incredible Hulk*, Guillermo del Toro's *Hellboy II: The Golden Army*, and Christopher Nolan's *The Dark Knight* (all 2008) aptly demonstrate this. All are comic book films, in which the real is obliterated by a haze of computer generated effects, cardboard characters, and conflicts that demand, and get, a predictable resolution. This is noir without risk, or reward; overblown playthings for a generation raised in fear.

If one wishes to visit the Statue of Liberty today, one must board a ferry in Manhattan as a similar face recognition surveillance system takes one's picture and instantaneously compares it to a database of terrorism suspects compiled by the United States government (Dixon 2003: 84). Most people seem willing to accept this loss of privacy as a consequence of living in a perpetually threatened world. As one visitor to the Statue of Liberty, David Miller from Madison, Alabama, noted of the surveillance system, 'I've got nothing to hide, and neither should anyone else . . . we're going to have to give up some freedoms so that we can continue to have freedom' (as quoted in Dixon 2003: 85). Predictably, others disagree with this assessment, including the American Civil Liberties Union (ACLU), but even in 2007, in the post-9/11 era, dissenting voices are all but drowned out by the frenzied rush to document and categorize every aspect of our existence.

And yet how effective is all this continual monitoring? It seems to me that much of the surveillance proceeds along class lines. I often recall colleague Stephen Prince's comment to me when we were going through security at Vancouver airport that the entire process was just 'window dressing,' in view of the fact that numerous maintenance workers, guards, and various officials seemed to drift through the gates with varying degrees of impunity, to say nothing of the fact that only a percentage of the plane's cargo was being examined in detail. The wealthy and privileged can now charter private jet craft to take them from point A to point B with little, if any, interference.

As Peter Zimmerman, former science advisor to the Senate Foreign Relations Committee from 2001 to 2003, told Steve Coll of *The New Yorker* on 12 March 2007, 'I think there are [. . .] people who, given [the right material] could think of very creative and malicious ways to use it. Why hasn't it happened? The answer is we've been lucky' (Coll 2007). In the same article, Coll recounts the case of five suspect cargo ships bound from Sri Lanka to the United States, which authorities suspected of transporting nuclear materials for terrorist groups. As Coll relates,

> The United States Coast Guard stopped [. . .] two New York-bound ships in territorial waters, about ten miles offshore; from that distance, if there was a nuclear weapon on board a detonation would cause relatively little harm. Scientists boarded the vessels, shouldering diagnostic equipment, but these ships [. . .] turned out to be clean; as it happened, the offending vessel was on an Asian route, and its cargo was scrap metal mixed with radioactive materials that had been dumped improperly. The entire episode, which was not disclosed to the public, lasted about two weeks. (Coll 2007)

How can such surveillance be conducted in all possible cases of infraction? The simple answer is that it can't; sooner or later, someone, with something, is going to get though. As Coll notes,

> In the United States, between 1994 and 2005, the N.R.C. recorded sixty-one domestic cases of stolen or lost isotopes in amounts that would clearly be useful to someone making a dirty bomb [and] it is not clear whether the commission's records describe all or even most of the problem cases. (Coll 2007)

In the early stages of the 2008 American presidential campaign, the politician and actor Fred Dalton Thompson, best known for his continuing role on the television series *Law and Order*, was running for the office of President of the United States. In Ben Goddard's film *Last Best Chance* (2005), he has already attained that office, and is saddled with the unenviable task of preventing nuclear terrorism in the United States, working with a system so porous that failure is almost inevitable. Surrounded by a group of advisors who seem overwhelmed by their task, the fictional president portrayed by Thompson, one 'Charles B. Ross,' fights to sift through an avalanche of conflicting reports, 'chatter' on the Internet, and interdepartmental intrigues because, as he puts it, 'I don't want us sitting on our butts if something's about to happen.'

But in the end, despite cooperation from the Russian government (a prospect that seems increasingly remote these days), all his vigilance is to no avail. Through a complex web of international negotiations, a group of terrorists manage to assemble a nuclear device in Canada, and then smuggle it across the border at an isolated location, right under the noses of customs officials. At the same time, bombs are smuggled in from other locations, and President Ross admits to his staff that 'I don't know how many there are, where they are, or what I can do to stop them.' The film ends with the implication that one or more of the devices will soon be detonated on US soil.

Last Best Chance is quite frankly a propaganda piece, which plays (not surprisingly) like a somewhat more ambitious episode of *Law and Order*, complete with 'date and location' intertitles, and it was distributed free to anyone who asked for a copy. Funded by the Nuclear Threat Initiative, with additional support from the Carnegie Foundation and the John D. and Catherine T. MacArthur Foundation, it is earnest and yet fatalistic in its world view. In press materials for the film, Fred Dalton Thompson commented that,

> I got involved in *Last Best Chance* because of its potential to make preventing nuclear terrorism a higher priority. We need an all-out global effort to

lock down nuclear weapons and materials so that the line I deliver in this film about al Qaeda becoming a nuclear power never comes to pass.

But this supposes that al Qaeda is one distinct entity, rather than a large group of splinter organizations and viral factions, all of whom are seemingly intent on the destruction of the West. The threat of nuclear terrorism in the United States today is at once real, ubiquitous, and, I would argue, sadly inevitable. When we participate in post-apocalyptic computer or video games or other moving-image doomsday scenarios, interactive or passive, we consciously or unconsciously affirm the possibility of such a catastrophic event. No one can deny that the results of such a nuclear terrorist attack would be both devastating and lingering, whether one target is hit, or multiple ones.

The age of innocence and technological primitivism posted by such films as Guy Hamilton's *Goldfinger* (1964), in which Auric Goldfinger (Gert Frobe) plans to nuke Fort Knox to increase the value of his own holdings in gold, is both remote and now even nostalgic. There is nothing comforting in the scenarios offered by *Last Best Chance*, *The Sum of All Fears*, and other contemporary nuclear thrillers that now proliferate on television, DVD, the Internet, cell phones, laptops, and conventional theatre screens. This is the end game, the next step down the road towards the collapse of a traditional system of governments, checks and balances, assignable accountability, and identifiable combatants.

Yet one can also argue that, with the use of inexpensive camcorders, including the new, throwaway one-use camcorders, cell phones, and the like, the moving image, while still controlled as a commercial medium by a few conglomerate organizations, has become a truly democratic medium. It is impossible to hold back the flood of images created by these new technologies, and in the coming century, these images will both inform and enlighten our social discourse. Still, the surveillance cameras now used in many New York nightclubs to provide low-cost intrusive entertainment for web users can only proliferate; there is no surcease from the domain of images that shape and transform our lives.

Human life is both cheap and expendable; *Halo III* (2007) is, at the time of writing, one of the most popular video games on the market, and consists of little more than continuous and grueling combat. CNN, Fox, MSNBC, and the other cable news channels have now become almost interchangeable, dealing in a steady diet of disaster, murder, destruction, violence, and societal failure. Scandal has replaced news, and violence, as in Myanmar, has supplanted legitimate rule. Hundreds of thousands of innocent civilians are starving in Darfur. The Russian army recently tested what they described as 'the father of all bombs,' for which there is 'no match in the world,' as Vladimir Putin (Russian president, and then, from 2008, prime minister) managed to cling to power with a series of carefully staged political maneuvers (Blomfield 2007). Perhaps most ominously, the White House recently issued National Security Presidential Directive 51, as Ron Rosenbaum reported in Slate.com. According to Rosenbaum,

> the directive, issued without any review by Congress or the Supreme Court, gives the president authority to decide when an emergency has occurred, and to do whatever he deems necessary to ensure continuity of government, whether it's to cancel upcoming elections, suspend the Constitution, or launch a nuclear attack on the enemy [. . .] NSDP-51 even has two secret clauses that the administration won't disclose to anyone, including congressional oversight committees, on the grounds of 'national security concerns.' (Rosenbaum 2007)

This alarming directive, rife with the possibility of abuse, coupled with the current administration's continual saber rattling on the threat posed by Iran's nascent nuclear program – Bush's pronouncements about an imminent 'World War III' (Conason 2007); Cheney's blunt assertion that 'we will not allow [original emphasis] Iran to have a nuclear weapon' (Stolberg 2007) – only adds to the general atmosphere of unsettling anxiety.

Reality television routinely traffics in humiliation and degradation – self-inflicted or otherwise – while the scenarios of numerous television shows, as back as the 1950s, have habitually depicted the world on the precipice of destruction. It could be that, as in the Cold War, we will continue to be 'lucky.' But when one looks at all the evidence, both cinematic and factual (each mirroring the other in a plethora of disturbing connections), the question of nuclear terrorism becomes a stark reality. This, then, is the place where this text ends, in a consideration of the limits of time, the limits of our shared future. But it is not yet the end of moving-image discourse, or the coming permutations this discourse will make manifest.

In the twenty-first century, the world of noir has become our life, our shared mode of televisual discourse, the world that we most embrace. As it migrates from the theatre screens that used to hold our undivided attention, to the world of the Internet and video gaming, its contours have deepened and become more pronounced. Many people now 'live' online twenty-four hours a day, seven days a week, and exist only to be taken out of their actual temporal reality and 'live' in an alternative one. The issue of noir has become the core of our existence, in alarmist newscasts, the dire predictions of paid pundits, and in the substitution of speculation for fact. At one point, noir could be contained. Now, it exists everywhere.

Even the government admits that human life today is cheaper than ever.

As Seth Borenstein of the Associated Press reported on 18 July 2008, in the *Huffington Post*,

> It's not just the American dollar that's losing value. A government agency has decided that an American life isn't worth what it used to be. The 'value of a statistical life' is $6.9 million in today's dollars, the Environmental Protection Agency reckoned in May – a drop of nearly $1 million from just five years ago. The Associated Press discovered the change after a review of cost-benefit analyses over more than a dozen years [. . .] When drawing up regulations, government agencies put a value on human life and then weigh the costs versus the lifesaving benefits of a proposed rule. The less a life is worth to the government, the less the need for a regulation, such as tighter restrictions on pollution. Consider, for example, a hypothetical regulation that costs $18 billion to enforce but will prevent 2,500 deaths. At $7.8 million per person (the old figure), the lifesaving benefits outweigh the costs. But at $6.9 million per person, the rule costs more than the lives it saves, so it may not be adopted.

Is it any wonder we feel so alienated, when our own government blithely assures us that our lives are not really worth that much after all, if their value doesn't work out on a cost benefit basis? As that most noir of all superheroes, Batman (Christian Bale), in Christopher Nolan's deeply despairing *The Dark Knight* (2008), says to his butler, Alfred (Michael Caine), in desperation, 'people are dying. What would you have me do?' To which Alfred gives the only reply possible: 'Endure. You can be the outcast.' In today's world, we are all outcasts, waiting for a rescuer who will never arrive.

In the world of film noir, our lot is to continually seek the phantom reassurance of a new social construct that can never fulfill our spectatorial desires. Lost in a wilderness of conflicting images, moving ever faster, with quicker and quicker editing until the unit of the cinema shot itself collapses, we are finally stripped of any fugitive identity we may have thought we possessed. Where will we go when we discover that we no longer exist? What will we do when the illusion, finally unable to bear the weight of its own construction, collapses in a double inversion of its figurative linkages?

The disavowal of the self that noir represents cannot survive without the continual production of images to support it, work that is going on now with a renewed, desperate intensity because the economic and social stakes are so much higher. What will replace the discrepancies of action that constitute straight discourse in contemporary cinema? For the moment, it seems that we are destined ceaselessly to repeat the past, hoping to find there some semblance of security and safety. The alternative seems too terrible to contemplate. What will we do when we are forced, at last, to see ourselves?

Appendix: A Gallery of Classic Noir 'Heavies'

Many of the actors mentioned here in specific categories 'crossed over' to different categories, sometimes even playing heroines or heroes. In all cases, of course, these categories are highly subjective, but I have tried here to list these actors for the characteristics for which they are best known.

Cold Heavies

Citizen Kane, Kiss Me Deadly	Paul Stewart
Gilda, The Missing Juror, Alias Nick Beal	George Macready
The Four Skulls of Jonathan Drake	Henry Daniell
Six Hours to Live, Dick Tracy vs Crime, Inc.,	John Davidson
Calling Homicide, Colorado Ambush	Myron Healey

Gross Heavies

Farewell, My Lovely	Kate Murtagh
Ruthless, The Maltese Falcon	Sidney Greenstreet
Hangover Square, I Wake Up Screaming	Laird Cregar
The Racket, Five Against the House	William Conrad
The Big Heat, To Have and Have Not	Dan Seymour
The Intruder, Underworld USA	Robert Emhardt
Vera Cruz, Violent Saturday	Ernest Borgnine
Whatever Happened to Baby Jane?	Victor Buono
The Big Combo, The Tarnished Angels	Robert Middleton

Hoods

Lady From Shanghai, Baby Face Nelson	Ted de Corsia
The Big Heat, Point Blank	Lee Marvin

Hard Guy, Machine Gun Mama	Jack LaRue
Claudelle Inglish, Comanche Station	Claude Akins
Gilda, The Lady and the Mob	Joe Sawyer
The Scarface Mob, Riot in Cell Block Eleven	Neville Brand
Vice Squad, The Big Heat	Adam Williams
Blood Money, Derelict	George Bancroft
Machine Gun Kelly, House of Wax	Charles Bronson
The Rise and Fall of Legs Diamond	Ray Danton
The Undead, Magnum Force	Richard Devon
Kiss Me Deadly	Jack Elam
Kiss of Death, No Way Out	Richard Widmark

Sharpies and Smoothies

Scarlet Street, Walk a Tight Rope	Dan Duryea
Dementia 13, The Naked and the Dead	William Campbell
Laura, House on Haunted Hill	Vincent Price
Rebel Without a Cause, Juvenile Jungle	Corey Allen
Red Ball Express, The Screaming Skull	Alex Nicol
North by Northwest	Martin Landau
The House of Fear, Secret Beyond the Door	Paul Cavanagh

Brains Heavies

The Asphalt Jungle	Sam Jaffe
The Fortune Cookie, Experiment in Terror	Ned Glass
Flash Gordon, Mystery of Marie Roget	Charles Middleton
Drums of Fu Manchu, Edge of Darkness	Henry Brandon
The Manchurian Candidate, Al Capone	James Gregory
Saboteur, The Colossus of New York	Otto Kruger
The Asphalt Jungle	Louis Calhern
Spellbound, Suspicion	Leo G. Carroll

Action Heavies

The Crimson Ghost	Kenne Duncan
Shadow of Suspicion	George J. Lewis
Alias Billy the Kid, The Vampire's Ghost	Roy Barcroft
The Dark Corner, The Glass Key	William Bendix
Nightmare Alley, Mysterious Intruder	Mike Mazurki
Club Havana, Hold That Ghost	Marc Lawrence

The Big Combo, A Man Alone	Lee Van Cleef
Combat Squad, I Saw What You Did	John Ireland
Kiss Me Deadly, Run of the Arrow	Ralph Meeker
The Big Knife	Jack Palance
The Haunted Palace, The Intruder	Leo Gordon
Woman on the Beach, Fallen Angel	Charles Bickford
The Garment Jungle, Ten Wanted Men	Richard Boone
Charade, The Dirty Dozen	George Kennedy
99 River Street, Chicago Confidential	Jack Lambert

Psychos

Psycho, The Fool Killer	Anthony Perkins
Strangers on a Train	Robert Walker
The Killing, Revolt in the Big House	Timothy Carey

Fall Guys

Phantom Lady, Stranger on the Third Floor	Elisha Cook, Jr
Strange Fascination, The Other Woman	Hugo Haas
Slave Ship, The Scarlet Claw	Arthur Hohl

Establishment Heavies

Murders in the Zoo, Beggars in Ermine	Lionel Atwill
Apology for Murder, Swing Parade of 1946	Russell Hicks
Terror by Night, The Phantom of 42nd Street	Alan Mowbray
The Brasher Doubloon, The Racket Man	Florence Bates
Lady From Shanghai, Patterns	Everett Sloane
The Brighton Strangler, The Pearl of Death	Miles Mander
Flight to Mars, The Damned Don't Cry	Morris Ankrum
Dangerous Business, Black Gold	Thurston Hall
The Earl of Chicago, City That Never Sleeps	Edward Arnold
The Night Key, Scarlet Street	Samuel S. Hinds
The Unknown Guest, Power of the Press	Victor Jory
The Dunwich Horror, Boomerang	Ed Begley, Sr
The Garment Jungle, Party Girl	Lee J. Cobb
A House is Not a Home	Jesse White

Mad Scientists

House of Frankenstein, Black Friday	Boris Karloff
The Devil Bat, The Ape Man	Bela Lugosi
Revenge of the Zombies, Five Bloody Graves	John Carradine
The Black Raven, The Flying Serpent	George Zucco

Corporate Backstabbers

Don't Make Waves, Hysteria	Robert Webber
Underworld USA, Walk on the Wild Side	Richard Rust
Address Unknown, The Town Went Wild	Charles Halton
Advise and Consent, The Phenix City Story	Edward Andrews
Chamber of Horrors, A Fine Madness	Patrick O'Neal
The Bad Seed, Vertigo	Henry Jones

Slatterns

Lady in a Cage, Chubasco	Ann Sothern
Little Tough Guy, Undercurrent	Marjorie Main
Fall Guy, Road to Alcatraz	Iris Adrian

Harpies

Scarlet Street, The Suspect	Rosalind Ivan
The Wizard of Oz, Thirteen Ghosts	Margaret Hamilton
The Dark Corner, Kitty	Constance Collier
Behind Locked Doors	Kathleen Freeman
Detour, Dangerous Blondes	Ann Savage
Johnny Guitar, The Exorcist (voice only)	Mercedes McCambridge
One More Tomorrow, The Youngest Profession	Marjorie Gateson
Destiny, Night Club Girl	Minna Gombell

Anti-Maternal Figures

My Reputation, Above Suspicion	Cecil Cunningham
A Stolen Life, Murder in Times Square	Esther Dale
The Little Princess, The Lady and the Monster	Mary Nash
Madame Racketeer, The Casino Murder Case	Alison Skipworth
Little Caesar, School for Girls	Lucile LaVerne
The Son of Dr Jekyll, The Wolf Man	Doris Lloyd

The Boogey Man Will Get You, Arson, Inc.	Maude Eburne
The Two Mrs Carrolls, Love From a Stranger	Isobel Elson
House of Strangers, All Mine to Give	Hope Emerson

Femmes Fatales

Scarlet Street, The Woman in the Window	Joan Bennett
The Black Widow, San Quentin	Carol Forman
My Favorite Blonde, The Spider Woman	Gale Sondergaard
Hot Cars, The Counterfeiters	Joi Lansing
Lady in the Lake, The Unsuspected	Audrey Totter
Born to Kill, Raw Deal	Claire Trevor
Dangerous Intruder, What a Blonde!	Veda Ann Borg

Racially 'Other' Heavies

The Conqueror, Francis of Assisi	Pedro Armendariz
I Loved a Woman, Devil and the Deep	Paul Porcasi
One Eyed Jacks, Flaming Star	Rudolfo Acosta
Killer's Kiss, Crime and Punishment	Frank Silvera
Crime Doctor's Gamble, Dillinger	Eduardo Ciannelli
Experiment in Terror	Ross Martin
The Manchurian Candidate	Henry Silva
Counter Attack, Mission to Moscow	Ivan Triesault
The Leopard Man, Strange Conquest	Abner Biberman
Japanese War Bride, Blood on the Sun	Philip Ahn
Devil Goddess, Don Winslow of the Navy	Frank Lackteen

Sexually 'Other' Heavies

The 5,000 Fingers of Dr T	Hans Conreid
Laura, The Dark Corner	Clifton Webb

Works Cited and Consulted

Acker, Kathy. 'The End of the World of White Men,' *Posthuman Bodies*, Judith Halberstam and Ira Livingston (eds). Bloomington: Indiana University Press, 1995: 57–72.

American Technion Society. Advertisement. *The New York Times*, 13 June 2007: A12.

Ansen, David, with N'Gai Croal, Corie Brown and Donna Foote. 'You Oughta Be in Videos,' *Newsweek* (24 January 2000): 61, 63–4.

'Apply to Be On Extreme Makeover: Home Edition Today!,' 'The Vitale Family, Season 2, Episode 23,' website, <http://abc.go.com/primetime/xtreme-home/casting.html>. 1 June 2005.

Auty, Martyn and Nick Roddick. *British Cinema Now*. London: BFI Publishing, 1985.

Backstreet, Jack. 'Biography for Ben Judell,' <http://www.imdb.com/name/nm0431879/bio>. 31 May 2007.

Bailey, F. G. *The Prevalence of Deceit*. Ithaca: Cornell University Press, 1991.

Baudrillard, Jean. *The Illusion of the End*. Trans. Chris Turner. Stanford: Stanford University Press, 1994.

Baudrillard, Jean. *The Gulf War Did Not Take Place*. Trans. Paul Patton. Bloomington: Indiana University Press, 1995.

Bergan, Ronald. *Jean Renoir: Projections of Paradise*. Woodstock, NY: Overlook Press, 1992.

Blair, Bruce G. 'What If the Terrorists Go Nuclear?' *CDI Terrorism Project*, 1 October 2001. <http://www.cdi.org/program/document.cfm?documentid=1348&programID=32&from_page=../friendlyversion/printversion.cfm>. 13 October 2007.

Blomfield, Adrian. 'Russian Army Tests the Father of All Bombs,' *The Telegraph* 13 September 2007. <http://www.telegraph.co.uk/news/main.jhtml?xml=/news/2007/09/12/wbomb112.xml>. 5 October 2007.

Bogdanovich, Peter. *Fritz Lang in America*. New York: Praeger, 1967.

Bogdanovich, Peter. 'Edgar G. Ulmer Interview,' in *Kings of the Bs: Working Within the Hollywood System*. Ed. Todd McCarthy and Charles Flynn. New York: Dutton, 1975: 377–409.

Bok, Sissela. *Secrets: On the Ethics of Concealment and Revelation*. New York: Vintage, 1989.

Borde, Raymond and Etienne Chaumeton. *A Panorama of American Film Noir 1941–1953*. Trans. Paul Hammond. San Francisco: City Lights, 2002.

Borenstein, Seth. 'American Life Worth Less Today: AP,' The Huffington Post 10 July 2008, <http://www.huffingtonpost.com/2008/07/10/american-life-worth-less_n_112030.html>. Accessed 18 July 2008.

Boyreau, Jacques. *Trash: The Graphic Genius of Xploitation Movie Posters*. San Francisco: Chronicle, 2002.

Brody, Richard. 'Auteur Wars,' *The New Yorker* 7 April 2008: 56–65.

Brottman, Mikita. *Hollywood Hex: Death and Destiny in the Dream Factory*. Creation: London, 1999.

Brown, Corie and Joshua Hammer. 'Okay, So What's the Sequel?,' *Newsweek Extra: A Century at the Movies* (Summer 1998): 116–18.

Bunn, Austin. 'Machine Age,' *The Village Voice* (4 August 1998): 27.

Cagin, Seth and Philip Dray. *Born to Be Wild: Hollywood and the Sixties Generation*. Boca Raton, FL: Coyote, 1994.

Cameron, Ian and Elisabeth Cameron. *The Heavies*. London: Praeger, 1967.

Cameron, Ian and Elisabeth Cameron. *Dames*. London: Praeger, 1969.

Cantor, Paul A. 'Film Noir and the Frankfurt School: America as Wasteland in Edgar Ulmer's *Detour*,' in *The Philosophy of Film Noir*. Ed. Mark T. Conard. Lexington: University Press of Kentucky, 2006: 139–62.

Caputo, Raffaele. 'Film Noir: 'You Sure You Don't See What You Hear?'' *Continuum: The Australian Journal of Media and Culture* 5.2 (1990), <http://wwwmcc.murdoch.edu.au/ReadingRoom/5.2/Caputo.html> 26 March 2008.

Cassidy, Marsha F. *What Women Watched: Daytime Television in the 1950s*. Austin: University of Texas Press, 2005.

Castle, William. *Step Right Up! I'm Gonna Scare the Pants Off America*. New York: G. P. Putnam's, 1976.

Cave, Dylan. '*Yield to the Night*,' *BFI Screen Online*, <http://www.screenonline.org.uk/film/id/521583/index.html>. Accessed 27 April 2008.

Chaffin-Quiray, Garrett. '"You Bled My Mother, You Bled My Father, But You Won't Bleed Me": The Underground Trio of Melvin Van Peebles,' in *Underground USA: Filmmaking Beyond the Hollywood Canon*. Ed. Xavier Mendik and Steven Jay Schneider. London: Wallflower, 2002: 96–108.

Coleman, Dennis. Unpublished interview with Martin Scorsese, 22 March 1991.

Coll, Steve. 'The Unthinkable,' *The New Yorker*, 12 March 2007. <http://www.newyorker.com/reporting/2007/03/12/070312fa_fact_coll>. Accessed 5 October 2007.

Commager, Henry Steele. *The Story of World War II*. Rev. edn. New York: Simon and Schuster, 2001.

Conard, Mark T. 'Introduction,' in *The Philosophy of Film Noir*. Ed. Mark T. Conard. Lexington: University Press of Kentucky, 2006: 1–4.

Conard, Mark T. (ed.). The *Philosophy of Film Noir*. Lexington: University Press of Kentucky, 2006.

Conason, Joe. 'Nuclear Hypocrisy,' Salon.com, 19 October 2007. <http://www.salon.com/opinion/conason/2007/10/19/bush_iran/>. Accessed 26 October 2007.

Costello, John. *Virtue Under Fire: How World War II Changed Our Social and Sexual Attitudes*. Boston: Little, Brown, 1985.

'D. Ross Lederman, Film Pioneer,' *Variety*, 30 August 1927, n.p. Collection Margaret Herrick Library, Academy of Motion Picture Arts and Sciences, Los Angeles.

'D. Ross Lederman (Obituary),' *The Hollywood Reporter*, 25 October 1972, n.p. Collection Margaret Herrick Library, Academy of Motion Picture Arts and Sciences, Los Angeles.

Debord, Guy. *Society of the Spectacle and Other Films*. London: Rebel Press, 1992.

Dimendberg, Edward. *Film Noir and the Spaces of Modernity*. Cambridge, MA: Harvard University Press, 2004.

'Direction Helps Good Story and Cast,' *The Hollywood Reporter*, 30 July 1934, n. p. D. Ross Lederman Papers.

Dirks, Tim. 'King's Row,' *Greatest Films Website*, <http://www.filmsite.org/kingr.html>. 26 March 2008.

Dixon, Wheeler Winston. 'The Digital Domain: Some Preliminary Notes on Image Mesh and Manipulation in Hyperreal Cinema/Video,' *Film Criticism* 20.1/2 (Fall/Winter 1995–6): 55–66.

Dixon, Wheeler Winston. *Visions of the Apocalypse: Spectacles of Destruction in American Cinema*. London: Wallflower, 2003.

Dixon, Wheeler Winston. *Lost in the Fifties: Recovering Phantom Hollywood*. Carbondale: Southern Illinois University Press, 2005.

Dixon, Wheeler Winston. *Film Talk: Directors at Work*. New Brunswick, NJ: Rutgers University Press, 2007.

Dixon, Wheeler Winston and Gwendolyn Audrey Foster. *A Short History of Film*. New Brunswick, NJ: Rutgers University Press, 2008.

Douglas, Ann. 'Night Into Noir,' *Vanity Fair*, March 2007: 438–43, 498–9.

Duncan, Paul. *Film Noir: Films of Trust and Betrayal*. Harpenden, England: Pocket Essentials, 2000.

Durgnat, Raymond. 'Paint It Black: The Family Tree of Film Noir,' *Cinema* 6 / 7: 49–56; rpt. in *Film Noir Reader*. Ed. Alain Silver and James Ursini. New York: Limelight, 1996: 49–56.

Ebert, Roger. Review of *The Penthouse*. *Chicago Sun Times*, 14 November 1967. <http://rogerebert.suntimes.com/apps/pbcs.dllarticle?AID=1967111...>. 4 April 2008.

Eck, Marcel. *Lies and Truth*. Trans. Bernard Murchland. London: Collier-Macmillan, 1970.

Eliot, Marc. *Walt Disney: Hollywood's Dark Prince*. New York: Birch Lane, 1993.

Elley, Derek. *The Epic Film: Myth and History*. London: Routledge and Kegan Paul, 1984.

Ellis, Robert. 'Ida Lupino Brings New Hope to Hollywood,' *Negro Digest*, August 1950: 47–9.

Epstein, Dan. *20th Century Pop Culture*. London: Carlton, 1999.

Everson, William K. *The Bad Guys: A Pictorial History of the Movie Villain*. New York: Cadillac, 1964.

Extreme Makeover: Home Edition website, <http://abc.go.com/primetime/xtremehome/show.html>. June 2005.

Fernett, Gene. *Poverty Row*. Satellite Beach, FL: Coral Reef Publications, 1973.

Fienup-Riordan, Ann. *Freeze Frame: Alaska Eskimos in the Movies*. Seattle: University of Washington Press, 1995.

'Film Baby Walks By Self: PRC Makes Big Strides With More Coin and More Stars,' *Daily Variety*, 16 October 1944, n.p. Collection Margaret Herrick Library, Academy of Motion Picture Arts and Sciences, Los Angeles.

'Film Merger Plan Revealed: PRC to Combine with Another Company,' *Hollywood Citizen News*, 3 August 1944, n.p. Collection Margaret Herrick Library, Academy of Motion Picture Arts and Sciences, Los Angeles.

Fink, Mitchell. *The Last Days of Dead Celebrities*. New York: Hyperion, 2006.

Flinn, Tom. 'Three Faces of Film Noir: *Stranger on the Third Floor*, *Phantom Lady*, and *Criss Cross*,' in *Kings of the Bs: Working Within the Hollywood System*. Ed. Todd McCarthy and Charles Flynn. New York: Dutton, 1975: 155–64.

Flynn, Charles and Todd McCarthy. 'The Economic Imperative: Why Was the B Movie Necessary?' in *Kings of the Bs: Working Within the Hollywood System*. Ed. Todd McCarthy and Charles Flynn. New York: Dutton, 1975: 13–47.

Flynn, Charles and Todd McCarthy. 'Interview with Joseph Kane, September 2, 1973,' in *Kings of the Bs: Working Within the Hollywood System*. Ed. Todd McCarthy and Charles Flynn. New York: Dutton, 1975: 313–24.

Foster, Gwendolyn Audrey. *Performing Whiteness: Postmodern Re/Constructions in the Cinema*. Albany: SUNY University Press, 2003.

Foucault, Michel. *Fearless Speech*. Ed. Joseph Pearson. Los Angeles: Semiotext(e), 2001.

Fox, Ken and Maitland McDonagh (eds). *The Virgin Film Guide*. 9th edn. London: Virgin, 2000.

French, Philip. *Westerns*. New York: Oxford University Press, 1977.

Friedrich, Otto. *City of Nets: A Portrait of Hollywood in the 1940s*. Berkeley: University of California Press, 1997.

'Fromkess Elected PRC President,' *Motion Picture Herald*, 22 July 1944, n.p. Collection Margaret Herrick Library, Academy of Motion Picture Arts and Sciences, Los Angeles.

Galan, Nely and Bronwyn Garrity. *The Swan Curriculum: Create a Spectacular New You With 12 Life-Changing Steps in 12 Amazing Weeks*. Regan Books, 2004.

Goddard, Ben (dir. and screenplay). *Last Best Chance*. Nuclear Threat Initiative, 2005.

Gomery, Douglas. '*They Live By Night* (Nicholas Ray),' in *Kings of the Bs: Working Within the Hollywood System*. Ed. Todd McCarthy and Charles Flynn. New York: Dutton, 1975: 185–96.

Graham, Don. *No Name on the Bullet: A Biography of Audie Murphy*. New York: Viking, 1989.

Grantham, Mark. 'Life on the Cheap with the Danzigers.' Manuscript in the BFI Archives.

Gray, John. 'Eli Roth Interview,' *Pit of Horror.com*, <http://www.pitofhorror.com/newdesign/promo/hostel/interview.htm>. Accessed 26 April 2008.

Grayson, Charles and Robert Hardy Andrews. Screenplay for *The Woman on Pier 13* (aka *I Married a Communist*). New York: Frederick Ungar, 1976.

Greenfield, Robert. *Timothy Leary: A Biography*. New York: Harcourt, 2006.

Griffith, Richard and Arthur Mayer. *The Movies*. New York: Bonanza, 1957.

Grossman, Gary. *Superman: Serial to Cereal*. New York: Popular Library, 1976.

'*Guest in the House*,' *The Internet Movie Data Base*, <http://www.imdb.com/title/tt0036886/>. 26 March 2008.

Hajdu, David. *The Ten Cent Plague: The Great Comic-Book Scare and How It Changed America*. New York: Farrar, Straus and Giroux, 2008.

Hardy, Phil. *Samuel Fuller*. London: Praeger, 1970.

Heher, Ashley M. and Caryn Rousseau. 'Police Investigate NIU Shooter's Two Sides,' 16 February 2008. APGoogle.com <http://ap.google.com/article/ALeqM5i72zW1WRLvclejGI5pefItEjKCAD8URNR302>. 16 February 2008.

Heller, Stephen and Michael Barson. *Red Scared!: The Commie Menace in Propaganda and Popular Culture*. New York: Chronicle, 2001.

Hertzberg, Hendrik. 'Rain and Fire,' *The New Yorker*, 3 October 2005. <http://www.newyorker.com/archive/2005/10/03051003ta_talk_hertzberg>. 5 October 2007.

Herzog, Don. *Cunning*. Princeton: Princeton University Press, 2006.

Hill, John. *Sex, Class and Realism: British Cinema 1956–1963*. London: BFI Publishing, 1986.

Hirschhorn, Clive. *The Universal Story*. New York: Crown, 1983.

The Hitch-Hiker. Pressbook. RKO Radio Pictures, 1953.

Hoover, J. Edgar. *Communist Target – Youth: Communist Infiltration and Agitation Tactics*. Washington, DC: House Committee on Un-American Activities, 1960.

Hope, Ted. 'Indie Film is Dead.' *Filmmaker* (Fall, 1995): 18, 54–8.

Houseman, John. 'Lost Fortnight: A Memoir,' in *The Blue Dahlia: A Screenplay by Raymond Chandler*. Ed. Matthew R. Bruccoli. New York: Popular Library, 1976: 7–23.

'Increased Film Budget Planned for PRC Product,' *Motion Picture Herald*, 30 June 1942, n.p. Collection Margaret Herrick Library, Academy of Motion Picture Arts and Sciences, Los Angeles.

'Interviews: *The Swan* – Interview with Andrea,' TVRules.net, 4 May 2004, <http://www.tvrules.net/modules.php?name=News&file=article&sid=4785 >. 21 May 2005.

Jewell, Richard B. and Vernon Harbin. *The RKO Story*. London: Arlington House, 1982.

Juno, Andrea and V. Vale. *Incredibly Strange Films*. San Francisco: V/Search Publications, 1986.

Katz, Ephraim. *The Film Encyclopedia*. 5th edn. Rev. Fred Klein and Ronald Dean Nolan. New York: Collins, 2005.

Kawin, Bruce. *Telling It Again and Again: Repetition in Literature and Film*. Boulder, CO: University Press of Colorado, 1989.

Keaney, J. L. *Film Noir Guide: 745 Films of the Classic Era, 1940–1959*. Jefferson, NC: McFarland, 2003.

Kermode, Mark. 'Review of *Hostel: Part II*,' *The Guardian*, 1 July 2007, <http://film.guardian.co.uk/News_Story/Critic_Review/Observer_review/ 0,,2116477,00.html>. Accessed 30 March 2008.

Keyes, Ralph. *The Post-Truth Era: Dishonesty and Deception in Contemporary Life*. New York: St Martin's Press, 2004.

Kinsey, Wayne. *Hammer Films: The Bray Studio Years*. London: Reynolds and Hearn, 2002.

Konow, David. *Schlock-O-Rama: The Films of Al Adamson*. Los Angeles: Lone Eagle, 1998.

Lait, Jack and Lee Mortimer. *USA Confidential*. New York: Crown, 1952.

Landy, Marcia. *British Genres: Cinema and Society 1930–1960*. Princeton: Princeton University Press, 1991.

Lee, Michael. 'Ideology and Style in the Double Feature: *I Married a Monster from Outer Space* and *Curse of the Demon*,' in *Horror at the Drive-In: Essays in Popular Americana*. Ed. Gary D. Rhodes. Jefferson, NC: McFarland, 2003: 67–77.

Leitch, Thomas. *Crime Films*. Cambridge: Cambridge University Press, 2002.

Leyda, Jay (ed.). *Voices of Film Experience: 1894 to the Present*. New York: Macmillan, 1977.

Lindsay, Cynthia. *Dear Boris*. London: Nick Hern, 1995.

Lucanio, Patrick. *Them Or Us: Archetypal Interpretations of Fifties Alien Invasion Films*. Bloomington: Indiana University Press, 1987.

Lyons, Arthur. *Death on the Cheap: The Lost B Movies of Film Noir*. New York: Da Capo, 2000.

McCarthy, Todd and Charles Flynn. 'Interview with Albert Zugsmith,' in *Kings of the Bs: Working Within the Hollywood System*. Ed. Todd McCartney and Charles Flynn. New York: Dutton, 1975: 411–24.

McCauley, Michael J. *Jim Thompson: Sleep with the Devil*. New York: The Mysterious Press, 1991.

McClelland, Doug. *The Golden Age of B Movies*. Nashville: Charter House, 1978.

McFadden, Tara Ann. *Pop Wisdom: A Little Guide to Life*. Philadelphia, Running Press, 1996.

McKie, David. 'Hollywood's Little Brother,' *The Guardian*, 9 September 2004, <http://film.guardian.co.uk/venice/story/0,15051,1300711,00.html> 3 April 2008.

Maltin, Leonard (ed.). *2003 Movie and Video Guide*. New York: Signet, 2002.

Mann, Denise. *Hollywood Independents: The Postwar Talent Takeover*. Minneapolis: University of Minnesota Press, 2008.

'The Marriage Circle,' cast sheet from episode of *Shotgun Slade*, 22–3 October 1959. D. Ross Lederman papers.

Meisel, Myron. 'Edgar G. Ulmer: The Primacy of the Visual,' in *Kings of the Bs: Working Within the Hollywood System*. Ed. Todd McCarthy and Charles Flynn. New York: Dutton, 1975: 147–52.

Meyer, David N. *A Girl and A Gun: The Complete Guide to Film Noir*. New York: Avon, 1998.

Meyer, William R. *Warner Brothers Directors*. New Rochelle, NY: Arlington House, 1978.

Miles, Barry. *Hippie*. New York: Sterling, 2003.

Miller, Clive T. '*Nightmare Alley*: Beyond the B's,' in *Kings of the Bs: Working Within the Hollywood System*. Ed. Todd McCarthy and Charles Flynn. New York: Dutton, 1975: 167–83.

Miller, Laurence. 'Evidence for a British Film Noir Cycle,' in *Re-viewing British Cinema 1900–1992*. Ed. Wheeler Winston Dixon. Albany: SUNY University Press, 1994: 155–64.

Milne, Tom. *Losey on Losey*. Garden City, NJ: Doubleday, 1968.

Mintz, John. 'US Called Unprepared for Nuclear Terrorism,' *The Washington Post*, 3 May 2005. <http://www.washingtonpost.com/wp-dyn/content/article/2005/05/02/AR2005050201454.html>. 5 October 2007.

Montgomery, Nancy. 'Army Reservist Undergoes Glamorous Transformation, Wins Swan Reality Show,' *Stars and Stripes*, 16 January 2005, <http://www.estripes.com/article.asp?section=104&article=25649&archive=true>. 1 June 2005.

Motion Pictures 1940–9: *Catalog of Copyright Entries: Cumulative Series*. Washington, DC: Library of Congress, 1953.

Muller, Eddie. *Dark City Dames: The Wicked Women of Film Noir*. New York: Regan Books/HarperCollins, 2001.

Muller, Eddie. *The Art of Noir*. Woodstock, NY: Overlook, 2002.

Muller, Tom. *Dark City: The Lost World of Film Noir*. New York: St Martin's, 1998.

Mulvey, Laura and Jon Halliday (eds). *Douglas Sirk*. Edinburgh: Edinburgh Film Festival/John Player and Sons, 1972.

Murphy, Audie, with David McClure. *To Hell and Back*. New York: Holt, 1949.

Murphy, Robert. *Sixties British Cinema*. London: BFI Publishing, 1992.

Nichols, Bill (ed.). *Movies and Methods: An Anthology*. Berkeley: University of California Press, 1976.

'Nuclear Terrorism,' *Union of Concerned Scientists*, 6 June 2007. <http://www.ucsusa.org/global_security/nuclear_terrorism/>. 5 October 2007.

O'Brien, Geoffrey. *The Phantom Empire*. New York: Norton, 1993.

O'Brien, Geoffrey. 'What Does the Audience Want?,' *The New York Times Magazine*, 16 November 1997: 110–11.

O'Brien, Geoffrey. *The Times Square Story*. New York; W. W. Norton and Company, 1998.

'Orders for Last Best Chance Exceed 42,000; Film Featured on Meet the Press, Nighttime.' Press release, *Nuclear Threat Initiative*, 14 July 2005.

Orr, Bob. 'Nuclear Terror,' *The CBS Evening News*, 13 June 2007.

Osgerby, Bill. 'Full Throttle on the Highway to Hell: Mavericks, Machismo and Mayhem in the American Biker Movie,' in *Underground USA: Filmmaking Beyond the Hollywood Canon*. Ed. Xavier Mendik and Steven Jay Schneider. London: Wallflower, 2002: 123–39.

Palmer, R. Barton (ed.). *Perspectives on Film Noir*. New York: G. K. Hall, 1996.

Parish, James Robert. *Hollywood Character Actors*. New Rochelle, NY: Arlington House, 1978.

Peary, Danny. *Cult Movies 3*. New York: Simon and Schuster, 1988.

'Penngrove Family Hit with Property Taxes After Extreme Makeover,' KESQ News Channel 3 website, <http://www.kesq.com/Global/story.asp?S=3116794>. 1 June 2005.

The Penthouse. Pressbook. Paramount Pictures, 1967.

Perry, William J., Ashton B. Carter and Michael M. May. 'After the Bomb,' *The New York Times*, 12 June 2007: A23.

Pettigrew, Terence. *British Film Character Actors: Great Names and Memorable Moments*. London: David and Charles, 1982.

Pinter, Harold. *Accident*, in *Five Screenplays by Harold Pinter*. London: Methuen, 1978.

Pitt, Peter. 'Elstree's Poverty Row,' *Films and Filming* 360 (September 1984): 15–16.

Place, J. A. and L. S. Peterson. 'Some Visual Motifs of Film Noir,' in *Movies and Methods: An Anthology*. Ed. Bill Nichols. Berkeley: University of California Press, 1976: 325–38.

Polan, Dana. *Power and Paranoia: History, Narrative and the American Cinema 1940–1950*. New York: Columbia University Press, 1986.

Polito, Robert. *Savage Art: A Biography of Jim Thompson*. New York: Vintage, 1995.

Pomerance, Murray (ed.). *City That Never Sleeps: New York and the Filmic Imagination*. New Brunswick, NJ: Rutgers University Press, 2007.

Porfirio, Robert. 'Interview with Dore Schary, 1905–1980,' in *Film Noir Reader 3*. Ed. Robert Porfirio, Alain Silver and James Ursini. New York: Limelight, 2002: 179–89.

Porfirio, Robert and Carl Macek. 'Interview with Joseph H. Lewis, 1907–2000,' in *Film Noir Reader 3*. Ed. Robert Porfirio, Alain Silver and James Ursini. New York: Limelight, 2002: 67–85.

'PRC Announces Takeover of Major Indie Producer: Reveals Theater Ownership,' *Daily Variety*, 3 August 1944, n.p. Collection Margaret Herrick Library, Academy of Motion Picture Arts and Sciences, Los Angeles.

'PRC Has Growing Pains: Record Year Marked by Five Forward Steps,' *Daily Variety*, 29 October 1943: 489. Collection Margaret Herrick Library, Academy of Motion Picture Arts and Sciences, Los Angeles.

'PRC Pictures Plans National Distribution,' *Motion Picture Herald*, 5 February 1944, n.p. Collection Margaret Herrick Library, Academy of Motion Picture Arts and Sciences, Los Angeles.

'PRC President Outlines Company's Expansion Plans,' *Hollywood Reporter*, 3 August 1944, n.p. Collection Margaret Herrick Library, Academy of Motion Picture Arts and Sciences, Los Angeles.

'Putin's Sly Power Grab in Russia,' *Newsday*.com 3 October 2007. <http://www.newsday.com/news/opinion/ny-opput035399688oct03,0,4352944.story>. Accessed 5 October 2007.

Rabinowitz, Paula. *Black & White & Noir: America's Pulp Modernism*. New York: Columbia University Press, 2002.

Ray, Fred Olen. *The New Poverty Row: Independent Filmmakers as Distributors*. Jefferson, NC: McFarland, 1991.

Redhead, Steve. *Unpopular Cultures: The Birth of Law and Popular Culture*. Manchester: Manchester University Press, 1995.

Renov, Michael. '*Leave Her to Heaven*: The Double Bind of the Post-War Woman,' in *Imitations of Life: A Reader on Film and Television Melodrama*. Ed. Marcia Landy. Detroit: Wayne State University Press, 1991: 227–35.

Review of *The Penthouse*, *Cahiers du Cinéma* 195 (November 1967): 77.

Review of *The Penthouse*, *Daily Cinema* 9424 (22 September 1967): 6.

Review of *The Penthouse*, *Kine Weekly* 3128 (23 September 1967): 11.

Review of *The Penthouse*, *Variety*, 1 January 1967, <http://www.variety.com/review/VE1117793932.html?categoryid=31...>. Accessed 4 April 2008.

Rhodes, Gary D. 'A Drive-In Horror by Default, or, The Premiere of *The Hideous Sun Demon*,' in *Horror at the Drive-In: Essays in Popular Americana*. Ed. Gary D. Rhodes. Jefferson, NC: McFarland, 2003: 53–66.

Rode, Alan K. *Charles McGraw: Biography of a Film Noir Tough Guy*. Jefferson, NC: McFarland, 2008.

Roland, William. 'Danzigers Sell Studio for £300,000,' *Evening Standard*, 26 October 1967, n.p. Cutting in the BFI Archives.

Rosenbaum, Ron. 'Who Will Rule Us After the Next 9/11?,' *Slate*.com, 19 October 2007. <http://www.slate.com/id/2176185/>. 26 October 2007.

'Ross Lederman A Director,' *Los Angeles Times*, 13 July 1927, n.p. Collection Margaret Herrick Library, Academy of Motion Picture Arts and Sciences, Los Angeles.

Sanders, Steven M. 'Film Noir and the Meaning of Life,' in *The Philosophy of Film Noir*. Ed. Mark T. Conard. Lexington: University Press of Kentucky, 2006: 91–106.

Sanger, David E. and Thom Shanker. 'US Debates Deterrence for Nuclear Terrorism,' *The New York Times*, 8 May 2007. <http://www.nytimes.com/2007/05/08/washington/08nuke.html>. 5 October 2007.

Schrader, Paul. 'Notes on Film Noir,' *Film Comment 8.1* (Spring 1972): 8–13; rpt. in Barry Keith Grant (ed.). *Film Genre Reader*. Austin: University of Texas Press, 1986: 169–82.

Schwartz, Ronald. *Neo-Noir: The New Film Style from Psycho to Collateral*. Lanham, MD: Scarecrow Press, 2005.

Schwartz, Ronald. *Noir, Now and Then: Film Noir Originals and Remakes 1944–1999*. Westport, CT: Greenwood, 2007.

Shone, Tom. *Blockbuster: How Hollywood Learned to Stop Worrying and Love the Summer*. New York: Free Press, 2004.

Silke, James R. *Here's Looking at You, Kid*. Boston: Little, Brown, 1976.

Silver, Alain and James Ursini. *Film Noir Reader 4*. New Jersey: Limelight, 2004.

Silver, Alain and Elizabeth Ward. *Film Noir: An Encyclopedic Reference to the American Style*. 3rd edn. Woodstock, New York: Overlook Press, 1992.

Silver, Alain, James Ursini and Paul Duncan (eds). *Film Noir*. Köln: Taschen, 2004.

Slide, Anthony. *De Toth on De Toth: Putting the Drama in Front of the Camera*. London: Faber and Faber, 1996.

Sontag, Susan. 'The Decay of Cinema,' *The New York Times Magazine* (25 February 1996): 60–1.

Stacey, Jackie. *Star Gazing: Hollywood Cinema and Female Spectatorship*. London: Routledge, 1994.

Stolberg, Cheryl Gay. 'Cheney, Like President, Has a Warning for Iran,' *The New York Times*, 22 October 2007. <http://www.nytimes.com/2007/10/22/washington/22cheney.html?ref=us>. Accessed 29 April 2008.

'Street of Terror,' cast sheet from episode of *Shotgun Slade*, 12–13 November 1959. D. Ross Lederman papers.

Suárez, Juan and Millicent Manglis. 'Cinema, Gender, and the Topography of Enigmas: A Conversation with Laura Mulvey.' *Cinefocus* 3 (1995): 2–8.

Taylor, Chris. 'A Painstaking *Fantasy*,' *Time*, 31 July 2000: 56.

Taylor, Kenneth. Letter to the author, 13 February 1997, and telephone interview, 2 March 1997.

Terrace, Vincent. *Encyclopedia of Television Series, Pilots and Specials 1937–1973*. New York: Zoetrope, 1986.

Thompson, Peggy and Saeko Usukawa. *The Little Black and White Book of Film Noir*. Vancouver, Canada: 1992.

Thompson, Peggy and Saeko Usukawa. *Hard-Boiled: Great Lines from Classic Noir Films*. San Francisco: Chronicle, 1996.

Tolstoi, Leo N. (Lev Nikolaevich). *Anna Karenina*. Trans. Louise and Aylmer Maude. Oxford: Oxford University Press, 1999.

'Treasure Trap,' cast sheet from episode of *Shotgun Slade*, 27–8 October 1959. D. Ross Lederman papers.

'TV Film Could Cause Hatred,' *The Chronicle*, November 1959, n.p.; clippings collection of the BFI, London.

Vaughn, Robert. *Only Victims: A Study of Show Business Blacklisting*. New York: Putnam's, 1972.

Velez, Andrew. 'Introduction,' Screenplay for *The Woman on Pier 13* (aka *I Married a Communist*). New York: Frederick Ungar, 1967: iii–iv.

Vermilye, Jerry. *Ida Lupino*. New York: Pyramid, 1977.

'Vote Today on 15 Million Combo of Pathé and PRC,' *Daily Variety*, 24 June 1944, n.p. Collection Margaret Herrick Library, Academy of Motion Picture Arts and Sciences, Los Angeles.

Wagner, Geoffrey. *Parade of Pleasure: A Study of Popular Iconography in the USA*. London: Derek Verschoyle, 1954.

Wager, Jans B. *Dames in the Driver's Seat: Rereading Film Noir*. Austin: University of Texas Press, 2005.

Warren, Patricia. *British Film Studios: An Illustrated History*. London: Batsford, 1995.

Waters, John. *Crackpot: The Obsessions of John Waters*. New York: Vintage, 1987.

Weaver, Tom. *Poverty Row Horrors!: Monogram, PRC and Republic Horror Films of the Forties*. Jefferson, NC: McFarland, 1993.

Weber, Cynthia. *Imagining America at War: Morality Politics and Film*. London: Routledge, 2005.

Weeks, Janet. 'Hollywood is Seeing Teen: Younger Set Favors Movies Above All,' *USA Today*, 22 December 1997: D1, 2.

Weinraub, Bernard and Geraldine Fabrikant. 'The Revenge of the Bean Counters: Studios Yell "Cut!" as Costs Spiral for Filmmaking,' *The New York Times*, 13 June 1999: Section 3; 1, 15.

Weiss, Ken and Ed Goodgold. *To Be Continued . . .* New York: Crown, 1972.

Weldon, Michael. *The Psychotronic Encyclopedia of Film*. New York: Ballantine, 1983.

Will, David. 'Three Gangster Films: An Introduction,' in *Roger Corman: The Millenic Vision*. Ed. David Will and Paul Willemen. Edinburgh: Edinburgh Film Festival, 1970: 68–80.

Williams, Tony. 'In the Science Fiction Name of National Security: *Cat Women of the Moon*,' in *Horror at the Drive-In: Essays in Popular Americana*. Ed. Gary D. Rhodes. Jefferson, NC: McFarland, 2003: 113–25.

Wilson, Maggie. 'On Location: *Ring of Fear*,' *The Arizona Republic*, 13 December 1953, Section 5, 1. D. Ross Lederman papers.

Wolgamott, Kent L. 'Fiction Writer Jim Thompson Got His Start at NU in Lincoln,' *Lincoln Journal*, 28 February 1991: 15.

Wood, Robin. 'Ideology, Genre, Auteur,' in *Film Genre Reader*. Ed. Barry Keith Grant. Austin: University of Texas Press, 1986: 59–73.

Yenne, Bill. *Going Home to the Fifties*. San Francisco: Last Gasp, 2002.

Index